NONE LEFT BEHIND

Charles W. Sasser

NONE

ST. MARTIN'S GRIFFIN ⚏ NEW YORK

LEFT BEHIND

THE 10TH MOUNTAIN DIVISION AND THE TRIANGLE OF DEATH

NONE LEFT BEHIND. Copyright © 2009 by Charles W. Sasser. All rights reserved. Printed in the United States of America. For information, address St. Martin's Press, 175 Fifth Avenue, New York, N.Y. 10010.

www.stmartins.com

The Library of Congress has cataloged the hardcover edition as follows:

Sasser, Charles W.
    None left behind : the 10th Mountain Division and the triangle of death / Charles W. Sasser. —1st ed.
        p. cm.
    ISBN 978-0-312-55544-3
        1. Iraq War, 2003—Campaigns—Iraq—Baghdad Region. 2. United States. Army. Mountain Division, 10th. 3. Counterinsurgency—Iraq—Baghdad Region—History—21st century. 4. Battles—Iraq—Baghdad Region—History—21st century. 5. Iraq War, 2003—Regimental histories—United States. I. Title.

    DS79.764.U6S37 2009
    956.7044'342—dc22

                                                                            2009028680

ISBN 978-0-312-61093-7 (trade paperback)

First St. Martin's Griffin Edition: November 2010

10   9   8   7   6   5   4   3   2   1

To the brave soldiers of the U.S. Army's 10th Mountain Division

ACKNOWLEDGMENTS

I would like to take this opportunity to thank all the fine soldiers who participated in sharing their experiences, filling in the gaps of history, and re-living with me the drama that appears in these pages. I am particularly grateful to Lieutenant Colonel Paul Swiergosz, who paved the way for my research and in the process became a friend; to Lieutenant Colonel Richard Greene, current commander of the 4/31st, who so graciously accepted me back into the Army fold and opened doors to greater understanding of his men and the 10th Mountain Division; to Mr. Benjamin Abel, 10th Mountain Division Public Affairs Office, who helped me begin the process; and to Mr. Harrison L. Sarles, Director, Army Public Affairs, for his understanding and stamp of approval.

While the core of this book is built around interviews with soldiers of the 10th Mountain, a variety of other sources also contributed: official U.S. Army military documents and After Action Reports; diaries; newspapers, books, and other published accounts; interviews with witnesses other than members of the unit and with other authorities. I wish to thank all these sources for helping make this book possible.

Thanks yet again to Mr. Marc Resnick, my editor at St. Martin's Press, who launched this project by sending me a news clipping; and to my long-time agent and friend, Mr. Ethan Ellenberg.

I would also like to express my gratitude to the following authors and published works, from which I drew inspiration and guidance in writing this book: *Warrior King*, by Lt. Col. Nathan Sassaman (w/Joe Layden, St. Martin's Press, 2008); *The Iraq War: A Military History*, by Williamson Murray and Maj. Gen. Robert H. Scales, Jr. (Harvard University Press, 2003); *Digital Soldiers: The Evolution of High-Tech Weaponry and Tomorrow's Brave New Battlefield*, by James F. Dunnigan (St. Martin's Press, 1996);

The Highway War, by Maj. Seth W.B. Folsom (Potomac Books, 2006); *The Last True Story I'll Ever Tell*, by John Crawford (Riverhead Books, 2005); *Dawn over Baghdad: How the U.S. Military Is Using Bullets and Ballots to Remake Iraq*, by Karl Zinsmeister (Encounter Books, 2004); *Counterinsurgency in Modern Warfare*, edited by Daniel Marston and Carter Malkasian (Osprey Publishing, 2008); *Baghdad at Sunrise*, by Peter R. Mansoor (Yale University Press, 2008); "Iraq's Forbidding 'Triangle of Death,'" by Anthony Shadid, *Washington Post* Foreign Service, Nov. 23, 2004; "5 Soldiers Named in Rape Case," CBS News, July 10, 2006; "The Massacre of Mahmudiya—The Rape and Murder of Abeer Quassim Hamsa," expose-the-war-profiteers.org, Dec. 22, 2008; "Post-Traumatic Stress Disorder Concerns," ABC News, Dec. 15, 2004; "Army Changes Tack in Treating Combat Stress," by Ryan Lenz, AP, June 4, 2006; "Final Rites for a Humble Kid," by Mark Berman, *Washington Post*, May 30, 2007; "Abducted Soldier Found Dead," McClatchy Newspapers, July 12, 2008; "Byron W. Fouty," Yahoo News, May 16, 2007; "Luck Runs out in 'Triangle of Death,'" by Cal Perry, CNN, Oct. 31, 2005; and the "Sermon by Reverend Jimmy Layne on Biblical History of Iraq, June 2007."

Finally, an extra special thanks to my wife, Donna Sue, who has suffered my writing of books throughout the years.

NONE LEFT BEHIND

INTRODUCTION

In the late spring of 2008, I rode my motorcycle from Oklahoma to the U.S. Army Military Academy at West Point, New York, where soldiers of the famed 10th Mountain Division were instructing officer cadets in the skills of warfare at a remote training area known as Camp Natural Bridge. The 2nd BCT (Brigade Combat Team) of the 10th Mountain had recently returned (November 2007) from a fifteen-month extended tour of duty in Iraq. It was the 10th's fourth combat deployment since 2001—three to Iraq, one to Afghanistan.

While interviewing soldiers at Natural Bridge for this book, I began to hear incredible and horrifying tales about the S-curves on Malibu Road. The 4/31st (4th Battalion, 31st Infantry Regiment) of the 2nd BCT had been assigned to pacify an area about twenty miles south of Baghdad known, appropriately, as "The Triangle of Death." The AO (Area of Operations) along the Euphrates River adjoined Anbar Province, the most violent and dangerous in Iraq. Of the more than 3,000 fatal casualties suffered by the United States in Iraq since 2003 and the start of the war, over 1,000 had died in this region. Chaos, anarchy, violence, and fear ruled.

To date, no Coalition troops had permanently penetrated all parts of The Triangle of Death. Delta Company of the 4/31st, roughly 150 infantrymen at full strength, assaulted into the AO to establish a Company FOB (Forward Operating Base) and two smaller patrol bases along a twisted four-mile length of Route Malibu that soon became known as the "S-curves." The gauntlet had been cast; the enemy immediately picked it up.

The courage and warrior fortitude of Delta and the 4th Battalion would be tried and tried again in The Triangle of Death where the hard, dirty, exhausted infantrymen of the 10th became a macrocosm of the war in Iraq. As one soldier put it, "We don't commute to work, it commutes to us."

1

The core of the book is built around dozens of interviews I conducted at Camp Natural Bridge and elsewhere with officers and soldiers of the 4/31st. As they shared their experiences with me, they made a single concordant request: "Please tell the story the way it really was." That I have tried to do.

It has often been noted that a thousand different stories may emerge from even a single shared event. Therefore, the recounting of events in this book may not correspond precisely in all instances with the memories of everyone involved. I have necessarily filled in narrative gaps by utilizing my own knowledge and experience with war and with men at war to re-create certain scenes and dialogue. After all, few of us remember past conversations word for word or past events in detail, especially if they occur under the stress and confusion of combat. Where re-creation occurs, I strived to match personalities with the situation while maintaining factual content. Where conflict, doubt, or hazy recollection arose, I selected the general consensus and went with that.

Actual names are used throughout except in those rare instances where names were lost due to imperfect memory or lack of documentation, where privacy was requested, or where public identification would serve no useful purpose and might cause embarrassment. In addition, all data has been filtered through the author. I am certain to have made errors in a work of this broad scope with so many men involved. While such errors may be understandable, I nonetheless take full responsibility and ask to be forgiven for them.

I apologize to anyone omitted, neglected, or somehow slighted in the preparation of this book. I do not intend to diminish your accomplishments or war records. It is merely that I had to focus on a smaller number of you in order to make this book manageable.

I am an old Army veteran, having served twenty-nine years (active and reserve), including a deployment as a Military Police First Sergeant during the 1991 Iraqi war, Operation *Desert Storm*. I thought I knew American soldiers, beginning with the Vietnam War era. What I encountered in the officers and soldiers of the 10th Mountain Division reinforced my faith in America. If we can field such magnificent men as these in times of peril, then all is still well with the nation.

ONE

Sergeant First Class Ronnie Montgomery never passed the large glass case at 4ᵗʰ Battalion headquarters on Fort Drum without stopping. Framed photographs of young men in uniform looked back at him, some smiling, others wearing the sober expressions of youth just out of high school and boot camp who were starting to realize that decisions have consequences. The memorial case had been almost empty fifteen months ago when the 2ⁿᵈ BCT (Brigade Combat Team) of the 10ᵗʰ Mountain Division deployed to Iraq. Now it was nearly full.

Montgomery, thirty-six, was a career six-footer with a broad face burned by the Iraqi sun and hair so high and tight that he hardly had any. His company alone, Delta, had contributed nine faces to the case. Not that they needed to be framed and displayed to be remembered. Who they were, what they were, was forever branded on the souls of those who survived the S-curves on Malibu Road in Iraq's Triangle of Death.

Manticore, as Montgomery recalled, was playing on the SciFi Channel in 2006 when the 10ᵗʰ Mountain began preparations to deploy its BCT to the Sandbox. The B movie proved popular among Fort Drum soldiers primarily because it featured a U.S. Army squad from the 10ᵗʰ. Tasked to locate and recover a missing news crew in a small Iraqi town, the squad arrives to find locals slaughtered by a mythical winged creature awakened from its long slumber by a terrorist leader determined to drive Americans from his land by any means. From the movie sprang a kind of dark proverb circulated among the soldiers: "In Iraq, monsters come out at night."

Fort Drum, the military post, home of the 10ᵗʰ Mountain Division, sprawled across a wide swath of real estate in the Thousand Island region of northern New York state thirty miles from the Canadian border, with the Great Lakes to the west and the Adirondack Mountains to the east. It was an old fort dating back to the early eighteenth century, but had been modernized over the years, even to include a runway for jet aircraft.

Montgomery began his army career here with the 10th fourteen years ago. Since then he had moved around a lot to other outfits and places— Panama, Belize, peacekeeping in Haiti, a combat tour in Kosovo. Along the way he gained a few stripes and lost a wife. What the hell. If the army wanted him to have a wife, it would have issued him one, as the old saying went.

It was good to be back at Drum. It was almost like coming home, even if for only six weeks before it, and he with it, moved out to the war zone. Things didn't seem to have changed much over the years. The 10th was still a plain light infantry outfit specializing in shooting and walking long distances carrying heavy loads. It maintained little connection with its old traditions as a "mountain" unit, other than for streets named after its World War II exploits at Anzio, Riva Ridge, and Mount Belvedere.

It had taken him three years to get this far. He had been assigned to a support platoon with the 101st Airborne when Operation *Iraqi Freedom* kicked off in 2003. The platoon was getting ready to deploy when he received a call from Brigade Schools.

"Sergeant Montgomery, you're going to drill sergeant duty."

"Don't tell me that. I got a forty-man platoon here and we're going to Iraq."

"Sorry, *Drill Sergeant* Montgomery."

The ultimate test for a soldier was combat duty. Most soldiers secretly wanted to be tested.

Montgomery hoisted the duffel bag containing most of his belongings to his shoulder—a rolling stone in the army collected little moss—and dropped it off at the NCO quarters before reporting in. It was a hot July afternoon when he took his papers and checked in at Personnel. A staff sergeant behind the desk looked down a list.

"You're going to Delta Company, Fourth Battalion," he said. "It's a new company just now forming. Looks like you'll be a plank owner." He grinned. "Good luck, Sergeant. And watch out for monsters."

Montgomery groaned. The way things usually happened, a new company received green boots right out of basic training and rejects from other units in the division required to contribute manpower. Trouble makers, sad sacks, shitbirds. No sergeant major or first sergeant worth his stripes shitcanned his best soldiers to another outfit.

"Delta has a few problems," was how First Sergeant Aldo Galliano put it when Montgomery reported for duty. He was a short, wiry-built Hispanic of about forty who looked like he knew his way around the army. "Sergeant Montgomery, your 201 file shows you served your last tour as a drill. I think that makes you enough of a son-of-a-bitch to whip Second Platoon into shape before we emplane for Iraq in six weeks. They're good boys. They just need direction."

It was Montgomery's experience as well that most guys just needed a push. Since he had been a drill, the Joes in Second Platoon expected things to tighten up—and they did. He took over as platoon sergeant hard-assed and no-slack hard. A soldier had to have discipline, especially in combat. He had to be the kind of guy who would be *right there* when he was needed.

"Get with the program, people," Montgomery warned. "We have to look out for each other. That's all we got, is each other. You remember that when you start acting like a bunch of shitbirds."

Private First Class Nathan Given, twenty-one, came to Second with an attitude. A tall, slab-sided kid from near Houston who never let anyone forget that everything grew bigger and better in Texas, he was forever neglecting to bring his pen to mandatory classes, showing up late for formations, and generally just all-around goldbricking and not taking up his share of the slack. Montgomery and the platoon leader, Lieutenant John Dudish, counseled him and turned him back into the platoon.

There were a few others like him in the company. Joes who either didn't give a shit, who had a chip on their shoulders, or who had rather be somewhere else, *anywhere* else. Corporal Begin Menahem over in Fourth Platoon had a legitimate beef. He had already served one combat tour in Iraq during the 10th's 2004–2005 deployment. He had had twenty-eight days remaining on his enlistment when the army's Stop-Loss policy barred him from being discharged. And now he was headed back to The Sand-box one more time.

"I was this close to getting out, man. *This close,*" he said, holding up as emphasis a thumb and forefinger pinched together with hardly any space between them.

In spite of it all, Montgomery sometimes admitted to himself in moments of honesty how much he loved the army and its pig-headed, boisterous, irreverent soldiers. Infantrymen—the grunt, the ground-pounder, the mud-eaters—were markedly different from any other arm of the military. They were like guard dogs protecting the master's house—brash men, proud, sometimes reckless, quick to take action and always ready to defend each other against the brass or the enemy.

They came in a variety of shapes, sizes, colors, creeds, and religions. Hard street kids from the concrete jungles of New York and Los Angeles; cynical suburbanites from Chicago; tough hillbillies from the Ozarks and the Appalachians; trust fund babies from Park Place and poverty-stricken bros from the ghettos; farm kids, computer nerds, jocks; from high society or low society or no society at all. A cross-section of all that was America.

Once they came together and jelled, they were like no other army in the world in their devotion to each other, in a brotherhood of arms that no outsider could ever understand. It was that sense of shared danger to come that formed Delta Company, new that it was, into the close-knit camaraderie of warriors about to ply their skills. Sergeant Montgomery could think of no other place he had rather be than about to lead a platoon in combat.

The six weeks until August and D-Day, when the 2nd BCT would go to meet the monster, passed in a frenzy of activity that gave little free time for the Joes to brood on what might happen to them in Iraq. Soldiers under orders to give up their lives if necessary wanted to believe that the petty rules and chickenshit of the peacetime garrison went by the way-side. Quite the opposite was true. Days on calendars fanned past in up-dating service records and wills and powers of attorney, in verifying next of kin information, in receiving immunizations . . . There was the constant up-training, classes to attend in ROE (Rules of Engagement) and other subjects, personnel and equipment inspections, equipment to be bundled for shipment . . .

As always, there was more work to be done than soldiers to do it.

The worst thing about deployment was the waiting, the painful dragging out of the inevitable, the frustration of not knowing exactly when.

"I'll be home in no time, honey. You'll see," men reassured their wives.

"Don't expect to hear from me right away," they said. "I don't know exactly where we'll be."

"If, God forbid, something happens," they said, "somebody from the army will get in contact to tell you what to do and how much money you'll get from the government."

This would be Sergeant Victor Chavez' third combat tour since 2001. He had gone home on a quick leave and married his sweetheart, Rebecca. He had to rush to get her into the system as his next-of-kin.

"We'll start life when you get back," she promised. "I'll be here waiting."

Specialist Jared Isbell's sweetheart told him the same thing. He didn't know if he believed her or not. He looked at her a long time. Then they kissed, and he looked at her some more before she turned away with tears in her eyes and left.

The atmosphere grew somber at the end. Small clusters of soldiers gathered outside their barracks in the summer nights to chain-smoke and talk in low tones. Sergeant Montgomery, divorced for nearly two years, could often be seen around Delta Company late at night, reassuring his platoon, letting himself be seen. During its last deployment in 2004–2005, the brigade suffered 29 soldiers killed in action and another 422 wounded.

One of Montgomery's section leaders, Sergeant Chris Messer, had a reputation for being something of a hardnose when it came to discipline and training. One night, he let his shell slip a little.

"Sergeant Montgomery," he said, "my little daughter is starting to talk. She can say 'Da-Da.'"

He looked off into the night.

"Da-Da," he repeated softly.

Earlier, he had shown Victor Chavez a small laminated card containing the words to the Prayer of Salvation.

"Victor, this is in God's hands now. Victor, I got a feeling I won't be coming back from this one."

Chavez looked at him, slapped him on the back. "Hey, man. Knock it off. You're coming back. We're all coming back."

The 2nd BCT of the 31st Regiment, over 3,500 soldiers, consisted of two infantry battalions, one reconnaissance/cavalry battalion, one field artillery battalion, one support battalion, and one special troops battalion of MPs, engineers, military intelligence and the like. As deployment date drew near, Lieutenant Colonel Michael Infanti, commander of the 4th Infantry Battalion (4/31st), stood in front of his men on the parade ground for the obligatory gung ho rally before going off to war. A sense of pride enveloped him. These were *his* soldiers. It was his job, his profound duty to use these men wisely in the nation's fight against a brutal enemy—and bring back alive as many of them as he could.

"I want all of you to be assured that no matter what happens," he concluded, "you are not alone on the battlefield. This I promise you: In the Fourth Battalion, no soldier will be left behind."

TWO

All new soldiers reporting in to the 10th Mountain Division were provided orientation packets. In addition to schedules of events and services and maps of the post, the packet included a history of the Division reaching back to 1916 and the Russian Revolution. The modern 10th Mountain Division (Light Infantry), "the most deployed unit in the army," sprouted out of two separate and seemingly disparate roots, the 31st and 87th Infantry Regiments, one of which served not a single day stateside for more than forty years.

As a result of a treaty ending the Spanish-American War in 1898, the United States gained possession of the Philippine Islands and established it as a commonwealth. In 1916, the 31st Infantry Regiment was activated at Fort William McKinley as part of the nation's defenses. Less than two years later, the 31st along with its sister regiment, the 37th, shipped out to the bitter cold of Siberia to fight off hordes of Red revolutionaries, Manchurian bandits, and Cossack plunderers trying to gain control of the Trans-Siberian Railroad.

Sixteen soldiers of the 31st won the Distinguished Service Cross and thirty-two were killed in a war few Americans knew was being fought. As a result of its service in icy Siberia, the 31st Infantry adopted a silver polar bear as its insignia and became known as the "Polar Bear Regiment," a designation it retains today.

The 31st returned to the Philippines in 1920 and remained garrisoned in the old walled city of Manila until 1932 when Japanese troops invaded China. The Polar Bear Regiment, reinforced by the U.S. 4th Marine Division, joined a British international force to protect Shanghai's International Settlement, after which it returned to Fort McKinley.

The invasion of tiny Finland by the Soviet Union in 1939 germinated the idea that led to the commissioning of the 87th Infantry Regiment. After Finnish soldiers on skis promptly whaled the Russians by annihilating two tank divisions, American skiing pioneer Charles Minot Dole began lobbying President Franklin Roosevelt to create a specialized mountain unit modeled after that of the Finns. General George C. Marshall, Army Chief of Staff, liked the concept and ordered the army to take action.

Skiers, trappers, muleskinners, and assorted other outdoor types volunteered in early 1940 to begin training on the slopes of Mount Rainier's 14,408-foot peak. The 87th Mountain Infantry Regiment was activated at Fort Lewis, Washington, on 15 November 1941, three weeks before Pearl Harbor.

The day after Pearl Harbor, Japanese bombers attacked military installations in the Philippines. A 31st Infantry soldier at Camp John Hay became the first casualty of the Japanese campaign to seize the islands. Enemy troops landed in both northern and southern Luzon in a rapid pincher movement to capture Manila. The 31st Infantry covered the withdrawal of American and Filipino forces to the Bataan Peninsula, fighting the invaders to a standstill for over four months.

Finally, starving and out of ammunition, the Bataan Defense Force surrendered on 9 April 1942. Of the 1,600 members of the 31st who began the Bataan Death March, roughly half perished either during the march or during the nearly four years of brutal captivity that followed. Twenty-nine Polar Bears earned the Distinguished Service Cross and one was recommended for the Medal of Honor, but the entire chain of command died in captivity before medal recommendations could be submitted.

In the meantime, the 87th Infantry Regiment was redesignated as the 10th Light Division (Alpine) and saw its first action in August 1943 during assault landings against Japanese who had occupied Kiska and Attu in the Aleutian Islands. In November 1944, it acquired its modern designation as the 10th Mountain Division and entered combat in Italy three months later.

The division fought its way across Italy, crossing the Po River and securing Gargano and Porto di Tremosine before German resistance ended in April 1945. The division earned fame in climbing unscalable cliffs in order to surprise and assault German positions.

Deactivated after the war, the division would be reactivated and deactivated three times during the next four decades. The 31st Infantry Regiment, however, remained on active duty status. General Douglas MacArthur assigned it to the 7th Infantry Division for occupation duty in Korea, where it remained until the occupation ended in 1948.

The regiment moved to the Japanese island of Hokkaido, but its stay was cut short by North Korea's invasion of the South in 1950. The 31st returned to Korea as an element of General MacArthur's invasion force at Inchon.

After Inchon, the regiment launched a second assault landing at Iwon, not far from Vladivostok, Russia. Polar Bear troops pushing toward the Yalu River suddenly encountered the Red Chinese Army sweeping down from Manchuria. Surrounded in a steel corridor of death, only 365 members of the task force's original number of 3,200 survived. Lieutenant Colonel Don Faith, who took command of what was left of the 31st Regiment after Colonel Alan MacLean was killed, also died trying to break out of the trap and lead his survivors to safety. He was posthumously awarded the Medal of Honor.

Battered and bloody and all but decimated, the 31st evacuated by sea to Pusan where it rebuilt and retrained, then plunged back into battle to stop the Chinese at Chechon and join in the counteroffensive to retake Central Korea. By 1951, the line more or less stalemated along the 38th Parallel.

For the next two years, the 31st slugged it out with Chinese and North Koreans across a series of cold, desolate hills that bore such names as Old Baldy, Pork Chop Hill, Triangle Hill, and OP Dale. By the time the war ended, the Polar Bear Regiment had suffered many times its strength in losses, and five of its soldiers had won Medals of Honor.

In 1957, the U.S. Army reorganized infantry regiments into battle groups. The 31st Infantry of the 1st Battle Group remained in Korea with the 7th Infantry Division while its counterpart, the 31st Infantry of the 2nd Battle Group, formed at Fort Rucker, Alabama. After 41 years, for the first time in its history, the regiment's flag flew over its U.S. homeland. Until then, it was the only regiment in the army never to have served inside the continental United States.

The Vietnam War was beginning to build up some steam by that time. In 1963, the army abandoned the battle group concept and brought back brigades, regiments, and battalions. The 4th Battalion of the 31st Infantry Regiment (4/31st) was activated at Fort Devens, Massachusetts, in 1965. Less than a year later, it was operating in Vietnam's War Zone D and around Tay Ninh near the Cambodian border. The 4th Battalion was part of the last brigade to leave Vietnam.

The Reagan buildup of the armed forces in 1985 finally merged the 31st Infantry Regiment with a reconstituted 10th Light Division to permanent status as the 10th Mountain Division (Light Infantry). No longer strictly "ski" or "mountain" troops, the division's strength lay in its ability to deploy by sea, air, or land anywhere in the world within 96 hours of being alerted, prepared to fight under harsh conditions of any sort.

Throughout the 1990s and early 21st Century, the 10th continued to add to its reputation for being the most deployed unit in the U.S. Army. Its list of tours in far-flung and war-torn regions circumnavigated the globe: Haiti, the Horn of Africa, Djibouti, Ethiopia, Bosnia, Somalia, the Sinai, Qatar, Kuwait, Kosovo, *Desert Storm* in Iraq, Afghanistan, Operation *Iraqi Freedom* . . .

During the Battle of Mogadishu in Somalia, made famous by the book and movie *BlackHawk Down*, the 10th Mountain provided infantry for the UN quick reaction force sent into the embattled city to rescue Task Force Ranger. Two division soldiers died in the fighting.

In 2001, 10th Mountain soldiers were involved in the famous rescue of downed Navy SEALs during Operation *Anaconda* in Afghanistan.

Four Brigade Combat Teams composed the 10th Mountain Division— the 1st BCT known as "Warriors;" the 2nd BCT "Commandos;" 3rd BCT "Spartans;" and 4th BCT "Patriots." During its 2004–2005 deployment to Iraq, the 2nd BCT assumed responsibility for the entire sector of western Baghdad, from Abu Ghraib and Monsour to the notorious "Route Irish" running from Baghdad Airport to the International Zone. The area harbored the largest number of enemy in the country, resulting in the highest concentration of casualties among American soldiers operating there.

And now, in August 2006, soldiers of the 10th Mountain Division were once again going into harm's way.

THREE

As a show of solidarity, of faith in a common mission, Iraqi Army soldiers in their dark-patterned combat uniforms stood formation with U.S. soldiers when Lieutenant Colonel Michael Infanti uncased 4/31st colors during a brief ceremony at Camp Striker in Baghdad on 17 September 2006. Standing at attention under the desert sun, every soldier in the battalion from the greenest private to the commander himself couldn't help being aware that this war had changed from the lightning strike of 2003 that brought U.S. troops all the way to Baghdad in a matter of weeks. Never in U.S. history before now had American forces been required to participate in large-scale urban fighting while simultaneously rebuilding the combat zone.

Iraq had descended into a sectarian hell in which thousands of Iraqis were being killed and millions more forced to flee the country. A particularly militant strain of Sunni Islam called Wahhabism flourished as the Sunni minority backed the insurgency in an effort to preserve the political power and economic benefits it had enjoyed under Saddam Hussein. Insurgents and terrorists were attempting to impose draconian Islamic law throughout the country. They carried out summary executions in the streets and villages of those who opposed them or cooperated with Coalition troops and the fledgling Iraqi government; conducted suicide martyr bombings against police stations, schools, and other public facilities; and posted cash bounties on the heads of Iraqi security personnel, National Guardsmen, and foreigners.

It wasn't unusual for a village to wake up and find the severed heads of its elders posted in the middle of the road. Even as the 4/31st prepared to move into its AO (Area of Operations), terrorists stopped a van at a checkpoint near Kharghouli Village, doused it in gasoline, and set it afire with the driver still inside. His crime: driving while Shiite.

American military forces were ill-equipped to cope with the new brand of urban warfare based on raw terrorism. No comprehensive doctrine existed for counterinsurgency outside relatively small units such as Army Special Forces. After the Vietnam War ended, the U.S. military focused training on rapid maneuver and combined arms, the so-called "Air-Land-Battle" concept that worked amazingly well in the quick "conventional" fight to liberate Iraq.

As the insurgency gained momentum after July 2003, U.S. troops pulled back into huge Forward Operating Bases (FOBs) far removed from the population and began executing "offensive operations" to destroy enemy forces. The U.S. military sallied forth daily in search and destroy missions against insurgents in civilian clothing whom they could rarely identify and whom the general population concealed and protected. American commanders launched large-scale sweeps to roll up enemy leaders and members, fired artillery to interdict insurgent activity, and used airpower to level the houses of those suspected of supporting the insurgency. After each operation, the Americans retreated to their consolidated FOBs and, instead of attempting to secure and hold ground, conceded the cities and countryside back to street gangs of insurgents.

Each division, brigade, battalion, and even company was left to its own devices on how best to secure and stabilize its AO, "doing its own thing." Predictably, the situation throughout Iraq deteriorated. Attacks against Coalition forces had grown from about 70 per day in January 2006 to more than 180 per day by the time the 10th Mountain's 2nd BCT arrived in-country.

The 2nd BCT commanded by Colonel Mike Kershaw was relieving a BCT of the 101st Airborne Division. To Lieutenant Colonel Michael Infanti's 4th Battalion and its four infantry companies fell the fertile area south of Baghdad, a hellish hotbed of subversion that had been appropriately dubbed "The Triangle of Death." During his long reign, Saddam Hussein had given this now-treacherous swath of land to loyal Baath Party members and close friends.

Infanti's AO encompassed roughly twenty square miles of terrain whose major feature, the Euphrates River, curved across the bottom to border the AO to the south, southeast, and southwest. The three towns of Mahmudiyah, Yusufiyah, and Latifiyah formed the apexes of The Triangle of Death. Yusufiyah, the regional township of Baghdad Province, lay fifteen miles south of Baghdad. It was a small center of about one hundred major buildings, fewer than ten of which were over five stories tall.

The road through Yusufiyah, designated as Route Sportster by the military, crossed the Euphrates River into Anbar Province at the Jurf Sukr Bridge. Control of the roads and the bridge allowed insurgents free movement into and out of Baghdad and Anbar.

Mahmudiyah, the larger of the three towns, was situated six miles to the east of Yusufiyah along a major north-south highway that connected Baghdad to Karbula further south. About three miles south of Mahmudiyah along the same road lay Latifiyah. Small, dirty, and impoverished, it was considered the most dangerous of the three towns.

Terrain around the towns was primarily river farmland broken into small family plots and sliced by numerous canals and irrigation ditches.

"It's a real mix of bad guys," 101st Airborne officers advised their incoming counterparts. "Thugs and criminals as well as insurgents. It's a crossroads for terrorists. They move in and out along lines that stretch in all directions."

Three 101st Airborne soldiers had been attacked near the Jurf Sukr Bridge three months before. One was killed outright while the other two were kidnapped. Four days later, their bodies turned up near the old Russian power plant on Route Malibu. They had been burned, beheaded, and booby trapped with explosives between their legs. The Mujahedeen Shura Council, a prominent insurgency group operating in the Yusufiyah enclave, claimed responsibility and released a video to Al Jazeera TV showing the soldiers being executed and mutilated.

"These people had rather kidnap soldiers than kill them outright," 101st officers explained. "Makes better TV propaganda. Al Jazeera is always eager to display terrorist atrocities to the Arab world—and the Arab world is always eager to view them."

This would be Lt. Colonel Infanti's second combat tour to Iraq. During the 2004–2005 deployment, he had served as deputy brigade commander.

That experience convinced him that the old methods of conducting the war simply weren't working. Having been promoted to battalion commander, with the autonomy that provided, he had utilized the "downtime" between deployments to study everything he could find on counterinsurgency. He discovered a paper issued by General Creighton Abrams nearly forty years before—the PROVN (Provincial Reconstruction of Vietnam) Report—to be particularly helpful. It recommended that soldiers *clear* areas of the enemy, then *stay* and *hold* those areas while living among the people. Pound hell out of the bad guys while at the same time protecting the locals in order that the communities could rebuild.

In Infanti's judgment, the key to winning lay in securing the population. The primary reason why the Iraqis weren't rising up to throw terrorists out of their country was because of fear. They remembered 1991 when the U.S. failed to follow through. People then who backed change suffered terribly. Why should the Americans have the stomach to see it through this time? People not only in Iraq but around the world, judging from the statements of politicians and international pundits, were already urging U.S. forces to withdraw, with the collateral effect of leaving those who assisted them to the mercy of terrorists and fundamentalists.

"The turning point will come when the Iraqis see we're going to stay and not run," Infanti argued.

He would try out his theories in The Triangle of Death. The 101st Airborne Division had already started the process by fighting its way into The Triangle as far as Mahmudiyah and Yusufiyah and establishing more-or-less stable FOBs. Infanti's battalion task force would push even further. Rather than conducting large sweeps and operating out of a central base, his soldiers would begin manning small patrol bases and battle positions in the heart of troubled areas where they could work directly with the people. Like police precincts. Or, more appropriately, like forts in the heart of "Indian Country."

Colonel Infanti was a tall, broad-shouldered, plain-spoken man of about fifty with a chiseled jaw and piercing eyes. He firmly believed in keeping his soldiers informed, from the highest level to the newest private. Only in knowing the raw facts could a soldier comprehend his position and the role he played in the "Big Picture." He had started laying out the mission for his men even before the battalion left Fort Drum.

"We can go in there and take over positions from the 101st Airborne, hole up, and get shot at for the next year," he had said, "or we can attack where these guys live. In doing this, we have to be realistic. We are going to take losses. This is probably the last time we're all going to be here together."

Now, at Camp Striker, Infanti made it even plainer that his 4/31st soldiers were not going to sit out the tour with their thumbs up their asses. They were going to take the fight to the enemy as soon as they settled in.

"The bad guys are *out there*. We have to go *out there* and live with them while we kick ass. Once we get started, we're not backing off. We have to prove to the people that we're here with them as long as they need us. This is your land now," he told his soldiers. "You defend it, you protect it, you bring peace to the people."

FOUR

In previous wars, you were on *this* side of the line. You shot anything or anybody out there on the *other* side of the line. In that respect, the modern soldier was not so different from the one of a century ago or, for that matter, from the Roman Centurion in first-century Judea. Today's ground pounder could readily identify with the American 1st Cavalry in Vietnam's Ia Drang valley, with the "Big Red One" slogging through Italy during World War II, or even with General Washington's troops crossing the Delaware. It was the foot soldier's task to find, fix, and kill the enemy while avoiding having the same thing done to him.

Things in this war, however, didn't seem all that simple. Rather than clarifying things, the new Rules of Engagement (ROE) left the Joes confused and uncertain, afraid that if they made a mistake and shot at the wrong time they might be charged with murder after the fact by people far removed from the reality of what things were really like.

"It's a question of proportionality of return fires if the enemy initiates contact with you," was how ROE classes went at Fort Drum. "If, on the other hand, you initiate the contact, the question you must consider concerns the collateral damage you may inflict."

Huh?

Sergeant Ronnie Montgomery broke it down for his Second Platoon. "That means you can't go around shooting up everybody. If some asshole takes a shot at you from a house, that doesn't necessarily mean you can blow it up or burn it down. Say a dozen ragheads use innocent civilians as a shield and open fire on us, we don't blast back and take the chance of harming innocent citizens."

"So what do we do? Let the fuckers kill us?"

"To win this war, we have to win hearts and minds," ROE instructors stressed. "We're dedicated to liberating the Iraqi people, not killing them. We accomplish that through kindness and understanding."

"And," someone added, "a 5.56 round through the head."

"That's a bad attitude to go over there with, soldier."

"You still haven't told us what we're supposed to do—let 'em kill us while we play nicey-nice?"

During the battle handoff and transition phase, Lt. Colonel Infanti's 809-member task force composed of his 4th Battalion, elements from the Iraqi Army, and small detachments from other U.S. units moved in with the 101st to occupy the FOBs at Mahmudiyah and at Yusufiyah, where Infanti would establish Battalion Headquarters before stretching out to build what would become the first Coalition presence in parts of The Triangle of Death.

FOB Yusufiyah consisted of a pair of large concrete-block buildings surrounded by ten-foot-tall cement blast walls and razor wire. An electrical fire had gutted one of the buildings earlier that year, forcing some soldiers and activities into large GP tents out in the yard. The surrounding terrain was mostly flat, desert-looking, with a few date palms growing along the banks of numerous canals. The town of Yusufiyah began outside the walls with a scattering of businesses and residences along a single thoroughfare.

FOB Mahmudiyah was similar to the one at Yusufiyah, except it enclosed more ground, the walls were higher, and a Bradley fighting vehicle blocked the gate. Iraqi flags, not American ones, flew over both bases and would fly over all new positions. After all, this *was* Iraq and not U.S. territory.

At first, things were relatively quiet, about like two fighters checking each other out from their corners before the bell rang. Here and there, hate-filled stares and graffiti splashed in red paint on a wall—DOWN TO USA—reminded the newcomers of the danger seething beneath the surface. The Joes were already apprehensive not only about the danger but also about what might be required of them and whether or not they could measure up to it. To that was added cultural shock. The "fertile crescent" was not nearly as fertile as GIs on their first combat tour to Iraq imagined it to be.

"Some people believe the Garden of Eden was located in the Tigris-Euphrates River Valley," observed PFC William "Big Willy" Hendrickson, twenty, who wanted to go on to college after he left the service and eventually teach history. "Can you believe it? We've invaded the Garden of Eden!"

Houses in the towns and villages belonging to the common people were mainly mud brick and cinderblock built low to the ground, tan or brown and rendered otherwise almost colorless by the scouring effects of sand and desert winds. The squalid structures contained little furniture and sometimes almost no food. Family members of all ages and sexes slept in single rooms on thin blankets spread on the floor, or on the rooftops when the night heat of summer became unbearable.

Running water was for the most part a luxury enjoyed by few, especially in the more rural villages and communities. Stripped-down Russian tanks sat jacked up on blocks in vacant lots, the Iraqi version of hillbilly pickup trucks in the Ozarks. Trash and garbage filled the yards and choked off streets. Raw sewage filled the air with the pungent odors of human refuse and decay. In the open-air markets—and every community had one—piles of skinned and boiled sheep heads attracted swarms of greenhead flies. Plucked dead chickens and skinned goat carcasses hanging from racks drew even more flies.

"How do you suppose they cook that stuff?" PFC Alfredo "Chiva" Lares wondered. He was a solidly built Latino from California who wanted to be a cop when he got out of the army.

"Nasty fucking stuff, ain't it?" his buddy PFC Robert Pool said. "Maybe they season it with flies."

Most of the Iraqi men wore Western clothing accessorized by dingy red-and-white *shemaghs,* the multipurpose headscarf adopted by Middle Eastern males. Children up to a certain age went bare-headed. Women were less than stylish in form-concealing robes, mostly black, with their heads and often their faces covered.

"Some of the young Iraqi girls are real hotties, but they grow up into old hags," soldiers of the 101st sagely advised their replacements.

PFC Byron Fouty was doubtful. "How can you tell the hotties from the hags, what with all the bed sheets they're wearing?"

People traveled by foot almost everywhere they went; nearly everything they needed was within walking distance. Cows, geese, donkeys, hairy goats, sheep, and children wandered about, rooting through trash and the occasional abandoned Toyota. Women and girls sometimes stood begging on the flat tops of their houses with their palms up and extended.

"Come on down here, honey," soldiers muttered to themselves. "We'll treat you right."

Polar Bear commanders and senior NCOs at all levels, from Brigade down to platoons, met with their 101st counterparts during the transition, picked their brains, sat in on war council briefings and conducted "left seat-right seat" operations in which incoming and outgoing peers pulled missions together before transferring command authority from one to the other. The relieved unit passed down voluminous briefing books, maps, operating procedures, patrol routes, and other essential intelligence, along with a set of fully functional bases in which vital preparations like security walls, food services, and blast-resistant barracks had largely been completed.

Inevitably, a lot of valuable information was lost whenever a new unit replaced a veteran one. Although some commanders made concerted efforts to preserve intelligence relating to local insurgent groups and pass it on, what usually happened was that incoming officers and analysts ended up developing their own leads and sources. It was like inventing the wheel all over again. There was just too much information to be digested in a short time.

One afternoon, Sergeant Ronnie Montgomery and his counterpart linked up with a four-vehicle route reconnaissance and familiarization patrol from Yusufiyah to the Jurf Sukr Bridge. Much of the road to the Euphrates was dirt or gravel before it reached the bridge and turned into the bleached macadam designated as Route Malibu by army planners. Malibu Road curved alongside the river from roughly south toward the north.

Montgomery had expected the Euphrates to be a great waterway like the Mississippi or the Nile. Instead, it was rather narrow, often shallow, muddy, and so slow moving in many places that it was practically stagnant. How could such a sorry excuse for a river have ever spawned "the cradle of civilization"?

The little convoy stopped at the bridge. Malibu Road had earned a sinister reputation for itself.

"This is as far as we go," Montgomery's counterpart announced. "We get blown up every time we go there—so we stopped going."

Montgomery got out of his hummer, fired up a cigarette, and stood looking up the road. Built into a bed from the surrounding lowlands, it didn't strike the sergeant as particularly ominous, not in the full light of day. But thick groves of date palms, eucalyptus trees, and patches of reeds higher than a man's head lined either side of the road where there were no farm houses. Shifting patterns of shadow might easily conceal killers waiting for troops to venture into their domain.

"We'll drive any road in Iraq," said the 101st sergeant, squinting into the forbidden lands, "but when we're called to drive Malibu, we're scared. You will never control that road. If you try, all of you will die."

FIVE

When he was a kid growing up in New Mexico, PFC Sammy Rhodes used to lie on the summer banks of a pond and watch the dragonflies quick-dart here and there, hovering sometimes above a lily pad or sprig of water weed sticking up above the surface. They were long-bodied, slender little insects with wings that beat so fast they blurred silver. Black Hawk helicopters reminded him of giant dragonflies, only darker with guns and rockets.

The two choppers on the pad at Jusufiyah turned over their engines. Blades curving toward the ground from their own weight began to build up centrifugal force and straighten out. Red-and-green running lights winked on and off in the darkness; they would black out once the aircraft lifted off and reached altitude, remain blacked out until the two birds had airlifted Delta Company's First Platoon onto the outskirts of Kharghouli Village. For most of the men, tonight's would be their first combat mission.

They were nervous about it, as well as curious. They smoked cigarettes, the butts winking like fireflies as they sucked on them, brightening and illuminating the tension in young faces. Mostly they were quiet now, waiting. Platoon Leader Lieutenant Allen Vargo and Platoon Sergeant Charles Burke were all over the field, working with squad and section leaders to get everything lined out, make sure the loading order was a go.

"Stand by!" Specialist Alexander Jimenez shouted above the roar of turning rotors. One of the platoon's two section leaders, Jimenez, twenty-five, was a muscle-building Latino from Michigan and, now on his third combat tour in Iraq, the platoon's saltiest vet. The guy never seemed to lose his sense of humor, no matter what. He could even tell jokes in Arabic, a language he had taught himself during previous deployments.

"Stand by. Don't worry, children. *Papacito* will take care of his babies. I even change diapers."

According to the operations order, bad guys were infiltrating through Khargouli and Rushdi Mulla to Baghdad, back and forth from across the river and out of Anbar. All over the AO, 4th Battalion companies were engaged in similar air assaults in first efforts to cut off the movement avenues, or at least put a kink in them preparatory to establishing company FOBs and patrol bases.

Second Platoon's helicopters had already lifted off into the night sky and disappeared with a movement of shadows and a rush of rotor wind. That meant First Platoon was next. As soon as both elements were on the ground again, First Platoon would set up its anvil on one side of the village against which Second Platoon would smash any enemy combatants it happened to run out when it swept through the settlement searching for weapons caches and rolling up or shooting suspected terrorists. S-2 (Intelligence) had provided the commanders of each element with a list naming high-value targets believed to be working in the area.

What the night was really about, everyone supposed, was to let the locals know there was a new sheriff in town. The Polar Bear could be nice, or the Polar Bear could be hard-assed. Peace and freedom began with superior firepower.

Word came down. The troops of First Platoon began to load, shuffling toward the waiting birds. Jimenez had once proposed, not altogether facetiously, that every GI be issued a personal squire to help him get in and out of vehicles, much like those who accompanied armored knights of old to hoist them into their saddles.

"And yours will probably be named what? Sancho Panza?" Jimenez' buddy, Specialist Shaun Gopaul, joked back.

It took the modern American soldier in Iraq longer to get ready for combat than any previous GI in history. A doughboy in World War I or a dogface in World War II or Korea drew on a pair of fatigues or woolens, buckled on his webgear, put on his "steel pot," picked up his Springfield or M-1 Garand, and he was ready to go out and fight. A grunt in Vietnam sometimes donned a flak jacket. But it wasn't until the end of the twentieth century that the military became more concerned with the protection of individual soldiers on the battlefield. A Joe in Iraq sometimes wore or lugged around as much as 150 pounds of "battle rattle." With that kind of weight, the infantry *had* to become mechanized. Units weren't about to go foot slogging over the Italian Alps or marching all the way across Germany.

Today, the well-dressed combat soldier started with a set of flame-retardant, heavy-duty digital-patterned ACUs (Advanced Combat Uniform) and rough-out tan boots. To that he added an armored vest padded with Kevlar SAPI plates that protected his front and back, both sides, shoulders, throat, armpits and, with the addition of a special flap, his family jewels. Theoretically, the armor would stop most shrapnel and bullets up to 7.62mm, the standard round for the Russian or Chicom-made AK-47 rifle used throughout much of the world. That meant the enemy now tried to aim his shots at the face, arms, or legs.

Optional knee pads protected against crawling and scrambling around in the rubble of a battlefield, not against bullets.

The FLK (Full Load Kit), or "flick," took the place of the old LBE (Load-Bearing Equipment) webgear used since World War I. It was a vest worn outside personal body armor for toting ammo, grenades, and other battle essentials. It was designed in such a way that a flip of the skirt while in the prone position placed everything within easy hand's reach.

The modern soldier's assault pack wasn't that much different from those carried into battle as far back as the Civil War. Nor was the nature of its contents, only their character: plastic bottles of water; an extra MRE (Meal, Ready to Eat) or two; fresh socks and underwear; a weapons-cleaning kit; extra ammo; shaving kit; a paperback novel; a couple of to-be-reread letters from back home; and a few other items that might be needed or might make life a little more comfortable.

A Kevlar ACH (Advanced Combat Helmet), or "nitch" as it was called, topped off the ensemble. No previous American grunt had ever gone to war so heavily laden.

On top of everything else, Sammy Rhodes, twenty, lean with long muscles on a modest frame, carried his squad's "two-forty," a 7.62mm

M240B machine gun that was the updated version of the old M60 used in Vietnam. It was a solid, dependable weapon with range enough to reach way out there and touch about anything. It weighed over twenty pounds with a belt of ammo in its feed tray.

Rhodes' mouth was dry, his tongue like a cactus in a bed of sand, as his squad loaded onto the waiting aircraft. Who would have ever thought he'd be flying in a dragonfly? Around him, his platoon mates kept up a running patter to conceal the apprehension they were all experiencing. Apprehension, hell! They were scared to death, and they were scared their buddies would know they were scared. They were also excited.

Dan "Corny" Courneya, a nineteen-year-old PFC from Michigan, crowded onto the canvas seating next to Rhodes. "This ain't no place for a Polar Bear!" he shouted to be heard above the noise. "Do you see any snow?"

"So this is war, huh?" marveled Christopher Murphy, a short, squat little PFC carrying a SAW (Squad Automatic Weapon). He squeezed in on the other side of Rhodes.

"Not much different so far from an FTX (Field Training Exercise) back at Drum, huh?" Rhodes said, surprised that the cactus in his mouth let him sound so calm.

Platoon Sergeant Burke stood up in the cargo compartment and waved his arms to be noticed. All the lights were off, except for the aircraft instruments, which provided scant illumination.

"All right, people. Keep your eyes open and the noise down when we hit the LZ. We're in bad guy country. This is what we came for. *Hoo-ra!*"

War was hell, or so the old vets like to say. Up to this point, Rhodes' first time out, it wasn't so much hell as, well, *strange*. And scary. Glory and a place in history were okay; everybody wanted a piece of it. But mostly what Rhodes wanted was to avoid spilling his guts in Iraq. It was a bit disconcerting to consider that his sleeping bag might also serve as a body bag if he were killed.

SIX

The two choppers descended over the midnight land, coming in fast and steep to a stubbly grain field about 400 meters from the outskirts of Khargouli Village. Few lights shone from the houses this time of night, only a pinprick in a window here and there. Insomniacs perhaps. The field looked vacant through the two-dimensional, grainy-green imagery of the optics soldiers wore for night vision.

Sammy Rhodes leaned forward in his canvas seat to look out the chopper's open door as the bird flared and hovered a few feet above the ground. The next thing he knew, everything went into overdrive. Guys were slapping each other on the butt, arm, or leg to rush them out the doors. The pilots were in a hurry. Choppers were at their most vulnerable to small arms fire and RPGs during troop airlift operations.

Rhodes leaped into the darkness, stumbled under the weight of his heavy weapon and gear when he hit the ground, and went to his knees. He scrambled to his feet, weapon ready, his heart pounding so hard in his chest he thought everybody in Khargouli could hear it. Immediately, the Black Hawks lifted up in a black wind tunnel and were gone, behind them on the field the awful, ringing silence that followed an air assault after the machines were gone and there was nothing left but men.

Lieutenant Vargo and Sergeant Burke got the patrol into overwatch and it moved out toward the sound of a dog yapping in its sleep and a rooster crowing. In the air hung the stench of animal dung and human feces and garbage, unmistakable indications of a settlement nearby. In their NVs (night-vision devices) and body armor, the guys looked goggle-eyed and bulked up to unbelievable proportions. Soldier noises of breath coming in gasps and gear rattling sounded loud enough to summon every hajji with a homemade bomb and a rifle from here to Baghdad. Rhodes imagined an ambush waiting behind every bush.

Moving in the dark toward the back approach to Khargouli, the patrol negotiated neglected fields and weaved through a maze of levees, ditches, irrigation canals, and reed patches. Dusty country lanes bordered by tall, vertical-thatch fences and crude, mud-walled huts helped point the way. Lieutenant Vargo coordinated the effort through constant radio contact with Second Platoon.

A narrow canal temporarily halted the platoon near the rear of the town. It seemed shallow enough. Through NVs, Rhodes watched Murphy, Joe Anzak, and several others ease into water up to their waists and wade on across, weapons above their heads.

Rhodes didn't think to follow the footsteps of the others. He searched for footing at his own crossing and waded in, hoisting the heavy two-forty above his head. The water reached his chest. Four or five more steps and he would be across.

Suddenly, the bottom of the canal fell out from underneath his boots. Weighted down with Kevlar, the machine gun, extra ammo and grenades, he sank instantly in ten feet of water. There was no way he could stay afloat, much less attempt to swim. As he went under, the first thought that came to mind was that, on his first day at war, he was going to drown in a canal filled with Third World shit and filth.

But he was determined not to drown without a struggle. As the warm water closed over his head, he kicked off the grassy bottom and lunged, reaching with one hand and holding onto the machine gun with the other. The lieutenant would have his ass if he lost it.

He reached as far as he could, desperately grasping with his hand, the only part of him above water. He caught a fistful of grass and reeds. He pulled and, to his dismay, felt the grass break free in his hand.

The next thing he knew, arms were dragging him out of the canal. A couple of men had thrown themselves belly-down in the reeds and grabbed his arm at the last possible moment. He lay on his back looking up at the black sky while he spluttered and gasped for breath.

"You are one lucky Joe that we saw your hand before you went under for good," Murphy said, kneeling over him.

Rhodes didn't feel so lucky. He coughed up water. "I swallowed some of that stuff. What kind of bugs and shit you reckon I'll get?"

Murphy chuckled. "Your dick'll probably fall off."

Sergeant Burke hurried back. "Keep the chatter down, for God's sake. What do you think this is, a Girl Scout outing? Rhodes, next time you want to go for a swim, take off your clothes. Let's move out. We got a job to do."

Rhodes was peeved. Hell, he was pissed off. He almost drowned and what did he get? Nothing but more shit from the sergeant.

Movement the rest of the way was slow and dangerous as the patrol approached the rear of the village. Lieutenant Vargo set up his blocking force on an extended line across a cleared field next to a road that presented the most likely avenue of escape for anybody the boys of Second Platoon might flush out.

By this time, Rhodes was shivering from his unscheduled submersion. Air in the desert could be surprisingly chill at night. Under instructions from the lieutenant, he set up his machine gun to cover a foot path leading out of the darkened village and settled down to watch and wait, dripping water and hugging himself against the cold.

From over to his right flank, he overheard a whispered exchange as Sergeant Burke repositioned Murphy and PFC Timothy Grom. By this time, Rhodes was so fucking miserable he could give a fuck about anything. It was a long time until the sun came up again, and everything was so quiet he doubted anything was going to happen. This was probably a dry hole, and that was fine by him.

Sergeant Burke went on down the line. Grom and Murphy were still shuffling about in the dark, finding a place of cover and concealment to continue their vigil, when a rifle shot almost caused Rhodes to jump out from under his nitch. He heard the unmistakable crack of a bullet zipping past his two buddies.

For an instant, he thought it might be an AD, accidental discharge. Except it came from somewhere in the village. Although he had never heard an AK-47 discharged, he knew the sound of a 5.56 M-4—and that wasn't it.

Murphy and Grom hit the ground as though poled with an ax, Murphy swearing and excited and crawling fast on his belly toward the nearest tree, like a crippled insect. Grom lay where he fell with his face buried in the dirt. This was the first time either of them had been shot at, the first time the platoon had drawn fire.

"Grom! Grom, you hit?" someone called out.

"Naw, man."

"Just lay there, buddy. He can't see you in the weeds."

"I think I pissed my pants."

Sergeant Burke raced along the front. "Hold your fire. Don't anybody shoot. We got people in the town."

That wasn't the only reason to hold fire. Hajji knew the rules of engagement under which the Americans operated better than the new kids on the block did. That was how he reduced his chances of being caught and punished. Shoot and scoot. That was his MO. Use a residential neighborhood, a mosque, or some other public place into which no American GI would dare return fire. Pop off a round or two and then haul ass.

This was fucked-up, Rhodes thought, *when they could shoot at you but you couldn't shoot back.*

"Break! Break! Break!" The L.T. (lieutenant) was on the radio with Delta HQ and Second Platoon. "Contact! We have contact. One sniper. Stand by."

Excitement surged through the platoon, but it didn't last long. In fact, the contact, such as it was, was almost a disappointment after all the buildup prior to the start of the mission. Just the single shot and after that, aside from the barking of dogs inside the town, nothing else. Second Platoon on its way through Khargouli rousted a couple of teenagers sneaking around with a jug of hooch.

It wasn't much of a war so far.

That is, it wasn't much of a war unless *you* were the one getting shot at. Then it was *war* whether it was one shot or a barrage. Murphy seemed surprised and indignant that someone had actually tried to kill him.

"The son-of-a-bitch shot at me! Did you see that? The bastard tried to waste me."

"We need to get the motherfucker," Grom said, furious and scared at the same time.

"Relax," Corporal Jimenez counseled. "This is just the beginning. You'll get your chance for payback."

By now, all PFC Rhodes wanted was to get this shit over with and go home. The first night in battle hadn't been kind to him. First, he damned near drowned. Then the hajjis started taking potshots. He had a feeling things were going to get much worse before they got better.

SEVEN

By the time of Operation *Desert Storm*, the first Iraqi war in 1991, the four-wheel-drive, wide-bodied High-Mobility Multipurpose Vehicle M998 or updated M1114 (HMMWV, "hummer," "humvee") had largely supplanted most light trucks within the U.S. military, including the old workhorse quarter-ton Jeep used since World War II and the Vietnam-era APC (Armored Personnel Carrier). At least seventeen configurations of the heavy-duty vehicle were now in service, ranging from cargo/troop carriers and ambulances to automatic weapons platforms and TOW missile carriers.

The army had drafted final specifications for the HMMWV in 1979 after concluding that militarized civilian trucks no longer satisfied tactical requirements. The hummer first saw combat in Operation *Just Cause*, the U.S. invasion of Panama in 1989. Over 10,000 were employed by Coalition forces during Operation *Iraqi Freedom* beginning in 2003.

Like the quarter-ton Jeep, the original hummer was designed for operations behind friendly lines and therefore was not armored against intense small arms fire, much less against machine guns and RPGs. It was not until after the Somalia disaster that the army recognized the need for a more protected vehicle to be used in urban combat.

AM General, a subsidiary of American Motors Corporation, began limited production of a fully armored humvee in 1996, the M1114. Only a few of those were available prior to the invasion of Iraq in 2003. "Up-armor" kits were installed instead on the original prototypes. These kits included armored doors with bullet-resistant glass, side and rear armor plates, and a ballistic windshield.

Where up-armor kits were unavailable, inventive soldiers improvised "hillbilly armor" out of scrap metal. In December 2004, Secretary of

Defense Donald Rumsfeld came under harsh political criticism for failing to provide better-equipped trucks. As a result, most hummers in the war zones were either immediately up-armored or replaced. By the time the 10th Mountain Division deployed its 2nd BCT, nearly all hummers in Iraq were the new, improved version.

The M1114 held up well against most small arms fire and lateral IED (Improvised Explosive Device) attacks where the blast was distributed in all directions. They offered less protection from a blast directly beneath the truck, such as buried IEDs and land mines. None of the soldiers was eager to test it either way.

Just after sunrise and the beginning of another sweltering day in early October, HMMWVs assigned to Delta Company, 4th Battalion, were lined up in front of the empty fire-gutted building at Yusufiyah, waiting for the anti-IED vehicles "Iron Claw" and "Husky" to link up. Delta Company was moving out in force. Officers and senior NCOs had been briefed and rehearsed over the last several days. As with other 4th Battalion companies, Delta was about to occupy and hold ground in its own AO—the four-mile stretch of treacherous highway known as Malibu Road that twisted in concert with the Euphrates River. Every soldier had already heard the disconcerting rumors about how the 101st Airborne feared to travel that route.

The Polar Bears had made their presence and intent known in a series of preemptive raids and air assaults. Now it was time for the companies to put Colonel Infanti's theories into practice—that only by living among the people and protecting them could the war be won. Delta would eventually occupy a Company FOB and two patrol bases or battle positions on the road. The grand strategy, as Buck Sergeant E-5 Joshua Parrish understood it, was for Delta to tame its AO step by step. Advance, occupy, or construct a "fort," hold and pacify the area, then move on down the road and do it again.

Parrish's Fourth Platoon, commanded by Lieutenant Joe Tomasello with Platoon Sergeant Louis Garrett had been tapped to occupy the first patrol base in the AO. Company, along with Iron Claw and Husky, would escort the platoon in, after which the Fourth would be left to hold its own ground. Parrish was a bit apprehensive, not knowing exactly how the local insurgents might react. Surely they wouldn't be foolish enough, or suicidal enough, to attack a heavily armed, heavily armored platoon.

Sergeant Joshua Parrish, Fourth Platoon's First Squad leader, had been working with his dad remodeling a house in Glenfield, New York, when terrorists flew hijacked airliners into the World Trade Center and the Pentagon on 11 September 2001. That very same day, even before the WTC finally imploded in toxic clouds of dust and smoke, he rushed right down to his local army recruiters and enlisted. It was his duty as an American to do *something*. He was nineteen years old and one year out of high school. Five years later, he was still in the army and still doing *something*.

He was a slender young sergeant, an inch over six feet tall, with cropped light brown hair, eyes that looked either gray or hazel according to the light, and a scar on his upper lip that gave him a wise, old-vet look. Conscientious and responsible, he had shaken his squad out of their racks as soon as he received the movement warning order at 0500. In the town outside the walls, muezzin were broadcasting their eerie, warbling calls to first prayers.

Corporal Begin Menahem and a new private named Pitcher were now tarping over a trailer hooked up to Parrish's vehicle. The trailer was full of MREs and water. No one knew exactly how long the platoon might have to survive *out there* on its own before it could occupy Delta's first position. Hopefully, no more than a few days. Intel sorts had tentatively selected a site in the first big curve of the road.

Lieutenant Tomasello came by while Sergeant Parrish was talking quietly with Menahem and several others from his squad. Tomasello was in his late twenties, broad-shouldered and almost Parrish's height, with a ruddy complexion and a friendly, open manner. The Joes liked him and respected his leadership.

"What do you think, Sergeant Parrish?" he greeted, looking down the length of the parked convoy with its turrets bristling in fire power.

"My boys are ready, sir. The sooner we start, the sooner we finish."

Tomasello clapped him on the back, eliciting a hollow sound from the SAPI plates in his armor.

"Keep them on their toes, Sergeant. We want to take everybody home with us when we leave."

EIGHT

The advance onto perilous Malibu was painstakingly slow, requiring nearly the entire day to penetrate even the modest distance from Battalion HQ at Yusufiyah to Route Malibu and the first big S-curve that twisted with the river. Malibu was fill road, which meant it had been elevated above the surrounding countryside to prevent its flooding and erosion. Clusters of houses, villages of sorts, thinned out on either side to small goat and sheep spreads and patches of wheat and barley or citrus orchards.

Incredibly enough, where there were no houses or cultivation was *jungle*. Beds of reeds as tall as a man's head insinuated themselves around and through swampy canals and irrigation ditches. Towering date palms grew so thickly that they blotted back the sun and produced premature shadows ominous in their depths. Ancient eucalyptus with their gnarled, lighter-hued boles and up-thrust roots resembled the broken bones of giants and trolls. Who knew how many terrorists might be hiding in there, watching with their dark eyes and plotting?

Pedestrians walked up and down the road, except in the heat of the day when most sought shade. Women in long, flaring burkas glanced shyly at the American invaders. Men in their *shemaghs* looked the other way. Whenever the procession halted for a few moments, usually because Husky had sensed a buried IED that had to be unearthed and disarmed, smaller kids ran directly up to the trucks, laughing and skipping and curious, and had to be warned off.

Everything was new and unfamiliar and therefore suspicious to the Americans. They had all heard the horror stories—of female suicide bombers and of kids as young as eight running up to a humvee and tossing a live grenade through the window. Only a few days earlier, a tank belonging to the 1ˢᵗ Cavalry had pulled to the side of the road near JSB (Jurf Sukr Bridge) to let one of its crew get out and take a leak. Along came a hajji rolling an old automobile tire. He looked harmless enough. The crew had grown careless.

The tire was full of explosives ready to go off on a remote electronic signal. As soon as the Iraqi was near enough, he hurled the tire against the tank and took off down a weeded canal. The explosion ripped tracks off the tank and busted the turret gunner's eardrums. The Joe taking a leak got up, dusted himself off, and vowed not to take another piss for the rest of his time in Iraq.

Husky led Delta Company's convoy. It resembled a road grader with a very sensitive metal detector up front instead of a blade. Whenever it sensed a metal object buried in the road that could be an IED, the operator marked the spot with paint and summoned Iron Claw to come forward.

Iron Claw—officially designated as "Mine Protected Vehicle—Buffalo"— was layered with armor so thick that it was nearly impervious to blasts short of a bunker buster. It carefully unearthed the suspected IED with its moveable iron arm and claw. Once the bomb was exposed, an EOD (Explosive Ordnance Disposal) team that accompanied Iron Claw moved in to disarm and remove it.

Several IEDs were discovered and neutralized along the short route, providing the men of Delta with their first look at what would become their prime nemesis. Most were salvaged 105 or 155 howitzer casings filled with dynamite or black powder and rigged with pressure-detonating wire. Others were lengths of pipe stuffed with a crude but effective homemade mixtures of diesel oil and ammonia nitrate fertilizer—poultry manure. Before the war began, The Triangle of Death had contained many of Saddam's major arms depots. Anticipating an insurgency, radical Sunnis had immediately raided the depots and appropriated the weapons, everything from 82mm mortars and machine guns to thousands of grenades, RPGs and AK-47s. If anything, the Islamic insurgency was well armed.

The sun hung low in the western sky by the time the slow-moving procession reached the big crook in Malibu Road. Company Commander

Captain Don Jamoles took Lieutenant Joe Tomasello off to one side near a rather nice house—at least by local standards—that sat among palms about fifty meters off the north side of the road, right in the bend. They smoked cigarettes, looked at the big house, and talked.

When Tomasello returned to Fourth Platoon, he said, "We have to hold what we got for tonight. This is where we'll build the first battle position on Malibu."

On this rock I will build my . . . fort?

Iron Claw and Husky rumbled on up the road, followed by the rest of Delta Company. Soon, they were gone and Tomasello's platoon of about twenty men was alone in The Triangle of Death, on what was considered the most dangerous road in Iraq, and the sun was going down. Corporal Menahem couldn't seem to shake *Manticore* from his mind. Monsters come out at night.

Tomasello circled his wagons, blocking off the road. There wasn't any traffic anyhow; checkpoints all over the AO restricted vehicles to military and emergency transport. Each of the four hummers backed up to a common center on the blacktop, each facing outbound to cover its own quadrant, bristling with .50-cals and M240B machine guns, 5.56mm SAWs, MK-19 40mm grenade launchers, carbines, sidearms and knives. An awesome amount of firepower for so small a unit. Even a conventional infantry company would think twice about attacking it.

That was little consolation, however, to the Joes in the trucks about to spend their first night surrounded by the enemy, deeper into the AO than any platoon had ventured before, gone where no man had gone before. For all they knew, they had been left with their asses hanging out ready to be chewed off. This was frontier in every sense of the word.

Private Michael Smith, who was always joking around, suggested they should have hooked up two or three more trailers filled with mortars and tanks instead of MREs and water. Lieutenant Tomasello ordered everyone to eat and get out and take a piss before nightfall. Nobody would be allowed to get out of his truck and take a chance on getting picked off by a sniper until after daybreak.

"Either do it now or pee in your pocket," he said.

"I'll pee in Smith's pocket," Pitcher said.

Although a hummer looked square and solid and roomy, like a souped-up Jeep on steroids, five or six soldiers and all their gear and weapons crammed into one left little room for stretching out to get any rest. Not that they were likely to sleep anyhow, even off-watch. They were too hyped.

The distant echo of a muezzin summoning the Muslim faithful to prayer reminded the Americans of how very far away they were from home. A half-baked moon rose through the date palms and eucalyptus that lined the road. It was October and nights were becoming cooler, especially along the river. Sergeant Joshua Parrish, manning the turret in his vehicle, commanded a view of the Euphrates River sheened by the moonlight. Fog rose in ghostly tendrils from the water. He could almost feel hostile forms creeping up on him.

Also in his vehicle were Michael Smith, Pitcher, PFC Justin Fletcher, and Corporal Menahem. Parrish constantly swiveled the .50-caliber machine gun, searching, watching. The others stared out into the gathering darkness, even those who had removed their NVs, ostensibly to get some sleep.

"Mayhem?" Smith whispered.

"Yeah, man?" Menahem said. Delta's First Sergeant Aldo Galliano had dubbed him "Mayhem" for no particular reason other than the similarity to his actual name. It stuck. From Florida, Mayhem, twenty-two, was of average size with an olive Mediterranean complexion and quick, dark eyes.

"This ain't no place for a good Southern boy," Smith said.

Smith was asking him if he was scared without actually coming out and saying it. It was so dark in the vehicle by this time that faces even close up were blurs against a darker curtain.

"I'm scared spitless," Mayhem admitted, interpreting the code. One thing about Mayhem, he never hid behind any phony macho.

"Naw, man," Fletcher said. "Know why? Yea, though we walk through The Triangle of The Valley of Death, we shall fear no evil—'cause we the baddest motherfuckers in *this* valley."

"You got that right."

They gripped their weapons and peered out the windows into the forest of shadows creeping closer all around them. Mayhem remained silent. *He* was scared; he had been in Baghdad during the 10th Mountain Division's last deployment in 2004–2005. Only a fool or a greenhorn wasn't scared.

The moon shone weak and pale, stars cold and distant. A cow lowed somewhere, answered by sheep bleating from somewhere else.

"You know," said Smith, "one of these days we're all gonna be back at Fort Drum having some beers and we're gonna look back on this shit and just laaaugh."

"Maybe so," Pitcher agreed. "But right now all this shit does is suck."

"You gotta love this job," Sergeant Parrish joked half-hearted from the turret. "Guys—"

He froze.

"Hold everything. I thought I heard something."

Tension shot right out the top of the hummer. Parrish scanned through his NVs. After a few minutes, he relaxed.

"It's okay. It's a fucking goat."

"Light him up. Barbecue the bastard," Pitcher proposed.

"Now look what you've done," Smith said plaintively. "I've gotta piss."

"Quit being a pussy. Suck it up. You know, the way I look at things, I'd kill every bitch and her son from here to Baghdad if it'd get me home a day earlier."

Looking through NVs made everything liquid and surreal. There wasn't much to see anyhow, what with the foliage and shadows. This land along the Euphrates was nothing like the desert most of the soldiers imagined Iraq to be. It was a very scary place where you couldn't afford to let down security. Ghosts of night fog creeping through the trees became, in the imagination, terrorists and bombers plotting, scheming, waiting for the right time to attack. The brush of a breeze through palm fronds, the snap of a falling twig, the sleepy chirrup of a night bird was enough to make soldiers flinch and look nervously about.

Hardly anyone dared doze off. Bad guys could sneak right up on the trucks and no one would know it until they were right *there*.

Around midnight, the sound of a distant explosion reverberated across the land, further escalating tension inside the trucks. Mayhem wasn't supposed to be here, not this time. Except for Stop-Loss, he would have been a civilian by now, hanging around the beaches back in Florida ogling the foxes in their teeny-weeny, itsy-bitsy bikinis.

He thought about going home at the end of all this and never coming back to this shitbag country where the babes covered up their faces, hajjis shot off AK-47s in the air every time they got drunk, and where American soldiers in The Triangle of Death were the biggest targets in the world.

NINE

For the first platoon to venture onto Malibu Road and *stay*, daybreak seemed an eternity coming. But arrive it did at last, as all things in time do, with a burst of color that first illuminated the sluggish stretch of Euphrates River visible from the curve in the road. After touching the river gently, slow sunlight melted yellow butter over an expanse of forest and undergrowth before touching the roofs of the few houses in the vicinity and reaching the covey of four humvees arrayed in defensive posture on the blacktop.

Corporal Mayhem Menahem opened his eyes when the sunlight caressed his face through the window. He blinked, surprised that he had managed to doze intermittently between watches after all. He looked out and saw an Iraqi man way down the road herding a flock of sheep from one side to the other, a scene from the Old Testament, including the crooked shepherd's staff the man carried. The muezzin were calling the faithful to prayer at the mosque on down the road, a five-times-a-day event. The magnified voices sounded like racing go-carts.

Things appeared so much less threatening in the full light of day than they had last night when most of Fourth Platoon soundly expected the enemy to hit them. A few even considered the possibility that they might never see another sunrise. Michael Smith, doing his turn in the turret, shifted to a more comfortable position and grinned down at Pitcher sitting behind the steering wheel. Both of them seemed a little abashed that, in the darkness, they had succumbed to their fears and imagination. Hell, there wasn't a damn thing out there after all, was there?

"How many armies over the centuries do you suppose have seen the sun rise like this over the Garden of Eden?" Mayhem mused.

"I really don't give a rat's ass," Smith decided. "What I need is a hot cup of coffee."

They ate in shifts, half on watch while the other half heated canteen cups of coffee over heat tabs and rummaged through the trailer for MREs. They stood around inside the circle of hummers flapping their arms against the morning chill that would quickly become a morning scorcher, farting, yawning, joking a little, and behaving in general the way soldiers do in an all-male environment.

Even before everyone finished eating, Iron Claw escorted up a convoy of army engineers with chainsaws and axes, along with an IA (Iraqi Army) interpreter who would remain with the platoon. Lieutenant Tomasello put everyone not pulling security to work with the engineers clearing timber and brush on the river side of the road where they would erect blast walls and stretch tents for Delta Company's first battle position along the road. It was going to be a primitive site at best—living in tents with few amenities. By comparison, the Battalion FOB at Yusufiyah was the Waldorf Astoria. Sergeant Parrish dubbed the budding patrol base Fort Apache; Smith referred to it as the Alamo.

From his experience of having been to Iraq once before, Mayhem questioned the tactical advisability of building in the curve of the road, which limited visibility in both directions. Lieutenant Tomasello agreed with him, but it wasn't their decision to make. Work continued.

Neighborhood residents shunned the newcomers. A few ventured out onto the road to watch from a distance, but almost no pedestrian came by, unusual in a country where everybody was constantly out walking.

"What, no welcoming committee?" Michael Smith wisecracked.

"You probably won't be getting cake and cookies," Lieutenant Tomasello said.

Mayhem looked up from work once to wipe sweat and happened to notice a rare, lone pedestrian. He was big and young, maybe nineteen or so, with his head bare. He wore baggy, filthy trousers and a shirt that might once have been any color but was now a dingy gray. His most striking characteristic, however, was the way he walked. He weaved back and forth, dragging one crippled leg and leaning forward sharply with each step to throw the bad leg forward. *Scrape, Thunk! Scrape, Thunk!* Stalking down the road in the gait of a physically challenged T-Rex.

A short while later, along came a gawky teenager on a rusty bicycle, pumping along bare-headed wearing sandals and a robe even dingier than the crazy legs guy's shirt. That was it until in the afternoon when the owner of the rather nice house down the road and his skinny son timidly took the initiative to come over. Mayhem observed them standing at the edge of the road, smiling and looking interested. He went up to them, along with Lieutenant Tomasello and the IA terp (interpreter).

The kid looked about thirteen or fourteen, wiry and strong. The father was short and rather stocky with a broad face, a scraggly beard, amicable brown eyes, and that perpetual smile. He said his name was Abu Ahmed Rafi Ibrahim Al-Hasan Al-Tikriti. Mayhem blinked. The terp, whose name was Sabah Barak, laughed softly and explained how, in Arabic culture, names were made up of a combination of the names of a man's grandfather, father and given names, along with tribal affiliations. *Abu* at the beginning meant a man had a son. Simply by looking at a man's name, you could tell to whom he was related, where he was from, and even where his loyalties lay.

The kid's name was Nezham. That was enough for his size.

Both appeared genuinely glad to have the Americans move into the neighborhood. Insurgents, the father explained through the terp, were vicious beasts that killed anyone who opposed them, including women and children and unborn babies. Americans would drive them out so the people could live in peace. Mayhem didn't know how much of that to believe, having learned from his previous tour to trust no Iraqi completely. If the guy was legit, he had a set as big as basketballs. Sooner or later, the insurgents would make him pay for consorting with foreign soldiers.

Abu Ahmed and Nezham went beyond lip service and volunteered to help in clearing the woodlot. For the next two days, they labored cheerfully alongside the soldiers in clearing a substantial portion of the woodlands. Fourth Platoon soldiers slept better at nights in their trucks in front of Abu Ahmed's house, having grown to trust him. They assumed he would notify them of anything suspicious. They also felt less vulnerable after having survived that first crucial night. They were also exhausted from playing lumberjack.

The engineers were about ready to start putting up blast walls when brass showed up from Battalion and declared that the blind curve was a shitty place to build a patrol base. Mayhem snorted in disgust. If the assholes at Battalion had had their heads out of their rectums, they could have saved everybody a lot of work and several tense nights forted up in trucks.

The brass strode across the road with Lieutenant Tomasello to look over Abu Ahmed's house. It was the same scoured dirty brown as most ordinary Iraqi houses, one story tall, with a flat roof that had a lip around the edges about three feet tall and two feet thick. Larger and nicer than most houses in the area, its five rooms would be quite adequate for a platoon base. It sat about fifty steps off the road in a grove of palms, but the open roof allowed views over and through the palms to an expanse of the road in either direction.

"It'll do," the officer from Battalion declared. "Cut down the trees and erect a blast wall around it."

So this was how they were going to repay Abu Ahmed and his son for their toiling—by kicking them out of their house?

TEN

Surprisingly, Abu Ahmed took his dispossession cheerfully enough. Of course, the U.S. would certainly compensate him generously. Some of his neighbors showed up with flat-bedded bongo trucks, and the Americans helped load the family's few possession onto them. The departure was cordial enough. Ahmed, his son Nezham, and all the neighbors with trucks insisted on shaking hands with every American.

While this was going on, the man with the crazy legs stalked past. *Scrape, Thunk!* He stopped and looked, then kept on going. *Scrape, Thunk!* Ahmed made a screwing motion with his finger against his temple.

"He is not right," he said through Sabah Barak, the interpreter. "He was once shot in the head."

By Americans or by insurgents? Mayhem wondered.

War is such that just when you begin to forget you're in one, it comes back to bite you in the ass. Mayhem's squad and several of the Iraqis, including Ahmed and his son, were gathered in the road saying last farewells when, suddenly, the air filled with the bloodcurdling whistle of an incoming mortar round.

"Holy shit! *Incoming!*"

Corporal Mayhem and Pitcher the new SAW gunner were standing next to their humvee with skinny little Nezham when the first round impacted only a few yards away, erupting in a fireball. The blast knocked Mayhem off his feet. As he slammed to the road, he heard shrapnel and road debris ricocheting off the truck. From the corner of his eye, he glimpsed the Iraqi boy being lifted off his feet and flying through the air like a foul ball until he landed on the other side of the road.

Soldiers scrambled for cover, some running for their armored chariots, other diving underneath them as mortar rounds exploded in a concentrated area around the vehicles, filling the air with sound and fury, smoke, fire, and shrapnel.

A shelling could be a terrifying event, especially if you were out in the open and explosions were walking all around and over you and there was nothing between them and you except God. Mayhem thought he might dig a hole with his fingernails right into the concrete.

He lifted his helmeted head an inch off the blistering blacktop. What he saw only a few feet away filled him with shock. Pitcher lay face down on the road, bloodstains on his back, his legs and arms working like an insect pinned down with a needle through its torso. Casting aside concerns for his own safety, seeing only a fellow soldier in trouble, Mayhem crawled to him as shells continued to stomp around in terrible eruptions all over the road.

"Medic! Medic!"

Doc Bryan Brown, the platoon's African-American medic and, at twenty, one of the youngest soldiers in the platoon, appeared magically at Mayhem's side. Cool and composed as he was, no one would ever have suspected he was under fire for the first time. Together, the two soldiers dragged the wounded SAW gunner to the cover of the nearest hummer. Blood dribbled from his nose and ears and his vest and trousers were ripped, exposing more injuries. Flying shrapnel had caught him in full flight and did a job on him. He was still alive and conscious.

"Mayhem . . . *Mayhem* . . . ?"

"Hang in there, dude. You're going to be all right."

"Am I going to die, Doc? *Am I dying?*"

"Easy there, Pitcher," Doc Brown cooed, ripping open field dressings while still lying on his belly. "Your plates took most of it. You won't die, do you hear me, man? I won't let you die."

It ended almost as quickly and unexpectedly as it began. Smoke hung heavy in the air among the trucks, swirling. The air tasted bitter from burnt cordite. Men called out to each other. Questions, reassurances.

A 60mm mortar was a relatively short-range weapon, which meant the fire had to originate from somewhere nearby, either from in the woods along the river, probably on the far side, or from among the scattering of huts down the road. Whichever, the perpetrators were already gone, fading away into the countryside like barracuda into the sea. No one had gotten so much as a shot at them. And, of course, it wouldn't do any good to call in artillery or mortars; there were no firm targets, and Americans never indiscriminately dropped hell into built-up areas.

Abu Ahmed discovered his fallen son. His wailing penetrated the ringing in Mayhem's ears. It was enough to make angels cringe.

Neither Pitcher nor Ahmed's boy were mortally injured, although both would be in recovery for quite some time. A QRF (quick reaction force) from Battalion rushed in and evacuated them to the Green Zone in Baghdad. Fourth Platoon never saw Pitcher again. He had a million-dollar wound. But for his armor, he would probably have gone home in a box.

The smoke laid, the sun shone bright again, and Iraqis down the road came out of their houses to stare. Mayhem stood in the road, blinking and filled with helpless rage. Delta Company had suffered its first casualty on Malibu Road. Insurgents had drawn first blood—and there wasn't a damned thing the platoon could do about it. The fuckers down there standing in the road must have known what was coming down, who the attackers were—but they were too frightened to say anything. None of them trusted the Americans to stay and protect them.

"That," Lieutenant Tomasello commented drily, referring to the mortars, "was the official welcoming committee. Does it make everyone feel at home?"

ELEVEN

Although the ordinary Iraqi did not support insurgency or al-Qaeda terrorists, he had lived under an oppressive government for so many years that he found it safer to stand back, keep his mouth shut, and wait for the Americans to leave—which they would do sooner rather than later. People were being forced to choose among three conflicting sides, either of which left them in the middle. They could side with the occupying infidels and their promise of freedom and democracy; they could revert back to the Sunni-dominated terror and tyranny of the old regime; or they could submit to Islamic fundamentalists and their petty, cutthroat society.

The minority Sunnis, who composed less than forty percent of Iraq's population and now most of its insurgents, had been Saddam's favorites. They had the most to lose by the coming of the Americans and Saddam's overthrow. Sunni tribes outnumbered Shiites in The Triangle of Death, one of the only regions in the country where that was true. Their hatred of the Shiite-dominated government in Baghdad motivated them to allow insurgent groups of all stripes, most recently al-Qaeda affiliates, to roam freely through the area.

A couple of factors acerbated the situation, the first being a seemingly endless supply of weapons looted from Saddam's old ammunition depots, the other the collapse of the economy after the Coalition invasion.

While only a relatively small hard-core cadre of Sunni fundamentalists and foreign bomb makers and sympathizers plotting and operating in a particular area had little chance of winning militarily, their aim was not to win in that manner. Instead, their intent was to destabilize the society by creating an atmosphere of generalized fear and chaos. They were nihilists who held nothing sacred, least of all the lives of those who got in their way.

Feared by most Iraqis, they were nonetheless not especially respected, liked, or trusted.

"Gunfire is like a symphony orchestra to us," declared a Jihad fighter captured by Bravo Company, 4th Battalion. "We cannot live without war and Jihad. *Allahu Akbar!* You Americans love Coca-Cola; we love killing and dying."

Lt. Colonel Infanti and his XO, Major Mark Manns, had held a long conversation about the reluctance of people in The Triangle to cooperate with American forces.

"How can we make them more afraid of us than the insurgency?" the commander asked rhetorically. "They all lie to us."

"They're scared to death."

Infanti nodded. "That's because they know we're not the ones going to take them out in the alley and put a bullet through the backs of their heads. They know we're temporary and that if we leave before the job is done, they'll still be here on their own with the bad guys, who will take them out in the alley."

Insurgency cadres amplified their power through coercion or by offering bounties on American soldiers and opponents among the Shiites. Attacking Americans had turned into a cash crop, often carried out by penniless young Iraqi men who formed loose-knit gangs to kill and to plant IEDs. There was little difference between them and U.S. inner-city gangs like the Crips or the Bloods.

It was relatively easy money. A bold or foolish youth could earn as much as $200 for shooting an RPG at Americans, double that amount for sniping with a rifle, half for planting an IED—with bounties doubled or even tripled if an assault resulted in the deaths of Americans that made headline news. Where did the money come from? Intelligence sources said it came from Iran and Syria and from terrorists groups like Hamas, Hezbollah, and al-Qaeda.

While Iraqi streets might bustle with commerce during the day, at night the people all hurried home and locked their doors. It was better for them to hear no evil, see no evil, and speak no evil against the insurgents.

Monsters came out in the dark to kill Americans. Thugs, criminals, and foreign fanatics turned the country into a free-fire zone.

During the final two months of 2006, Lt. Colonel Infanti's 4th Battalion established twenty-three FOBs and patrol bases in The Triangle. Of these, three belonged to Delta Company, all erected on that four-mile stretch of narrow, brittle blacktop known as Malibu Road. After Fourth Platoon took over and occupied Abu Ahmed's house and designated it Patrol Base 151, other Delta platoons occupied 152 down the road less than a mile away and then 153 on further north and west. Captain Don Jamoles selected 153 as headquarters for Delta Company and designated it as FOB Inchon.

Patrol bases 151 and 152 were single story, flat-roofed houses typical of Iraqi dwellings in the region. Inchon was a massive concrete and mortar structure, two floors tall, imposing and even luxurious. The owner, a Sunni, must have once held high favor in Saddam's regime to have been so well rewarded.

Four bedrooms upstairs and four downstairs were turned into soldier bunkrooms. Grounds outside proved sufficient to erect commo tents, build makeshift latrines, and park a fleet of humvees. Three reinforced guard towers were built on Inchon's roof, one each on the northeast and southeast corners and one on the south overlooking an expanse of date palms leading to the banks of the river. As at 151 and 152, blast walls four feet thick and ten feet high topped in razor wire soon surrounded the base, lending it more than ever the appearance of a cavalry fort on the American frontier in the early 1800s. Windows were sandbagged against mortar and rocket attacks so that life for soldiers inside was almost like being in caves.

The mortaring of Delta's Fourth Platoon initiated the battle for Route Malibu. Delta Company occupied the forts and began patrolling, making its presence known and felt on what was readily acknowledged as a lawless frontier and the most active area in The Triangle. During the weeks ahead, the troops would conduct hundreds of routine patrols, raids, and traffic stops. At the same time, Civil Affairs officers held weekly meetings with sheikhs and other community leaders to discuss improving schools, roads, irrigation canals, community centers, and other infrastructure. It was a mammoth project, but Colonel Infanti kept stressing that the only way to win was with boots on the ground seen out among the people. America would lose if he allowed his soldiers to hide behind their thick walls and razor wire.

This approach to war meant GIs patrolling their sectors may as well have worn targets on their front and back sides. They were fairly well on their own in squads and platoons, with very little air or artillery support. Even though Battalion commanded four 81mm mortar and 105mm howitzer batteries strategically placed throughout the AO, and Brigade had helicopter gunships and fast movers, they were seldom used because of the potential for "collateral damage" to Iraqi citizens.

Patrols were virtually assured of getting hit every time they left the walls of their fortresses. Attacks occurred almost daily somewhere within the AO, if not on Malibu Road itself. IED booby traps blew up passing vehicles. Snipers, mortars, and insurgent fighters began taking a toll. For the Americans on Malibu, each day and night was something to be dreaded and feared, a condition that exacted a heavy psychological penalty from soldiers tasked to drive out insurgents and bring peace and stability to The Triangle of Death.

TWELVE

First Platoon's convoy of four trucks was headed east toward Mahmudiyah on a long-route recon of Sportster Road when it came upon four IA
soldiers smoking and joking in the middle of the road. Lieutenant Allen
Vargo called a halt at a safe distance. Iraqi soldiers and interpreters assigned to work with Delta Company had proved trustworthy so far, but
no one knew these guys. Every now and again, a suicide bomber dressed in
IA or police uniform wormed his way into a chow hall or something,
touched himself off like a rocket, and wasted a whole shitpot full of friend-
lies. You could never afford to get complacent or careless in a guerrilla war.

"Jimenez, go up there and see what those assholes are doing," Vargo
instructed. Jimenez' command of the Arab tongue had proved valuable.
Terps were often in short supply or busy elsewhere.

Specialist Alex Jimenez clambered out of the hummer and approached
the uniformed Iraqis with a grin. The guy never seemed to have a bad day.
He returned to report that the IAs had located a buried IED and were
there to keep watch over it until somebody came up to dismantle it. Except it was getting near nightfall and the IAs were going to leave. You
weren't going to catch *them* out in the dark.

Lieutenant Vargo radioed Company HQ for guidance.

"*Delta One-Six,*" HQ responded, "*remain at the site and secure it until
EOD arrives.*"

The IA took off, leaving First Platoon at the scene as the shadows
lengthened and the sun turned a sick red preparatory to dropping out of
sight.

"Delta X-Ray, is EOD still enroute?" Vargo requested of HQ.

"*Negative, One-Six. They got tied up. You'll have to RON* [remain over-
night]."

Apparently, you weren't going to catch EOD out in the dark either.

"Tied up, my ass!" Sergeant Anthony Schober exploded. "Them fuckers are afraid of the night."

"And you're not?" Jimenez chided him.

The prospect of playing sitting ducks overnight had about as much appeal as undergoing a root canal without Novocain. Lieutenant Vargo circled the wagons into a defensive posture and placed everyone on fifty-fifty alert. There were a few little brown houses further down, open fields on one side of the road with a few hairy goats bleating around, and an orchard on the opposite side with an irrigation ditch full of water between the hummer and the groves.

"Rhodes, don't go near the water," Platoon Sergeant Charles Burke teased. Rhodes had become the butt of good-natured kidding since the night he almost drowned.

"Sar-jent, basically the only way I'm going to take so much as a bath in this shitbag country is in my canteen cup."

The orchard provided the most likely avenue of enemy approach. Having been neglected, it was grown up with chest-high weeds and undergrowth. Vargo and Platoon Sergeant Burke discussed putting out OP/LPs (observation, listening posts) but decided that would be suicide. The insurgents knew the terrain better and had already proved their ability to sneak around like jungle cats. Better to hole up inside armor and wait for daybreak. Isolated in Indian Country made for some long nights.

Twelve hours later, the sun was coming up again after a surprisingly uneventful night, the muezzin in distant villages were go-carting, and HQ advised that Second Platoon was enroute with water and chow. First Platoon had gone through most of its supplies the day before and during the night. As for EOD, there were so many IEDs all over the AO that these guys were stretched thin and worn ragged.

Just when Lieutenant Vargo had about given up on Second Platoon, it rolled in with Platoon Sergeant Ronnie Montgomery's vehicle looking as though it had gone through the ashes of a forest fire. One front tire was wobbling and the windshield was coated with soot, except for a wiped-clean area that allowed the driver, Specialist Alfredo "Chiva" Lares, to see out.

The four-truck convoy had hit an IED on the way up Malibu from 152, likely command-detonated by some perp hiding in the bushes with a telephone wire and a battery. Nobody spotted the guy hauling ass in all the smoke and confusion. The bomb went off directly underneath Montgomery's truck in a burst of dirt, gravel, smoke, and road asphalt that jolted the passengers like pebbles in a can and made their ears ring. Fortunately, it hadn't been a big explosion and did little damage to the truck except knock the front tires out of balance and add a few more scars to its chassis.

Chiva Lares, the solidly built Latino from southern California who wanted to be a cop, had a sunny outlook on life that allowed him to laugh at life's little travails. He showed First Platoon guys the new dents in his hummer and ad-libbed a comical demonstration of the look on the redheaded Jonathan Watts' face when the IED went off. Everyone laughed with him, but nervously.

"I don't know how, but I knew it was coming," Lares said. "I swerved, but it was too late. It didn't hurt anybody, but, man, it sure caused some terminal cases of diarrhea."

Second Platoon moved on down the road toward a mission in Kharghouli—a hit on a suspected terrorist's house in cooperation with a QRF from Battalion. Some kids came out and waved at the trucks. Children out on the roadway waving and chattering and people going about their normal activities generally meant any American patrol in the vicinity was safe. But if the kids started running away with their fingers in their ears when they saw trucks coming, chances were something was about to happen.

First Platoon continued to wait on EOD. Rhodes rotated off his turret's .50-cal machine gun, relinquished it to Jimenez, and was relaxing in the back seat of his truck having a spaghetti-and-meat sauce MRE when he noticed somebody had tossed some litter in the road. Lieutenant Vargo had warned that if he saw one more soldier throwing trash out of vehicles, he would have the entire platoon policing up Malibu road with nails in sticks—although Rhodes couldn't see what difference one more piece of rubbish made in a country that already looked like a garbage dump.

Muttering to himself, he got out and picked up the empty MRE packet. A used MRE was almost as nasty as a used condom. He found a trash bag in the truck's back hatch and started to get back in the hummer when he noticed all the children who had been playing down the road were gone.

Just as he opened the door and bent to climb inside, he heard a loud crack from the overgrown orchard. Startled, he jumped back as a bullet struck the ballistic glass only inches away from his face, spider-webbing it but not penetrating. But for the glass, there probably wouldn't have been anything left of his head except a bloody pulp.

As he dived the rest of the way into the truck on top of Courneya and Gopaul, he heard the sharp spatter of automatic rifle fire coming from the orchard and the pinging of more bullets ricocheting off the truck's steel hull.

Holy fuck! The hajjis were right on top of them.

THIRTEEN

A sizeable number of Baghdad hajjis were popping up out of the brush in the orchard and rushing the trucks, blazing away with AK-47s. Not enough to describe as a horde, but still too many to count under the stress of the circumstances. Many of them wore black hoods and masks like executioners in the film clips Al Jazeera TV was always showing of Jihadists cutting off the heads of their infidel prisoners. Shouts and huzzahs rang from their throats, almost drowning out the clatter of their weapons.

"*Allahu Akbar! Allahu Akbar!*" God is great!

"Allahu Akbar *this*, motherfuckers!" Alex Jimenez roared back as, swiveling his turret toward the threat, he unlimbered his big .50-caliber machine gun with its steady, throaty *Chunk! Chunk! Chunk!* The .50-cal was designed for use against vehicles, not personnel. One slug through the block of a car engine exploded it. One slug into flesh and bone left nothing but scraps and offal.

For most of the men in First Platoon, this was their first time under fire. They responded to training and crisis, aware that they were in a fight for their lives, and returned fire with everything they had. Those not in turrets popped out of their trucks to seek firing positions behind them. The savage exchange thundered and howled with machine guns and SAWs surging to carry the awful melody while M203 grenade launchers worked counterpoint, geysering mini-detonations throughout the orchard.

Either the Jihadists weren't serious about the attack, or they had underestimated the resistance. The charge stalled and turned into a fixed gunfight, with both sides shooting at each other from behind cover. Sergeant Burke darted from vehicle to vehicle, all stooped down and scurrying with an M4 in his hands, checking on the men and encouraging them in their first battle.

"Everybody calm down!" he shouted. "Don't pull the trigger unless you got a target. If you ain't directly engaged on the orchard, I want you to orient south. I don't want any fuckers sneaking up on us from the rear."

As soon as he recovered from the shock of almost having his head blown off, Sammy Rhodes grabbed a SAW and scooted around to the front of the truck with nineteen-year-old Daniel Courneya right behind him, carrying an M-4 with attached M203 40mm grenade launcher. They raced past Lieutenant Vargo kneeling in the open door on the lee side of his hummer, yelling into the radio mike. They joined the fight, using the truck's hood as a shield.

A SAW, though a lighter weapon than the old faithful .50-cal or the newer two-forty, was still capable of dispatching an awesome swath of death and destruction. Rhodes stood on the trigger and raked the gun back and forth at muzzle flashes and enemy figures ducking and dodging among the trees and waist-tall underbrush, joining .50-cals operated by Jimenez and Specialist Brandon Gray in scything the underbrush into shredded mulch.

A hajji wearing a red-and-white *shemagh* screamed and threw up his arms. Another turned tail and bolted deeper into the orchard while Corny rained 40mm grenades down on his ass.

The radio net was alive with people shouting and screaming on both Company and Battalion frequencies. Captain Jamoles had to cut in to restore order.

"Break! Break! Break! Delta One-Six [Vargo], *this is Delta X-Ray* [Jamoles]. *Send your traffic . . ."*

"Roger. Contact! Contact! My platoon is caught in an ambush . . ."

"Roger that, One-Six. Tell me what you got out there. What do you need?"

"We're taking fire, X-Ray. Small arms . . . across the road in the orchard and next to us from the treeline . . . We can see them maneuvering. Estimate platoon-sized enemy personnel . . ."

Another overload jammed the company net.

"This is Delta X-Ray. Clear the net. Say again, clear the net. One-Six, what's the SITREP [Situation Report]*?"*

"We're handling them. They're pulling back from the orchard toward a canal and some houses . . . We're firing them up . . ."

"*One-Six, do not engage the houses* . . ."

"We're taking some fire from the built-up area . . ."

"*Repeat. Do not engage the houses. Do not pursue. Battalion QRF is on the way.*"

"Roger, X-Ray. Send in the cavalry."

The fight was over almost as soon as it began, a brief game of cat and mouse. As Delta Company soldiers were beginning to find out, short engagements of this nature were almost SOP with the Jihadists. Typically, they attacked with RPGs, AK-47s, and mortars to do as much damage as they could within a few minutes, then hauled ass because they knew reinforcements would be on the way. After dumping their weapons in a canal or other pre-determined cache location, they fled back to their houses and became Farmer Mustafas again, blending in because the locals were too intimidated to snitch on them.

Sergeant Burke ran by again. This time he was shouting, "Cease fire! Damnit, cease fire! Is anybody hurt? Is everybody okay?"

Unbelievably, no one had been hit, although most were pretty shook up. Rhodes took a deep breath and stood cursing to himself, swatting at flies, and staring at the shattered window that had saved his life. Corny was pale and blinking at the now-silent orchard, almost as though he found the preceding minutes hard to accept as having happened. Lieutenant Vargo looked pissed; he had been so busy with the radio that he hadn't got off a single shot.

PFC Joe Anzak walked over. He was a real horse of a guy, a hard-charging martial artist with a belt in Judo. He licked his thumb and touched the hot barrel of his M4 as though testing it to see if it would sizzle. He grinned.

"We lit up them fuckers," he said. "I saw we got a couple of them. Who's gonna bury 'em?"

"Not us," Byron Fouty said. "Muslims bury their own. It's part of their religion."

"They drag off their dead," Jimenez added, still in the turret, watching. "Probably won't be anything out there except an IED waiting for us."

The platoon felt pretty good about itself, even cocky in its adrenalin high. The only damage was to the trucks—tires shot out, shattered glass, bullet dents, and dings in the armor.

"We showed them assholes."

"Yeah, man. They won't be so eager to take us on again."

"We the killer platoon, that's what. We're killers."

"Get some local security out," Lieutenant Vargo ordered. "Keep your heads down. This might not be over yet."

"It was pretty hairy for a moment there, L.T.," Chris Murphy said, still riding his excitement. "Real intense."

"Yeah, well. For a dirtbag, thrown-together bunch of misfits and shit-birds, you guys did good. You proved you can drop the hammer. Give me a cigarette and we'll call it a win."

Rhodes showed Murphy the shattered window that had stopped the bullet meant for his head. First, he had almost drowned. Now this.

"It'll be a miracle if I make it through, Murph," he said.

The QRF assisted First Platoon in searching the battlefield. The insurgents had left nothing behind except trampled terrain, empty cartridge casings, and some blood trails leading deeper into the orchard and out along an overgrown canal. Rarely were bodies or other evidence found at a contact site. A separate Jihad squad always accompanied fighters to police up the battlefield of casualties and dropped equipment.

It was getting late by the time search squads had pounded on all the doors in the vicinity. Like always, no one knew anything about the insurgents; they must be out-of-towners, strangers. Right, and if you believed that, there was some beachfront property in Kharghouli for sale. The QRF flex-cuffed a couple of guys and took them back to Battalion for questioning and to test for gun powder on their hands. First Platoon never learned the outcome.

EOD arrived a few hours before nightfall to defuse the bomb in the road. Almost twenty-four hours late, First Platoon continued its route recon to Mahmudiyah. To add insult to injury, Sammy Rhodes' vehicle hit a second IED at a curve in the road. The massive concussion swept through his body and lifted the front of the truck off the ground, almost flipping it over backwards. It seemed everyone was shouting at once, but from a distance since Rhodes could hardly hear after the blast. He was also half-blinded from dirt flying up from the floorboard. The smell of engine coolant and battery acid made him choke.

The entire platoon breathed a big sigh of relief when it finally reached the FOB at Mahmudiyah without a single casualty other than eyes irritated by dust and ears stopped up from explosions and gunfire. Murphy commented how Someone must be looking over them.

Rhodes was still thinking about the shattered glass.

FOURTEEN

For several weeks after "the occupation" of Malibu Road, resupply for Delta Company's isolated platoons proved to be hit and miss. Supply convoys venturing onto the blacktop were frequently blown up, mortared, or waylaid by crazy martyrs, resulting in long delays while tow trucks pulled damaged humvees back to Battalion HQ at Yusufiyah for repairs. Sometimes, insurgents cut the road, blasting out impassable trenches in an effort to keep Delta isolated and vulnerable.

Guys began to complain, as soldiers will, that they were under siege, that al-Qaeda was trying to starve them out, and that Battalion didn't give a damn. Eating leftover MREs wasn't all that appetizing, especially if they had been opened that morning or the day before.

"Nothing's too good for Dyin' Delta—and nothing's what we're getting."

One morning after Sergeant Joshua Parrish offered to eat his combat boots if somebody had an extra bottle of hot sauce, a thousand-pound bomb blew up with an ear-shattering, house-rattling boom down the road from 151 and changed the day. It exploded directly in the bend of the big curve where Fourth Platoon RON'd its first long night in the AO and not far from where the Joes had labored two days chopping down trees before somebody in authority changed his mind and they took over Abu Ahmed's house instead and turned it into a battle position. Thinking themselves under attack, soldiers of the Fourth and Second Platoons, who were working together out of the PB for the week, grabbed their weapons, threw on body armor, and rushed outside to defend the perimeter. The sight of a nuclear-like mushroom etched against the near horizon stopped them in awe.

"*Holy shit!*"

So far, they had seen nothing that big, just the smaller IEDs that rattled bones, busted vehicle tires, and bent axles. An explosive that powerful would do a whole lot more. They hoped it wasn't a harbinger of things to come.

The blast blew a crater eight feet deep and the width of the road. As far as anyone could tell, the bomb had probably been buried there quite some time, including the night Fourth RON'd at the curve. Some of the guys went into mild shock for days afterwards every time they thought of what could have happened to the platoon if the bomb had cooked off while they were parked right on top of it. Its sheer size was enough to put everyone's teeth on edge for the rest of the day.

Michael Smith's first thought when he recovered was of resupply. He groaned. "No fucking chow today," he predicted.

Each patrol base kept a security force behind the walls at all times to defend against attacks and takeover. Lieutenant John Dudish's Second Platoon was pulling security while Lieutenant Tomasello's Fourth was on the day's schedule to patrol for insurgents and meet and greet the locals to win hearts and minds and the war while avoiding IEDs and ambushes. Everyone felt as though he had survived a close call with the big bomb and probably shouldn't even be alive.

With that kind of overall distracted mood and the resulting drop in morale in the platoons, leaders of both elements got together and decided to call a work holiday. The platoons would hold a backyard barbecue. Captain Jamoles needn't know. Fourth Platoon would go patrolling as required—but only to the nearest open-air market in Kharghouli.

Tomasello loaded up his men and set out. Morale picked up immediately. The expedition took on a festive air. Heavily armed and armored GIs descended upon the market in a rush that caught vendors and, hopefully, any insurgents in the area by surprise. Some of the platoon watched the trucks while Tomasello, Platoon Sergeant Garrett, and Mayhem Menahem quickly made their selections in order to be back on the road again before the local outlaws got over their astonishment and cooked up a little something of their own.

The choice of delicacies, as Mayhem noted sarcastically, was enormous. Dried or boiled goat heads, river fish in various stages of putrefaction, dead chickens and live chickens, geese flopping on the ground with their legs tied, whole sheep carcasses hanging in little open sheds, and kid goats tied up bleating by their necks, all garnished by swarms of black flies attracted to the stench. Women wearing *hijabs*, men standing around in dirty white robes, and barefooted, filthy kids stared at the soldiers.

Tomasello nixed a live goat. "Who's going to butcher it? You, Mayhem?"

"I'm no country boy. Doesn't Doc Brown have a scalpel?"

"He'd cure it and keep it for a pet."

Sergeant Garrett rejected home-grown vegetables. "Do you know what they use for fertilizer?"

They finally settled on live chickens, scrawny, bare-assed specimens with their legs tied to keep them from getting up and running off. Tomasello paid for them—a real bargain, he decided—and they threw the squawking birds in back of one of the humvees and took off in a cloud of dust.

Back at 151, the platoons confronted the issue of how to prepare live chickens, starting with butchering them. Sergeant Ronnie Montgomery and several other country-bred boys who had served in poverty-stricken rural areas of the world like Kosovo and Haiti demonstrated how to wring a chicken's neck. Grab it by the head and swing the bird vigorously at arm's length until the body separated from the head, whereupon the dying chicken kicked and spasmed all over the yard, spewing blood from its ruptured jugular.

PFC Nathaniel Given, who had been a bit of a minor fuckup at Drum before deployment, released his victim too soon. Head intact but twisted over to one side, it jumped up and ran drunkenly all over the enclosed grounds, pursued by a lynch mob of roaring, laughing GIs who finally cornered it and assisted Given in completing the execution.

Finally, the first task completed, some of the guys gathered up wood and built an open fire. Sergeant John Herne of Second Platoon and Sergeant Parrish of Fourth volunteered as cooks to roast the chickens. Colonel Sanders, Sergeant Montgomery declared, could have done no better.

The barbecue and games ended at sunset, everyone having stuffed himself with fresh meat. Mayhem watched the Iraqi sun go down from the flat roof of the house and listened to the calls for the faithful to come worship at the 109 Mosque down the road. Other than the thousand-pound spontaneously ignited bomb, which didn't count as an attack, no one had shot at him all day, and no vehicle had got blown up. It was therefore a good war. The land lay quiet and peaceful all around as though it had never been touched by violence.

FIFTEEN

Lieutenant Colonel Michael Infanti was a Mustang officer, a former enlisted man who had worked himself up through the ranks to earn a commission. As such, he brought with him a special affinity for young soldiers that kept him constantly on the move circulating among his companies, checking on the men, letting himself be seen taking the same risks they did, reconfirming with deed and word the spirit and letter of their mission in Iraq—that the 4th Battalion would live among the people, in the midst of danger, in order to prove it was here to stay until peace and stability returned to the AO. There would come that turning point, he insisted, when it would begin to come together.

A job in the military was one of only a few that entailed ordering someone to go out and possibly die. To Infanti, the lives of his men were his sacred responsibility, a truth the casualty cards he carried in the breast pocket of his ACUs never allowed him to forget. Casualty cards kept a running account of the soldiers of the 4/31st who were either killed or wounded in action. The longer the 2nd BCT remained in Iraq, the thicker grew the deck of cards. He sometimes took out the little stack and shuffled through it, trying to remember the boyish faces that went with the cards.

Although Infanti was too young to have served in Vietnam, he remembered hearing 'Nam vets speak resentfully of how colonels and general officers would live in air-conditioned mobile homes while their troops dug holes and huddled in the rain. He swore his men would never talk about him like that.

At FOB Yusufiyah, he lived in an old steel shipping container that had previously been used by ocean-going freighters, although other facilities offered better accommodations, even with one of the buildings having been gutted by fire. His TOC (Tactical Operations Center)—communications, operations, Intelligence—was housed next door in a GP (General Purpose) Large tent that allowed easy access. He insisted on being awakened any time something happened day or night within the AO.

His battalion second-in-command, Executive Officer Mark Manns, and Battalion Command Sergeant Major Alexander Jimenez, who bore the same name as Specialist Jimenez in Delta Company but to whom he was not related, worried about their commander. After all, due to his penchant for sharing danger, Infanti's was one of the first trucks in 4th Battalion to hit an IED.

It occurred on Sportster Road while the Colonel, as he was generally called, and his PSD (personal security detail) were on their way back to Yusufiyah following an impromptu inspection of Delta Company's Inchon on Malibu Road. Infanti's hummer triggered an IED whose blast bent the frame of the vehicle and slammed it against his knee. He ended up in a support brace that he would have to wear for at least a year or until the Polar Bears returned home and he took the time for more definitive medical treatment.

"Sir, you don't have to be out there *every* day," Major Manns argued.

Infanti was a stubborn man. "The soldiers have to know that we don't talk the talk while they're out there walking the walk," he said.

Infanti had had that same obstinate unbending streak during the previous 2004–2005 deployment when he was Brigade Deputy Commander. Manns and CSM Jimenez had heard all the stories from Corporal Shane Courville, a medic who had been with Infanti then and returned with him as his PSD medic this time.

Courville was big enough to toss a wounded man over each shoulder and jog off the battlefield with them. The big man had in fact carried soldiers out of harm's way on at least six previous occasions, one of whom was Infanti on a November afternoon in 2004.

Infanti's convoy was speeding down the overpass leading into the city of Abu Ghraib to distribute blankets to a local school before winter set in when Captain Jennifer Knowlden noticed that the streets were suspiciously deserted. The disappearance of children was always a warning.

An IED went off underneath Knowlden's lead vehicle and sandblasted out the windows. Infanti heard the whooshing report of an 85mm rocket-propelled grenade belching from the mouth of an alley to his right. It caught the commander's truck near the right front door, the concussion tossing it sideways in the street and popping open the doors.

Although disoriented and almost unconscious from injuries to the back of his head, Infanti leaped out of the smoking truck with his M-4 blazing against black-hooded RPG gunners hammering the stalled convoy from the alley and from the cover of a nearby wall. Rockets crisscrossed the street, screaming and etching smoke. One struck the pavement and skidded underneath a hummer where it detonated in a ball of red flame, jolting the truck completely off the ground. Another targeted the last unscathed vehicle in the convoy and ripped off a tire. A third penetrated the rear hatch of Captain Knowlden's disabled truck and lodged in its cargo of blankets without exploding.

In the midst of all the smoke, noise, and confusion, Knowlden saw Colonel Infanti collapse in the street next to his truck, seemingly unconscious or mortally wounded. His adrenaline had finally worn off. Knowlden got on the radio, yelling for the medic who always accompanied a commander's patrol. The call was unnecessary. Courville was already racing through the smoke toward Infanti.

Even though Captain Knowlden had herself been injured in the IED explosion, she scrambled out to help the big medic. Just in time, it seemed, for a second IED detonated underneath her truck, ripping off the back hatch and sending it flying end over end through the air. Fortunately for the other passengers, they had abandoned the truck to return fire against attacking insurgents.

Still under fire, Courville hoisted his unconscious commander off the pavement and stuffed him into the back seat of his damaged vehicle where, at least partially protected by side armor, he began to treat him for head injuries.

As usual, the contact didn't last long. The ambushers hauled ass, leaving in their wake four damaged or disabled humvees, two wounded Americans, and a number of injured civilian bystanders caught in the crossfire. Colonel Infanti suffered from a serious concussion and other cuts and bruises, but, characteristically, insisted on staying with the brigade until it was recalled to Fort Drum.

During his battlefield treatment of the wounded officer, Courville used scissors to cut off Infanti's clothing to check for additional injuries. Infanti had put on a new uniform that morning. From then on, every time the Colonel got ready to circulate, he lifted an eyebrow at the medic in mock rebuke.

"Corporal," he joked, "this is a brand-new uniform I'm wearing."

"Yes, sir. I've got a brand-new pair of scissors."

SIXTEEN

Each patrol base had its obligatory coffee brewer operating on a generator in the common area. Sergeant Ronnie Montgomery started stripping off his battle rattle as soon as he entered the big house at Inchon; Delta's four platoons rotated periodically among the three outposts. Somebody had propped Brenda the Bitch on a chair at the card table. She was a blow-up, anatomically correct, life-sized doll one of the Joes had ordered from *Hustler* magazine as a joke on Joe Anzak. Montgomery poured himself a cup of coffee, tasted it, and made a face. Guys were always receiving exotic coffees in care packages from home. A half-dozen or so different brands sat at the table among spilled creamer and empty sugar packets.

"Is it too much to ask that we stick to just one kind of coffee?" he grumbled. "An average cup of coffee shouldn't be too much to ask for."

He seized Brenda by the tit and tossed her at a worn-out sofa salvaged from only God knew where. He collapsed in her chair at the table and was scowling at his coffee cup when the rest of Second Platoon straggled in from maintenance on their hummers. Second had been out most of the night on a wild goose chase over in Kharghouli, nothing but dry holes.

Joe Anzak grabbed Nathaniel Given in a quick headlock as soon as Given came through the door. Second was currently sharing Inchon with First Platoon and Delta's HQ element.

"What's up, faggot?" Anzak said. "Anything exciting happen last night?"

Given slipped free and rained fake punches into Anzak's midsection. "Naw, man. Same ole same ole. You know, rescuing damsels in distress and saving the world from the manticore. I got to get some sleep. If you guys are going out, wake me for chow when you get back, okay?"

"You have it. See you in a few hours."

"No *feaky-feaky* with the ladies."

On his way through, Specialist Dar-rell Whitney (spelled Darrell, but pronounced Dar-rell) rescued Brenda from the floor where Sergeant Montgomery had tossed her. He copped a feel.

"Ain't *feaky-feaky* the reason we got Brenda?" he said.

Joe Merchant grabbed *him* in a headlock. "What's with you black boys, always fucking with the white girls?"

"That's *African-American men* to you, honky," Whitney shot back, slipping free.

"Whatever. Get your hands off Brenda. It's my turn to sleep with her."

"She is such a whore."

Soldiers in an all-male environment could be remarkably disgusting. Day-to-day life at the forts was an eclectic mixture of *Animal House*, Doctor Phil, and *One Flew Over the Cuckoo's Nest*. Life might be more or less expendable outside the walls, but inside existed at least a modicum of security where guys could let down a little.

The patrol bases were never really quiet, not with soldiers working 24-hour shifts and always coming and going—on-going shifts walking doggedly out to their vehicles to replace soldiers who staggered in to their bunks looking drained from the bone-deep weariness of day-after-day tension, but nonetheless gamely trying to keep up each other's spirits. The forts had about them the feel of old bus stations coupled with the odd stench of occupation most would always associate with the war—the putrid odors of burning garbage and human excrement, of diesel fuel, open MRE packets, sweat, and musty clothing.

The bunkrooms were mostly kept near pitch dark because of shift work. They resembled cluttered and fusty caves strewn with resting bodies as from some apocalyptic disaster scene. Sandbags, sheet metal, and planks of wood barricaded the windows against the enemy as well as against sunlight. Only a few diligent rays found their way through cracks to the sleeping soldiers within.

Off-time, what little there was of it when men weren't sleeping or eating, was consumed with taped music, reading, cards, Nintendo and computer games, laptop music, and the grabassing and clowning around of young men away from home, some for the first time. Men got tight with others they might not have even spoken to under different circumstances, forming a closeness and loyalty that time and distance would never break.

Guys like Anzak and Jimenez had the capacity to raise the mood of entire squads and platoons. They were always joking around, never seeming to let things get them down, seldom a bad word to say to or about anyone. A bunch of guys back from patrol would start comparing stories about whatever action may have occurred, debating about who shot what and how close they had come to getting wasted. Before the mood had a chance to get dark and the guys started brooding, Jimenez might flash one of his million-dollar grins, throw himself onto the old torn-up sofa, and plunge into a joke that only he could tell to its fullest benefit.

"These two Arab fuckers boarded a flight and sat down in the window seats with a 10th Mountain soldier in the aisle seat. The Polar Bear kicked off his shoes and was settling down when one of the Arabs says, 'I need to get up and get a Coke.'

" 'Don't get up. I'm in the aisle seat. I'll get it for you.'

"As soon as the soldier got up, one of the Arabs spat a goober in his shoe.

"This happened twice more. The soldier knew immediately what had happened when the plane landed and he put on his shoes. He leaned over to his Arab seatmates.

" 'Why does it have to be this way?' he asked. 'How long must this go on? This fighting between our nations? This hatred? This animosity? This spitting in shoes and pissing in Cokes . . . ?' "

Joe Anzak remembered being away from home as a kid and some of the other kids bawling at night, wanting to go home. He hated that pussy shit, but he wanted to go home now and he could imagine how badly homesickness affected some of the other guys. It became his personal mission to take their minds off it, to keep them going. He could be a real character, making a big show of heading off to the latrine with a wag bag and a *feaky-feaky* magazine.

"I'm going to be busy for a while. Don't bother me."

Sometime, for the amusement and edification of the platoon, he would lean back on his bunk clad only in his underwear and light his farts with a cigarette lighter, shooting out blue flame. *"Incoming!"*

"Man, you're gonna burn your nuts off."

"Come on over here, sweets. I can hold you if you like. Lie down next to me and spoon."

In order to compensate for the isolation, to bring in a little order and civilization, everyone went all out in celebrating holidays, birthdays, and anniversaries. On Halloween, some of the guys camouflage-painted their faces and went trick-or-treating in their underwear and combat boots, dashing from bunk to bunk soliciting leftover MRE chocolate bars or care package candy. Birthdays and anniversaries required exchanging little gifts—a clean pair of socks, cherished MRE oatmeal cookies, somebody's last pack of American cigarettes . . .

No matter how hard they tried to forget the war, however, it had its ways of intruding. Chiva Lares' truck hit an IED on his twenty-first birthday. Robert Pool got mortared on his twentieth.

Specialist Pool, who wanted to be a psychiatrist one day, was tall and slender with light-brown hair and a wife waiting back in California. He had come up hard on the streets, more or less abandoned by his parents to make his own way. He got into pushing dope and was likely on his way to prison sooner or later when he met his wife and enlisted in the army. He liked to say he went from big man on the streets to big target in Iraq. In California, he was accustomed to punks holding grudges, but it took some real getting used to when people started trying to blow him up.

Victor Chavez sang *Happy Birthday, Dear Shitbird* to him while a couple of other guys burped in accompaniment. Then Third Platoon had to pull a mounted/dismounted patrol to search for roadside IEDs. Pool's squad, led by Chavez, did the dismount and was trudging through the weeds and underbrush about fifty meters off and parallel to the road when Pool heard the unmistakable bloodcurdling whistle of an incoming mortar round, then a loud *Thump* as the shell impacted on Malibu near the slow-moving trucks. The dismounted half of the platoon hit the dirt; the mounted half hunkered down inside their armor.

Four more rounds followed in quick succession, thudding up and down the road, geysering up black smoke, asphalt, and dirt, and filling the air with the terrifying whine of shrapnel. Good thing the Jihadists couldn't shoot for shit. During the lull that followed, Sergeant Chavez ordered his squad to break for the armored safety of the hummers.

Pool was huffing up the road bank toward the nearest truck when a shell streamed down like a Roman candle and hit the road directly in front of him. It was a dud. Instead of detonating and killing or wounding the entire foot squad, it bounced twice like a stone skipping on water and slammed into a house on the other side of the road where it finally exploded, blowing a hole in the poor farmer's house.

A couple of turret gunners spotted seven or eight Baghdads with AK-47s hot-footing it across the road about three hundred meters away. They were probably supposed to be the attack cleanup element but had chickened out when they saw the mortars had caused no damage. Third's gunners lit them up with .50-cals and two-forties. They vanished into the countryside. As usual, the QRF found little except a few blood trails and some poor bastard hiding in a house with blood on his trousers. He was taken to Brigade for questioning and detention.

The adrenalin was still pumping when Third Platoon returned to 152. Fourth Platoon on base security detail wanted to hear all about it.

"That was something else, man!"

"Sounds like it. Anybody hurt?"

"No problem. You ought to see the vehicles though. Ricochet dents all over them. It was fucking crazy."

"For a change, just one time, I'd like to see a good firefight initiated by us instead of by them."

"Happy birthday, Bobbie," James Cook said.

Pool hoped it wasn't his last.

Conditions at the patrol bases were decidedly primitive, especially at the outset. Men ate nothing but MREs supplemented by whatever they received in care packages and, infrequently, by kabobs they purchased from vendors or, as with Second and Fourth Platoons that time, chickens

from the local markets. On security watch, an infantryman did everything he could to stay awake and alert. He drank coffee, dipped tobacco,
figured out ways to smoke cigarettes without letting any light escape.

Sleep following a shift was more important than anything else—more
than money, happiness, or sex. Yet, it seemed sleep in the hot houses did
everything it could to evade a man. He would wake up rolling in sweat, get
up and drink Gatorade, then go back to his sweat-soaked sleeping bag to
wrestle with sleep some more. Some of the guys tried sleeping on the roofs
in the open air like most of the Iraqis did. Only, flies started swarming an
hour or two before daybreak, taking over from the night-shift mosquitoes,
making it impossible to sleep.

Under Colonel Infanti's guidance, conditions in the AO gradually improved. As he informed his battalion staff, "We want our guys to be able to
fight outside the wire, but when they come inside they have got to feel secure taking off their gear. They need reasonable chow, cool water, a comfortable place to sleep, toilet facilities, some down time . . . Make it happen."

A "meals on wheels" from Battalion eventually began delivering chow
to the outposts at least once a day, providing the truck didn't run over an
IED and have to be towed back. One afternoon, Staff Sergeant "Cookie"
Urbina and his kitchen in a trailer showed up at Inchon to whip up the
best meal any of the Joes had had in weeks. He had come to stay.

Cookie was around forty, a small man with a stout Hispanic accent.
His talent for creating gastronomic miracles with Raman noodles and
powdered eggs, spicing them up with condiments for a little variety, immediately made him the most popular soldier in Delta Company. On
chilly autumn nights he always had a hot pot of soup burbling on the stove
for whenever the men came back from the field. Sometimes he sent soup
cups out with them.

"I'd marry you today if you weren't so *damned* ugly, Cookie," Anzak
teased.

"Puck you, Joe."

For Thanksgiving, Cookie prepared a turkey dinner with all the trim-
mings, consumed by the men in stages as they came and went on their
duties. The war never stopped. Everyone looked forward to Christmas

when Cookie promised to pull out all the stops. Lieutenants Dudish and Tomasello offered to take their platoons on another shopping spree. A Christmas goose sounded nice.

Water for the troops was a life-or-death proposition in a climate where temperatures often reached triple digits, even in the winter. Bottled water supplied their needs at first. Coolers powered by small generators kept it almost cold. After a while, the outposts received large rubber donut-shaped storage tanks that supplied running water for the patrol bases. Eventually, there were even warm showers supplied by two hundred-gallon drums assembled on the flat roofs of the houses where the water could be heated by the sun.

Gasoline-powered generators provided energy for lights and computers—and eventually for air conditioning to cool off the bunkrooms and make life in the desert almost bearable. This luxury, however, did not arrive until the beginning of summer in 2007.

In World War II or Korea, as in most wars, the advance of an infantry outfit could be traced by the path of litter it left in its wake—cast off C-ration cans, food wrappers, empty ammo crates, greasy fire pits, half-filled-in latrine trenches . . . In Iraq, one of the first tasks of the new U.S. "green-conscious" army was to construct sanitary burn and waste disposal pits to eliminate litter. The tongue-in-cheek motto of the Green Army became a standing joke: "Leave the war cleaner than you found it."

"Wag bags" served as the dogface Joe's first toilet. Wag bags were simply heavy-duty trash bags into which a soldier did his duty. Then he tied a knot in the top of it and delivered it to a pit to be burned. Any violation of the practice was bound to cause a stir.

"Sir, I just seen a guy taking a shit out in the open."

"Wonderful. That's the kind of report Battalion needs. Did you offer him a Handi Wipe?"

Medics were in charge of sanitation and preventive medicine. The first shitters they built at the patrol bases were too high, so that legs dangled whenever soldiers sat to take their constitutionals. Later, pre-built wooden toilets were trucked in. They had metal buckets underneath the holes, like the ones used in the 1991 Operation *Desert Storm*, but wag bags still had to be utilized. This was accomplished by the soldier spreading his bag across the mouth of the metal receptacle, then afterwards escorting the filled bag to the burn pit as usual. No more Vietnam-era mixing diesel with wastes and burning out the cans.

Iraqi Army terps and soldiers stationed at the patrol bases with Americans turned out to be a major hitch in solving the sanitation challenge. Most lower-class Arabs wiped their asses with their bare hands and were accustomed to sleeping next to where they shat and shitting next to where they ate. The back yard enclosed by the blast wall at Inchon, where most of the IA were stationed, turned into a minefield from the terps taking their dumps right on the ground. Even after "porta-potties" were installed, the IAs still preferred the open ground or, worse yet, the plywood ledge next to the holes in the latrine.

The location of the mines was quite frequently pinpointed by the sound of angry cursing when a patrol prepared to exit the compound at night and some groggy GI stepped in a mess.

"I am going to profoundly *shoot* the next motherfucker I see drop his drawers—"

Life was lived according to the next patrol—and that produced an entirely new angle of routine in the lonely forts on Malibu Road. Between missions, some of the men went off to themselves in the dark and chain-smoked cigarettes, puffing away while their hands shook. Yearning to go home. Hell, yearning to go *anywhere* away from here.

"When this war is over," Sammy Rhodes said, "basically I am going to pack up my stuff and *walk* all the way down Malibu Road back to the real world."

"You're kidding, right, Sam? This war ain't ever gonna end."

"I don't think we should answer the radio anymore," Corny Courneya proposed. "'We're sorry. Delta ain't in at the moment. Please leave a message at the sound of the tone and we'll get back to the war when it's more convenient.'"

It was easy for hard, dirty, exhausted infantrymen to become cynical and angry. Guys' minds could get all weird, what with being away from home and wives and girlfriends and living together and picking up all the rumors about who was getting divorced, whose wife was leaving him, whose girlfriend was pregnant or diseased or "acting funny."

"Man, the bitch's letters have gone all freaky. What I think is she's screwing some other dude while I'm over here."

"My girlfriend has broke her hand. Either that or she's forgot how to read and write. I ain't got a letter from her in six weeks. What do you think, Anzak?"

"You always got me and Brenda the Bitch."

Specialist James Cook's daughter was two years old when he deployed. He was twenty-three years old, a skinny little guy, like a tough tree branch. He suspected his wife was running around on him.

"I can hardly picture what she looks like anymore," he said. "She'll be gone when I get home. My little daughter is growing up fast. She won't even remember who I am . . ."

"Home. What's that?" Justin Fletcher wondered.

Sergeant Chris Messer kept a picture of his wife and her last letter to him in his breast pocket, along with his laminated copy of the Prayer of Salvation. He memorized the letter, like he tried to memorize his wife's face and the sound of her voice. Whenever he got all quiet and withdrawn, someone would ask him, "Are you sick, man?"

"Naw," someone would answer for him. "He just misses his wife and wants to go home like the rest of us."

"Sergeant Messer thinks God's wrath has descended upon us for invading the Garden of Eden. Messer, will you pray for us?"

"Jeez cheez! What's a guy got to do around here to get some sleep?"

Everyone knew everyone else's private affairs. Chris Murphy was saving all his money in order to send his alcoholic mother to rehab and get her a decent place to live. Cournyea's mother was jealous of his fiancé Jennifer, complaining that he spent more time with her than with his own mother. Byron Fouty wanted to request reassignment to a medic slot in order to help people in Iraq like other medics were doing. Anthony Schober was going to buy a ranch in Nevada, although no one ever thought him to be a cowboy. Jared Isbell's girlfriend Kathy was breaking up with him. Alex Jimenez was distraught over having told a lie to his grandmother.

She had begged him not to return to Iraq for another tour of duty. He lied by telling her he was going on a training mission somewhere else and therefore would not be in any danger. She passed away while he was patrolling Malibu Road, without knowing the truth.

Delta Company possessed one satellite phone for use by its four platoons. Each soldier was allotted ten minutes each week to call home on it. Although it provided contact for couples who missed each other desperately, it could also be a double-edged sword by providing an avenue for conflict in relationships already frayed around the edges. The romantic notion was of yellow ribbons wrapped around trees and Sally waiting at home faithful to her man. The truth was a bit more complicated.

For some of the Joes, it was hard cleaning up their act after living with a bunch of soldiers and then trying to talk like a normal person on the phone with a wife or mother. They sometimes found they had nothing to say. Imagine calling home after a bad day in the war.

"Honey, it's great hearing your voice. Are you okay?"

"Uh, you know, same old stuff. Killing and dying. How about you?"

So many times, no one answered at the other end of the line. Disappointed husbands and fathers strayed into quiet corners to smoke cigarettes and stare into the darkness of their thoughts. It was easy to imagine all kinds of things.

SEVENTEEN

After having already been awarded two Purple Hearts for wounds suffered in battle, Lt. Colonel Michael Infanti was still on the move, albeit with one knee trussed for support. Delta's Second Platoon met Iron Claw and Husky at Yusufiyah for an IED sweep the length of Malibu Road from JSB (Jurf Sukr Bridge) through Delta's three outposts to the old Russian power plant. Colonel Infanti and the four trucks hauling his PSD hooked up with the procession as an opportunity for the commander to meet with soldiers in the field and get a look at how things were going. Malibu Road was still the most active region in the AO.

An E-4 Specialist named Martinez drove the vehicle occupied by the commander and a terp called Scarface. He pulled into the middle of the convoy, fifth truck from the front, third from the rear, ordinarily a relatively safe position. Two trucks back came CSM Alexander Jimenez' hummer. The highest-ranking officer in the battalion and the highest-ranking enlisted man never rode in the same vehicle, for obvious reasons.

Second Platoon Sergeant Ronnie Montgomery rode shotgun in the hummer directly ahead of Colonel Infanti's, with Lieutenant Dudish another position further up. Specialist Jared Isbell was Montgomery's driver. Section Sergeant John Herne, thirty, short and solid and the father of four children back in New York, sat in the turret behind a two-forty.

The trip from the first big curve in the road short of 151 where the thousand-pound bomb had spontaneously exploded was agonizingly slow, full of starts and stops while Husky crept along up front sniffing for buried explosives, followed by the Iron Claw and an EOD team. Dismounted patrols worked as outriders on either flank to keep an eye open for an ambush, although no one expected it due to the size of the column.

The convoy halted past the big S-curve while the crews of the counter-IED machines did their stuff. Isbell shook out a cigarette and offered one to Montgomery. They smoked while the sergeant gazed out his side window, thinking of the mission to Rushdi Mulla his platoon had drawn for later on—a high-value target suspected of the recent mortar attack against Lieutenant Fawley's Third Platoon. Going into Rushdi at night often generated contact.

Isbell leaned forward over the steering wheel and watched Husky nosing around in the curve ahead while the procession waited behind, engines idling. The brown walls topped with razor wire that marked 151 were visible not far ahead. Isbell's mind was on the lunch break that awaited them once they reached the compound. There was no ill wind in the air. The day was too sunny and bright for trouble.

Sergeant Herne reached his foot down from the turret and tapped Isbell's shoulder with it. "How about a cigarette, man?"

"I thought you gave up smoking, Sergeant Herne."

Herne grinned. "I didn't want to have to be the one to tell you this, Isbell, but you're a soldier and there's a war going on. I might not live for another fifteen minutes, so why should I worry about lung cancer fifteen years from now?"

Husky and Iron Claw roared and inched on down the road, the convoy trailing along. Chow time was just ahead.

By their very nature, IEDs always seemed to go off at the most unexpected times. Some clown hiding nearby with a cell phone or a car battery hooked up to a hot plate or some other makeshift contraption could set it off at will. That Husky overlooked this one may have been because it contained no metal parts, perhaps only chicken manure and diesel fuel packed solid in a cloth bag or several cloth bags. Whether Colonel Infanti was the specific target, or whether it was merely the luck of the draw would never be determined. If Infanti *had* been targeted for assassination, killing the highest ranking officer in the AO would have been a big coup for insurgents.

The convoy was paused almost in front of a farmer's residence and not far from a rural schoolhouse when the charge went off with a shattering bang and a burst of black smoke, an explosion of such enormity that it instantly turned sand to glass and shredded the air with shrapnel. The ground shook. Isbell thought his truck was going to bounce off the road. Montgomery thought he had taken the hit.

Back toward the rear, Chiva Lares had never encountered such a powerful bomb. To his astonishment, it exploded directly underneath the battalion commander's humvee and flipped it end over end through the air like the toy of a child throwing a tantrum. It landed smoking and sizzling upside down on the road's embankment.

Isbell saw it through his side mirror. "Oh, my God! It's upside-down and on fire!"

In the turret, Herne swiveled his two-forty back and forth, sweeping for a target against the blast that almost tore the nitch from his head, yelling at the top of his lungs, *"Shit! Shit! Shit!"* That was the deepest his thoughts ran.

Montgomery's first impulse was to secure the commander's vehicle before the enemy ran up and tossed in a grenade to finish the job. He flung open his door and, M4 in hand, dashed toward the demolished truck, past a crater blown in the road fifteen feet wide and eighteen deep. He couldn't believe how big it was.

The mangled body of Scarface, the Colonel's IA interpreter, lay crumpled on the roadbed, his legs twitching while a half-inch stream of blood spurted from his jugular. He was dead, he just didn't realize it yet.

Beyond, Specialist Martinez was pulling himself out of the wreckage toward a nearby tree from behind which he might hold off an attack and protect his commander. Dragging his crippled legs, he looked as pathetic as an injured bug.

Colonel Infanti remained strapped in the front passenger's seat, upside down with all his weight on his neck instead of his shoulders. Unable to move, he was choking to death from the pressure of his Kevlar throat protector while blood gushed from his eyes, ears and nose. Gasoline and other engine fluids trickled into the interior, soaking everything.

CSM Jimenez, a dark-skinned man with both guts and brawn, had already reached the truck and was attempting to tear open the door to get to Infanti. "Get him out before it explodes!" he yelled.

The door was jammed. The sergeant major demanded a Rat Hook to rip it off while Montgomery and other officers and NCOs organized a defense in the unlikely event of an attack. Everything was mass confusion until the Colonel was finally freed and medic Shane Courville started emergency life-saving measures. Infanti was barely conscious when Courville started clipping away with his scissors.

"Not again," he groaned.

"I'll save you the big pieces," Courville promised.

Soldiers enraged over the targeting of their commander stormed the schoolhouse and the little house near the road looking for the bomber or his accomplices. They busted through doors and kicked over furniture, adrenalin pumping, ready to shoot the first motherfucker who moved with bad intent, *wanting* some motherfucker to move.

Both buildings were abandoned; the occupants must have been warned in advance to clear out.

"Lovely people," a soldier commented. "Fuck this whole stupid country."

After the Iron Claw and its EOD crew hauled Colonel Infanti and Martinez to 151 for evacuation by Black Hawk helicopter, Sergeant Montgomery and Herne stood near the still-smoking crater in the road while medics prepared Scarface's body to be hauled away. He left a big puddle of blood slowly baking in the desert sun. Infanti's truck smoldered upside down by the side of the road.

Sergeant Montgomery offered Herne a cigarette from his supremely harsh Iraqi pack, Blue Death, which, at fifty cents, was a lot cheaper than Marlboros or Winstons from the military Post Exchange in the Green Zone.

Herne accepted. "Might as well enjoy my fifteen minutes now," he said.

EIGHTEEN

Lieutenant Colonel Mike Infanti vaguely recalled the chopper flight from Malibu to Baghdad. He lay strapped onto a stretcher next to another bearing Specialist Martinez. The big medic, Corporal Courville, attended their IVs, kneeling between them with his knees wide-braced against the helicopter's movement. Courville was speaking to him. So was Martinez. The Colonel tried to concentrate—but he was just so damned tired.

By the time he became fully cognizant of his surroundings, he found himself at the CASH (Combat Army Support Hospital) in Baghdad, flat on his back in the more-or-less modern ER. A doctor told him he suffered from shrapnel lodged in the back of his head, torn ligaments in the knee that was already bad, and a back injury the seriousness of which would not become apparent until much later.

Service doctors seemed most worried about possible severe head injuries. He had been knocked unconscious by the IED blast. Bleeding from his eyes, ears, nose, and mouth had almost stopped, but the pain was intense. Fluid buildup in his chest caused secondary concern.

"How long am I going to be stuck here?" he demanded.

"Sir, we'll have to do some more tests. The war'll go on without you."

Since he had now been wounded three times within a period of two years, his greatest fear was that the Pentagon would relieve him of his command, for his own good, and send him home. The Brass might not understand that out there in The Triangle of Death his soldiers were also getting blown up. They got patched up, went back to their little forts, maybe shaved and took a canteen bath, caught a bite to eat and a few hours sleep—and then they went right back out, knowing the chances of their getting blown up all over again.

That took guts, an *esprit de corps* of unbreakable bonds between men joined from facing misery and death together. Battlefield success depended upon unit cohesion like that. Infanti had promised his troops that *we* were going to stay, *we* were not going to be run out of the AO. How would it look to them if he took off now, for whatever reason?

Besides, what would the parents, wives, and children of his soldiers think, how much greater their own fears, if it became known that he had been evacuated from the combat zone? If the battalion commander could be blown up, what chance did the common privates and sergeants have?

A doctor with a clipboard returned to the ER. "Colonel, we're going to have to medically evacuate you for further diagnosis and treatment."

"To the States?"

"Yes, sir. We think that's the prudent thing."

"Screw prudent." Although in great pain, especially from his back, he swung his legs off the examining table and stood up. "Can you bring me another uniform? The medic cut mine off. I'm recommending him for a medal."

"Sir . . . ?"

"I'm not leaving my men."

And with that, he put on the bloody remnants of his old uniform, as a new one was not forthcoming, and hobbled out of the hospital. Within forty-eight hours after the IED exploded underneath his humvee, he was back at Battalion HQ in Yusufiyah changing to a fresh uniform in the large shipping container he called home. From then on, constant agony from an undiagnosed broken back allowed him only three or four hours' uninterrupted sleep a night. He walked with a painful limp. Sometimes, when none of his troops were about to see, he leaned on a cane fashioned from the branch of a eucalyptus tree.

And CSM Jimenez and he went right back out into the AO, moving to the sound of guns.

NINETEEN

Enemy snipers and mortar teams working the S-curves had wounded or taken shots at any number of American soldiers. So far, Delta Company had been lucky, *lucky*, and that was about all you could say for it. Sooner or later, guys were going to get killed. PFC Sammy Rhodes in First Platoon would already have been on his way home to New Mexico with an extra hole in his head if the ballistic glass in his hummer hadn't caught the bullet meant for him. As far as Sergeant Ronnie Montgomery could tell, Delta Company and the enemy were about even when it came to a casualty count—and the enemy kept putting more points on the board for his team.

A GI with a good arm could throw a rock from the flat roof of Patrol Base 151 and hit the Euphrates River. Battle Position 152 on down the road and out of sight around one of the S-curves set a bit further off the river, but it was still within mortar and rifle range of it. FOB 153, Inchon, was the most invulnerable of the three with its larger cantonment and its long two-story view of the Euphrates past the date palms. Even so, Jihad shooters using the river as a barrier to avoid pursuit were constantly harassing all three posts to keep the Americans on edge.

Montgomery cautioned his soldiers about standing around in open sight. When you had to get from one place to another, walk so as to use the trucks for cover. Stay low while on security guard up on the roofs. All an insurgent on the other side of the river had to do to see everything going on inside the walls of either 151 or 152 was to climb a tree. If he scaled it at dusk, the Manticore Hour, the roof watch probably wouldn't notice him in the gathering shadows. Don't be careless or stupid, Montgomery warned. Keep your eyes open. That was how you stayed alive.

Patrols sent to stake out the river met with little success. It was such a large area with so many places for a shooter to hide that, unless the patrols knew when and where he was going to show up, they had about as much chance of nailing him as a snowflake had of falling on the Sahara. It also proved unreasonable to expect soldiers to scurry from hole to hole like frightened mice while they were inside their forts. Certain housekeeping duties and chores had to be accomplished in spite of the threat.

Second Platoon leader Lieutenant John Dudish and Sergeant John Herne were supervising the cleaning of the latrine behind 152 when someone from across the river took a potshot at them, the bullet whipping by so close that both heard its supersonic passage.

A few days later, Specialist Robert Pool was pulling guard on the roof of 151 when Third Platoon Leader Lieutenant Westcott and Platoon Sergeant Ford came up to discuss where to place more barriers. The two were standing talking and looking out toward the river when a sniper drilled Westcott through the arm. The shooter disappeared before Pool could sight in on him. Westcott was medevac'd to the CASH in Baghdad and no one ever saw him again. Lieutenant Darrell Fawley showed up a few days later as a replacement; he was the platoon's third platoon leader in less than six months.

Specialist Jared Isbell was the next victim. Second Platoon was out in the S-curves between 151 and 152, keeping watch for suspicious activities when Isbell had to take a leak. He couldn't hold it any longer, couldn't tie a knot in it, piss in somebody else's pocket, or follow any of the other suggestions his teammates offered. He slipped out of his truck to do his business. It was his twentieth birthday. It seemed something was always happening to guys on their birthdays.

Wham! Isbell caught the slug right through the thigh before he heard the rifle shot that nailed him. Panicked, he ducked to the safety of the nearest truck, his leg going numb and blood soaking his ACU bottoms. Platoon gunners hammered the woods across the river with machine guns and M-203s.

The clean flesh wound put him out of commission for about a week. Doc Luke Bailey, platoon medic, placed him on quarters and bed rest and swabbed out his wound every day with a big Q-tip. Isbell lay around reading and watching movies and waiting for the other guys to come back in. They greeted him with a barrage of good-natured ribbing.

"He was shooting at your pecker, Isbell, but it was too small to hit."

"If that raghead had been a better shot, we'd be calling you *Miss* Isbell by now and raising the morale of the entire platoon."

"Just think of how much cash you could be making as platoon *gahob*."

Like the guy from the 1st Cav who climbed out of his tank to pee and got blown up by the hajji rolling an old tire, Isbell vowed never to take another piss outside for the rest of his life.

Specialist Dar-rell Whitney experienced the closest call of all.

Rotation watches on the roofs of the patrol bases were generally long and dull. A soldier could smoke an entire pack of cigarettes. Dar-rell Whitney was team leader for Second Platoon, wiry, twenty-five years old, and on his second enlistment of an army career. He relived O'Neal on the roof of 152 just as an autumn morning was fast warming up. He watched the sun crest over palm trees on the far side of the river and spread bright tentacles upon his little patch of the Fertile Crescent.

His eyes scanned trees and undergrowth along the river, but detected no movement or anything out of place. His greatest enemy were squadrons of flies that attacked in black droves, seeking moisture from his body. He waved his hands vigorously back and forth in an effort to drive them off. Through the swarms, he noticed that strange kid everybody called Crazy Legs hobbling by on the road.

Almost at the same instant, a distant rifle shot rang out from the direction of the river. Or at least Whitney *thought* he heard it. The bullet and the sound of the report reached him simultaneously and knocked him flat on his back, unconscious. The 7.62mm round struck his helmet just above his eyebrow. The tough Kevlar deflected the slug enough that it barely broke the skin along his hairline before blowing out the back of his nitch.

Stunned but not badly wounded, he was moving around, coming to, by the time Sergeant Montgomery and other platoon members raced onto the roof ready to do battle with monsters. Mere inches had kept him from emptying his brain into his Kevlar. Some of the men brought rags and water to clean up blood that was already attracting more flies, while Specialist Luke "Doc" Bailey patched Whitney's head.

Whitney made five GIs, counting Dudish and Herne, whom unseen snipers had picked out of Delta Company in a matter of days, none fatally or even seriously wounded as of yet. Whoever the shooters were, they seemed to know exactly when and where to select their targets in order to allow their escape before the Americans responded. They never showed up at any of the sites where patrols staked out in their range, but they were always back when the Americans withdrew. It was almost as though the insurgents had spotters out constantly watching the patrol bases and the U.S. soldiers who manned them.

The inability to clearly assess who was a threat and who wasn't complicated the situation in ways that caused immeasurable stress. It was nearly impossible to keep the players straight, to pick out the farmer by day who turned terrorist by night from the "good ol' boy" who remained a "good ol' boy" when the sun went down. The platoons were fed up to the eyeballs, pissed off, what with people getting shot at or blown up all the time while they were impotent to do anything about it.

It didn't matter to them that many of the Iraqis might consider them invaders. That wasn't the issue. Malibu Road had become their block, their home, and it wasn't right that those Jihad fuckers could come in and blow up their houses and shoot at them.

"Sarge, what the hell are we accomplishing here?" Montgomery's soldiers wanted to know.

"Killing bad guys until they're all gone."

"How many have we killed?"

"Some," he said. "The important thing is, how many of *us* have they killed."

"That's only because they can't shoot for shit. It's only a matter of time. We ought to bomb these assholes back to the stone age and let God sort 'em out."

"Kids and women too? That'll wins hearts and minds."

"I don't give a rat's patootie about their hearts and minds. I want to go home alive. I got a wife and kid."

The final straw came when insurgents tried to kill the battalion chaplain. He was the *chaplain*, for God's sake!

TWENTY

Chaplain Jeff Bryan, in his thirties, was a short, stocky captain with that compassionate, benevolent look that seemed standard issue among military men of God. Every opportunity that came along, he hooked up with a supply convoy to venture out onto the frontier to bring the Word to his flocks. He seldom held Sunday services as such. Instead, he assembled a congregation wherever he happened to be. Sitting on a bottom bunk in one of the battle positions with soldiers gathered around to read the Bible. Perhaps in a tent singing "Amazing Grace" in his clear baritone voice. *Wherever one or two gather in My name . . .*

Sergeant Chris Messer of Second Platoon grew especially close to the young chaplain. Chaplain Bryan made a point of stopping by Second Platoon whenever he entered the Malibu AO. Messer and Chaplain Bryan would hold long talks or study Scripture together. Messer carried a machete on his belt. Sometimes he sat sharpening the machete while they talked. The sergeant almost never smiled or laughed anymore; he looked grim and preoccupied and what time he wasn't out on patrol he was sitting by himself reading his Bible.

Messer's closest friend from since Fort Drum, Victor Chavez, thought Messer's intense piety had something to do with the premonition that he would never see his wife and baby daughter again. This was his second combat tour in the Sandbox.

"I never thought I would ever have to come back here," Messer confided in Chavez at the start of the deployment when they climbed off the B-17 at Camp Striker. "Victor," he said solemnly, looking straight into his friend's eyes, "I'm going to die here this time."

"No, man."

"Yeah. I am."

He was serious.

Chavez tried to talk him out of it. "You'll be good, you'll see."

"I'm pretty sure it's going to happen."

"Man, *I* might die here. Any of us might—but none of us can know."

Messer unsheathed his machete and looked at it. "*I* know," he said.

One afternoon when most of Second Platoon had downtime, all except the roof watch, Chaplain Bryan arrived to hold services. Since, as the old saying went, there were no atheists in foxholes, the platoon squatted and sprawled on the floor around the man of God. Afterwards, Messer walked the chaplain out of the house to the resupply convoy preparing to depart for Inchon.

On guard duty up on the roof, Specialist Joe Merchant happened to notice a rusty old Toyota cruising slowly by on the dusty road that ran parallel to the other side of the river. The vehicle stopped. Merchant focused his binocs on it. Jihadists armed with rifles, RPGs and 60mm tubes piled out of it in a rush, like a clown fire drill in a circus act. Merchant shouted a warning.

"*Incoming!*"

The hajjis had Merchant's position pinpointed. A couple of them opened fire on him with AKs, whipping and zinging rounds all around to drive him to cover, while the others quickly set up their tubes. Mortar rounds and rockets arced high in the sky, streaming smoke contrails, before they plunged back to earth and exploded in a wide pattern inside the compound. Men scrambled for cover.

By the time Merchant stuck his head up to unlimber his SAW, the attackers were scrambling back into their van and squealing tires, disappearing over a hilltop. Chaplain Bryan prayed thanks for his deliverance until his convoy sped out through the gate and headed down the road. Messer looked grimmer than ever.

Specialist Whitney noticed something unusual about the attack that apparently had escaped everyone else's attention. Lieutenant Dudish, Sergeant Montgomery, and some of the squad, team, and section leaders held an impromptu council inside 151 to try to come up with a plan to put an end to the harassment from across the river. Whitney spoke up.

"Do any of you remember the guy Menahem saw when Fourth Platoon first settled 151? The crippled retard?"

"Crazy Legs? He's always walking up and down the road. I guess he lives around here."

"Sarge, what I'm telling you is, I think he's not as retarded as he looks. You know how it always seems like we're being watched and how they know everything we do? We *are* being watched. Crazy Legs is a spotter. Wait, before you think I'm crazier than he is . . ."

"Mayhem said the guy walked by just before Fourth Platoon got mortared, the day Pitcher and that Iraqi kid got hit. That's the beginning. Somebody saw him on the road before the IED exploded underneath the Colonel's humvee. How do you suppose the Baghdads knew which vehicle the Colonel was riding in? Crazy Legs told 'em, okay? Crazy Legs was on the road when I got shot. Now, guess what? Steffan saw him about fifteen minutes before the mortars started falling on the chaplain. That's how they knew the chaplain was here."

Everybody went silent while they thought about it. It made sense to Sergeant Montgomery. The guy was exactly the sort the insurgents tried to recruit as martyrs and accomplices.

"We need some payback," Sergeant Herne proposed. "I say we start with Crazy Legs."

That couldn't be done. That would be classified as *murder*. According to ROE, a GI was allowed to shoot back only if he took direct fire. Even if a guy walked down the road carrying a weapon, you couldn't light him up unless he made a hostile move. Everyone in this part of the world owned an AK-47. It was a status symbol and as much a part of the culture as men squatting to urinate. Crazy Legs had done nothing overt.

"So what do we do?" Sergeant Nathan Brooks asked. "Stand around with our thumbs up our butts and let the pukes keep shooting at us? I'm telling you, Lieutenant Dudish, we're gonna have to waste that traitorous cocksucker."

Sergeant Montgomery was already working on a plan. "Look at it like this," he said. "Crazy Legs can be more help to us than to them. He's our early warning system as long as we understand that something is going down whenever we see him. The next time, we'll bring so much shit down they'll think they've fallen into a vat of it."

TWENTY-ONE

Crazy Legs weaved past on the road in front of Patrol Base 151. *Scrape-thunk! Scrape-thunk!* As luck would have it, Second Platoon had just pulled in from an all-day patrol over toward Latifiyah. The guys were still refueling when somebody spotted the odd-gaited Iraqi innocently going by and sounded the alarm. It was time to test the validity of Specialist Whitney's theory.

Lieutenant Dudish and Sergeant Montgomery grabbed Second Platoon, as many soldiers as were available of the twenty or so currently at the post, and rushed to the roof, careful not to expose themselves to Crazy Legs' scrutiny. Soldiers eager for some payback crouched out of sight behind the raised lip that enclosed the roof, every machine gun, grenade-launcher, and rifle cocked and loaded for manticore. The Joes were pissed off and on a hair trigger. It wouldn't take much to set them off. Excitement and an air of expectation crackled like static electricity through the ranks. For a war in which there was no clear way to measure progress, not even a body count, to finally get a chance to turn the tables on the insurgents marked a clear victory.

They waited.

"Crazy Legs must have a way of signaling that there are targets inside and exposed," Montgomery reasoned. Ordinarily, it took a returning platoon a half-hour or so to refuel and maintenance vehicles, which meant a number of GIs would be out in the yard at the same time. Perfect targets for mortars or rockets lobbed up and over the walls.

The bad guys should be coming any time now—if Whitney was right about Crazy Legs.

The dirt country road that hugged the opposite bank of the river lay well within the outer range limits of even M-4s, no more than 350 yards away. Eucalyptus and palms obstructed a perfect sight picture, but all-in-all some very unaware hajjis were going to get the surprise of their miserable lives if they showed up.

The sun would be down in another ten or fifteen minutes. Shadows were starting to lengthen. Evening mist oozed up from the slow brown waters of the Euphrates. The river was fairly narrow at this point.

Montgomery served as an observer while the rest of the platoon kept low. Just when he was beginning to conclude that it was a dry hole, that it was only a coincidence that Crazy Legs seemed to appear every time something was about to happen, he spotted a black sedan missing a front fender creep into view. It was full of Iraqis. It eased to a stop directly across the river from151, almost out of sight in the shadows beneath the spreading branches of a eucalyptus.

"We got action," he said. "Stay down. Hold it . . ."

Men clad in red-and-white *shemaghs* and grayish robes over trousers and combat boots—the new trademark of the murder squads who once ran around the countryside in black outfits calling themselves *Fedayeen Saddam*, "Saddam's Men of Sacrifice," jumped out of the sedan with RPGs and small M-224 60mm mortars. They ran into the undergrowth near the river bank to set up their weapons.

"They're right on the river," Montgomery relayed. "Twelve o'clock. On my signal, fire these fuckers up . . . *Now!*"

The roof of 151 lit up like a Christmas tree with the flickering of rifle and machine-gun fire. The sound trapped inside the walls was deafening, echoing as it crackled and rose into a fierce crescendo. M203 grenades spouted short in the water. Machine-gun rounds racing across the water before they chewed into the riverside foliage resembled schooling piranha.

It was remarkable. It was exhilarating.

The Baghdads didn't get off a single shot. They jumped up and ran for their lives, carrying or dragging their weapons and casualties with them. Two-forties and SAWs riddled the sedan, sparking and shattering, until it careened down the road and into the shadows of the night. A .50-cal would really have done a job on the car had there been time to set one up, leaving the insurgents stranded and at the mercy of the fierce fire from the roof. None of them would have escaped.

Spontaneous cheers, catcalls, and taunts erupted from 151. "Allahu Akbar *that,* motherfuckers!"

It felt good, *good,* to shove hot lead up their asses after all the Joes had suffered from them during past weeks. Soldiers of Second Platoon swaggered around like gunfighters as they recounted for the other platoons, in detail, how they had finally turned the tables on their tormentors—at least this one time.

"You should have seen it, man. We lit them fuckers up. They hauled ass like the back-shooting cowards they are. The Colonel's right. We *are* going to bring law and order to Malibu Road. Like Wyatt Earp and Doc Holliday in Dodge City. There's a new sheriff in town, boy, and he's walking tall."

TWENTY-TWO

Delta Company soldiers expected something to happen whenever they went out. They kind of got used to it, but at the same time they didn't. They kept going down that same treacherous stretch of road through and past the S-curves. Specialist Robert Pool got where he lay awake in his bunk and went through in his mind every curve and bend in the road from JSB past Patrol Bases 151, 152, and Inchon, past the 109 Mosque and the old Russian power plant, speculating on where and when he would get it and how bad it would be.

GIs knew the do's and don'ts of the war by this time. Platoon leaders and sergeants constantly preached caution. Don't cross footbridges and high traffic spots. Never take the easy road. Go around. Never let down your guard. Recognize the signs if you wanted to live.

One hot, windy afternoon, Specialist Brandon Gray walking dismounted point for First Platoon came upon a little footbridge spanning a drainage ditch. As he was about to cross, the wind riffled a thread of white cloth knotted on a tree next to the bridge. He jumped back, recognizing that that was how Jihadists marked their booby traps to warn locals to stay away from them.

Sure enough, there was an all-but-invisible trip wire stretched between two roots and across the approach to the little bridge. One end of the wire was attached to a 155mm artillery shell buried in the ground. It contained enough black powder to blow a crater in the earth big enough to bury the entire squad. One more step, Gray realized, and he would have stepped into eternity.

Sergeant Montgomery had witnessed his first IED when 2nd BCT initially took over from the 101st. A 1st Cavalry vehicle triggered an explosion that shoved the bottom of the hummer right up through the passenger compartment, igniting a fire and killing one trooper. Since then, three Air Force EODs had been blown up and killed in the AO. One was a female. They responded to check out a suspected site. When they climbed out of their truck to look it over, some turd hiding nearby with an old telephone set off a second explosion almost directly underneath their feet. And, of course, he was there the day Colonel Infanti's vehicle hit the IED and Scarface died.

Insurgents never seemed to run short of bomb making ingredients. Prior to 2003, Iraq had actually possessed more conventional munitions than the entire U.S. military, with something like six thousand ammo dumps in the country. Insurgents had carted off the contents of a large number of these before Coalition forces could secure them. Coalition forces had also left a large number of expended 105mm and 155mm howitzer shells lying around. Jihadists policed them up; stuffed them with black powder, ammonia nitrate fertilizer, or even chicken shit mixed with diesel fuel; stuck in blasting caps; and, lo, they had effective and deadly booby trap IEDs that could be set off by pressure plates, crush wires, or command-detonated with a garage door opener, a car alarm, or a wireless telephone.

There was little GIs could do to protect themselves against IEDs. Iron Claw and Husky couldn't be everywhere for every patrol. Second Platoon alone was blown up 47 times during the weeks after Delta Company occupied the patrol bases on Route Malibu. Fortunately, most of the explosives weren't powerful enough to do much more than rattle the GIs around like pebbles in a tin can and bust tires, windows, and axles. What the Joes feared was hitting a really huge bunker buster like the one that caught Colonel Infanti and killed Scarface. Or like the one that finally took out Iron Claw.

Fourth Platoon was on a route mission with Husky and Iron Claw in the lead when Sergeant Joshua Parrish overheard EOD on the radio suddenly shouting for everyone to get down and take cover. You knew something was coming when EOD panicked. *Boom!* The explosion blew the indestructible Iron Claw in half. Part of it flew over Parrish's hummer and landed on the other side of the road.

Delta trucks ran constantly, day and night. Soldiers on that single stretch of Malibu through the S-curves were being attacked more than any others in Iraq. It turned into a fishing game, but it was hard to determine who the anglers were and who the fish. Platoons always traveled in squadrons of at least four trucks, moving at about 25mph and spaced no closer than fifty meters apart, all heavily armed with mounted .50-caliber machine guns, two-forties, and M19 automatic grenade launchers. Steering vehicles through the perilous landscape was nerve-wracking and monopolized every last bit of a driver's attention. Like rats or cockroaches, insurgents kept sneaking up to the road after nightfall to plant more IEDs, which often resulted in wild Fourth of July displays of orange flame and dirty gray billows of smoke the next time a convoy drove by.

Getting blown up became almost a spectator sport. Every Iraqi in the vicinity disappeared just before something was about to happen. The kids were always the most obvious as they scurried for cover. As soon as the IED went off, however, jetting a spray of earth and smoke several stories into the sky, every hajji around crowded up with children in arms to see what the commotion was all about. Naturally, nobody ever saw anything. Deaf and dumb as a bunch of sand crabs.

After each attack, Americans and IAs pushed through the nearest villages and settlements rounding up every male of military age for interrogation. They ransacked houses for weapons and used metal detectors to probe yards for buried stashes. They questioned suspects in hopes of catching them in lies that could be leveraged into workable information on anti-Coalition terrorists in the area. It was sheer craziness. Pathetic-looking figures sitting cross-legged on the ground with burlap bags pulled over their heads and their wrists flex-cuffed behind their backs. They were either ballsy little bastards or else they were scared shitless at the prospect of being turned over to the IA, where the Queensberry Rules did not apply. Big NCOs manhandled them and conducted strip searches, voices barking orders.

"Stand up. Take off your pants."

Delta Company tried everything to stem the assaults—mounted and dismounted patrols, static watches, cordon-and-search raids, rewards, bribes, intelligence gathering . . . Nothing seemed to work. Week after week, it was more of the same: IED and mortar explosions, the chirping, whistling sounds of shrapnel shards spinning through the air; the screaming of rocket grenades launched from concealment; the sudden ring of a sniper's shot . . . And always the men felt they were being watched by dark plotting eyes. Someone proposed more than once that they assassinate Crazy Legs. At least get rid of *that* pair of hostile eyes. No way in hell could it go on like this indefinitely without the Joes losing their minds.

After a while, Sergeant John Herne was the only man in Second Platoon whose truck hadn't been blown up by an IED. The other Joes competed to see who would ride with him. Men wanted to rub his head for good luck. It got so bad that it sometimes took the army's Rapid Repair Road crew days to get around to filling up the numerous IED holes up and down Malibu Road. In the meantime, insurgents crept up and planted more IEDs in the bottoms of the craters in order to blow up the road crews when they finally came around.

That led to the establishment of 24-hour-a-day "crater watches" to guard the holes. Sergeant Chris Messer of Second Platoon protested.

"It's crazy to put a static watch out there," he scolded Lieutenant Dudish, his platoon leader. "We're asking for them to be ambushed and our guys wiped out."

"I agree with you, Sergeant," Burke said. "But we still got to do it."

Neither would know for several months yet just how precognitive Messer really was.

In spite of all the activity, Delta Company was fortunate. Although a number of soldiers had been shot or suffered concussions and various other IED injuries, no American had been killed so far. The Joes kept getting up, dusting themselves off, repairing their trucks, and returning to the fray.

TWENTY-THREE

The reason the 10th Mountain Division was deployed so much and to so many different places—and then to the angriest parts of those places— was because its soldiers were some of the best in the military. Even so, good soldiers could break under the strain of uncertainty, privation, fear, separation from home, and combat that was both nerve-wracking and strange in that the enemy was nowhere and at the same time everywhere. There were only so many times they could turn themselves on and off. It was like repeatedly heating and cooling a length of metal. The process eventually weakened the material over time until it ruptured from the strain.

Shaking hands, chatting up merchants, flirting with shy girls, and handing out candy and little presents to kids had been easy until about the eighth or ninth IED. After that, the soldiers began to have second thoughts. They still wanted to make friends, be good neighbors, but they lost the illusion that they could build a relationship one-sided. They became more curt with Iraqis, wary, suspicious, unable to let down their guard for even a moment lest the manticore that stalked Malibu Road get them.

At the same time, the longer American troops remained in the AO, the less cordial everyday citizens became. A lot of it had to do with resentment at the inconvenience of the occupation. Closing off roads to through traffic meant farmers had difficulty transporting their produce to market. Stopping people to check their ID cards and raiding in search of terrorism suspects further annoyed the population. Soldiers on Malibu could almost feel the hate in Iraqi hearts as they passed by in their armed and armored convoys. It seemed the people were merely waiting for the Americans to get fed up with the shit and go home. They didn't believe the Americans were here to stay until it was over and that they would have to cooperate with the Americans in order to bring about better days.

Colonel Infanti constantly reminded his troops that things were going to change. There would be a turning point. Persevere and stay strong, he encouraged. We're a team. Every soldier is important to the chain of command. We're suffering right along with you. Change is coming.

Yeah? When?

Mosques were behind much of the trouble, especially those controlled by Sunnis. Imams bitterly harangued their congregations about the invaders and prodded them to resist, creating even more insurgents.

"These sons of monkeys and pigs come to Iraq in the name of freedom, but they are poison that will change our lives. They will shave our beards; take the dresses and veils off our wives, sisters and daughters; seduce them and turn them into whores. We must ask Allah to rain darkness upon the American and Jewish pigs. Please, God, kill the Americans and Jews, destroy them and eject them from our country. Allahu Akbar! Allahu Akbar!"

Insurgents used the mosques as safe houses and there was little GIs could do about it except shoot the finger at the 109 Mosque every time they passed it. Raiding a mosque to disinfect it was out of the question; it would be like poking a stick into a hornets' nest at the response it would generate throughout the AO.

The trick to pacification lay in ridding the land of insurgents while weaning the people away from them. As far as American soldiers were concerned, the only way to get rid of fanatics was to kill them, wipe them off the face of the earth. They were little better than predatory animals. After all, what kind of men wired themselves with suicide belts and blew themselves up on Israeli school buses full of very young children? Who launched rockets indiscriminately into Tel Aviv churches, schools, and houses? Who hid out in caves to manufacture anthrax or the Bubonic Plague in order to wipe out the cities of those they considered infidels? Who would hijack airplanes full of innocent women, children, and babies and fly them into skyscrapers . . . ?

You had to know your enemy.

"We're here to help, don't you understand?" Army Civil Affairs officers pleaded with local sheikhs and community leaders. "If you don't stop bombing trucks and start fighting insurgents, things are going to get much worse."

No constructive aid or rebuilding projects could be launched until residents put a stop to the murderous assaults and the AO became less dangerous. PsyOps (psychological operations) soldiers went through villages and towns handing out leaflets or shoving them underneath gates and doors. Some of the handbills cautioned locals that attacks on Americans would be dealt with harshly. Others offered rewards for information on terrorists or weapons caches.

Trucks with loudspeakers drove through, blasting caveats against insurgent activity.

"Attention, men of Kharghouli. Three days ago, there was an attack on an American patrol near here. Attacks like that hurt innocent Iraqis, slow progress, and prolong the presence of Coalition forces in Iraq. You are responsible for security in your town. Provide us with information on those who commit such futile acts and help bring peace to your community. Do not confuse our restraint with weakness. Today we come as concerned friends. Do not make us come back as enemies."

A bang outside the town signaled another American hummer striking an IED.

TWENTY-FOUR

As the modern U.S. Army fought with computers and high-tech communications as much as it did bullets, Battalion maintained a section of ten trained specialists to keep all the digital electronics going and everybody talking to everybody else. Companies in the field called it the "geek squad," no disrespect intended. Computers and Internet or satellite phones were also the Joes' link with home and the outside world, which made the geek squad in high demand when something broke down. The most popular communications specialist in the section, at least in Delta Company, was a nineteen-year-old Speedy Four (Specialist Fourth Class) named Jenson Mariur.

Originally from Palau in the South Seas, the brown-skinned young soldier was forever optimistic, polite, soft-spoken, and eager to help. He could light up an FOB with a single grin. What made him even more popular with Delta was the fact that the soldiers could always persuade him to repair their PCs, video games and assorted other personal entertainment gear.

Mariur's popularity had its downside. The Delta platoon with a problem would jump on the radio and ask for him personally. "Hey, hey, dude. We're having a little trouble. When are you coming out? Just say the word and we'll send a convoy to Yusufiyah to get you."

The result of which meant another nervous trip running the gauntlet known as Malibu Road.

One afternoon, Delta Company's First Sergeant Aldo Galliano hightailed it in to Battalion with a convoy from Third Platoon to pick up tech support to install some new computer equipment for the Company TOC at Inchon. That naturally meant Mariur, who felt more than a little apprehensive about riding with the Top Sergeant's convoy.

Top Galliano was jinxed, an IED magnet. It seemed his caravan got hit almost every time he went out. Not just his convoy, *his* truck within the convoy. He had been blown up twenty times, so often he began to take it personally. It got where, as soon as he was clear of the explosion, he jumped out of his hummer with his ears still ringing, dust up his nose, and went into a contrived rage, kicking tires, ranting and raving like a bull charging a red flag.

"Them dirty, no-good, ragheaded, shit-eating, Baghdad sons-of-bitches . . . !"

"Tell us how you really feel, Top."

"I get it every damned time. What's with Herne? They never hit him. What's he doing, bribing 'em?"

Anyone in Delta who failed to experience one of the Top Sergeant's productions was missing an Oscar-winning performance, tales of which circulated among the troops with a great deal of laughter and joking. Men would be passing the stories down to their grandchildren, they were that entertaining.

Galliano was one hard-charging Latino, rather small and short with a broad face, thick shoulders, and a practical-joke sort of humor that made him as well-liked as he was respected. He could chew a hole in a soldier's boxers and make him like it. When he noticed how shaky Mariur seemed about taking the trip down Malibu with him, he really laid it on.

"Mariur, you can ride in the truck with me. I got some technical stuff I want to talk to you about."

"That's okay, Top. We'll have a lot of time to talk when we get to Inchon. Why don't I ride back here?"

"What's the matter, Specialist? You don't believe all them stories about me, do you?"

"Well . . ."

"What are you so pale about, soldier? When I get hit—"

"*When?*"

"Well, yeah. Have you ever been blown up before?"

Mariur had a feeling he was about to. He sucked it in and managed,

"Top, I sure wouldn't want to miss seeing you kick the tires out from underneath this old crate."

Galliano laughed. The convoy headed back for Malibu Road with Mariur seated next to the Top Sergeant behind the driver, the third vehicle back in a procession of four. The crazy road with all its potholes and patched-up IED craters reminded Mariur how vulnerable they were.

It was a lovely autumn day, not so hot as sometimes, with the sun shining brightly, kids in the fields herding shaggy goats, and muezzins revving up their calls for afternoon prayers.

"Any damage you do to government property comes out of your pay," Galliano noted slyly.

"Pardon?"

"Your ass is chewing a hole in the seat."

True to form, Top's vehicle detonated an IED just before the trucks reached Inchon. Mariur wasn't even surprised; he expected it. There was a loud bang, a puff of dirt, and pieces of shrapnel chipping at the vehicle's undercarriage. Although the scumbag who put it there buried it too deep to cause any real damage, the concussion was enough to knock the breath from Mariur's lungs. He had never felt more profound relief than when the convoy pulled through the gate at 153.

Aldo Galliano jumped out to go through his usual rant. As he was stomping around kicking tires, he glanced up to see Mariur standing with his hands in his pockets looking solemn and appreciative at simply having survived the trip. His eyes were open wide, the whites in sharp contrast to a patina of "black face" sweat, dust, and smoke. He looked totally out of place in a war zone. All he needed to complete the picture of geek was a bow tie and a pocket protector.

As for Mariur, he chuckled to himself from then on whenever someone described Galliano's hitting another IED. He couldn't help himself—picturing the little Top Sergeant out there somewhere on Malibu Road kicking hell out of his hummer and blackguarding loud enough so every "Baghdad motherfucker" in The Triangle of Death could hear him.

Delta Company's First Platoon prior to DUSTWUN. Indentifiable soldiers: Sergeant Rasheen Reevers (kneeling, right); Sergeant Charles Burke (standing, third from left); Sergeant Anthony Schober (standing, fourth from left); and PFC Joe Anzak (standing, fifth from left); PFC Christopher Murphy (standing on right end). *(Courtesy of Will Hendrickson)*

LEFT Lt. Col. Michael Infanti, commander of 4/31st, 10th Mountain Division, promised his soldiers a "turning point" in the war. *(Courtesy of Lt. Col. Michael Infanti)* **RIGHT** Specialist Brandon Gray, First Platoon, on patrol in the Triangle of Death. *(Courtesy of Specialist Brandon Gray)*

Second Platoon soldiers building defenses at Patrol Base 151 on Malibu Road. *(Courtesy of Specialist Brandon Gray)*

Second Platoon on patrol through date palms. *(Courtesy of Ronnie Montgomery)*

Lieutenant Joe Tomasello, Fourth Platoon Leader (front) and Specialist James Cook on patrol. *(Courtesy of James Cook)*

Soldiers of 4/31st drop a shell on a mortar fire mission from Yusufiyah. (*Courtesy of the U.S. Army*)

Captain John Gilbreath (left), commander of Delta Company 4/31st, and Major Mark Manns, executive officer of 4/31st, with an Iraqi civilian. (*Courtesy of Major Mark Manns*)

Delta Company soldiers unearthing an insurgency weapons cache. (*Courtesy of the U.S. Army*)

Battalion mechanics were kept busy repairing vehicles blown up by IEDs on Malibu Road. (*Courtesy of the U.S. Army*)

Lt. Col. Michael Infanti's Humvee after it struck an IED on Malibu Road. His interpreter was killed and Infanti suffered a broken back. (*Courtesy of Lt. Col. Michael Infanti*)

Corporal Begin "Mayhem" Menahem, an "IED Magnet," shown here with one of his trucks destroyed in an IED explosion. (*Courtesy of Corporal Begin Menahem*)

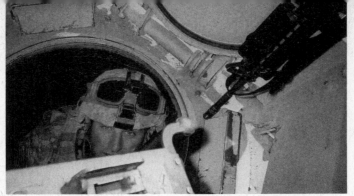

PFC Joe Anzak, a martial artist, put up a valiant fight at DUSTWUN before he was abducted. *(Courtesy of Specialist Brandon Gray)*

Iraqi Army interpreter Sabah Barack, slain by insurgents during the DUSTWUN attack. *(Courtesy of Specialist Brandon Gray)*

PFC Nathaniel Given on patrol prior to his being killed by an IED. *(Courtesy of the U.S. Army)*

1. Nathan Given. From one of the worst soldiers in Delta Company, he earned an award as one of its best just before he was killed at the DUSTWUN attack. **2.** PFC Byron Fouty, a shy, bookish soldier when he died at age 19 during the DUSTWUN attack. **3.** PFC Christopher E. Murphy tried to escape after his "crater watch" was attacked during DUSTWUN. He died entangled in concertina wire. **4.** Specialist Alexander Ramon Jimenez. He taught himself to speak Arabic before he was kidnapped by insurgents during the night of DUSTWUN. **5.** Sergeant First Class James D. Connell died at DUSTWUN weeks after he returned from home leave, after telling a family member he would never return. **6.** Sergeant Christopher Messer died according to what his precognitive dreams indicated. **7.** PFC Daniel W. Courneya was one of five Americans killed during the DUSTWUN attack. (*All photos courtesy of the U.S. Army*)

TOP LEFT Specialist Darrell Whitney with the helmet he was wearing when a sniper shot him. *(Courtesy of Corporal Begin Menahem)* **LOWER LEFT** Soldiers search house-to-house following DUSTWUN attack. *(Courtesy of the U.S. Army)* **ABOVE RIGHT** PFC Alfredo "Chiva" Lares stands inside the giant IED crater that insurgents created in an attempt to isolate Second Platoon. *(Courtesy of PFC Alfredo Lares)*

Headquarters company, 4/31st. *(Courtesy of the U.S. Army)*

TWENTY-FIVE

The Triangle of Death was like a house infested with rats and mice. Kill one or two or three, and a half dozen more popped up somewhere else. The Joes of Delta Company sometimes thought they must have tumbled down the rabbit hole into a world of lunacy. It might be better to have had a battle fully joined, such as the Marines fought at Fallujah, than to suffer constant attrition from deadly rodents sneaking and gnawing around.

ROEs dictated that you couldn't shoot an insurgent unless you actually caught him in the act of being a rat. That meant he was shooting at you or engaged in other obvious insurgent-like behavior. Delta's platoons were taking it in the shorts until they learned to use the rules of engagement to their own benefit.

"We have to be smarter than they are," Sergeant Montgomery said. Being smarter than the bad guys was how Second used Crazy Legs to significantly reduce the number of mortar and rocket attacks from across the river. Two or three times observing Crazy Legs and then ambushing the ambushers had almost put a stop to it. Maybe Second Platoon could do the same thing to those planting IEDs.

Some guy out in the middle of the night with a shovel and pick digging a hole in the road wasn't repairing the road. He was a legal target the moment he started digging, whether armed or not. Heretofore, soldiers had tried to capture them or run them off if they weren't packing heat. Lieutenant Dudish and Sergeant Montgomery, having received permission from Captain Jamoles to shoot to kill, launched a campaign to eliminate as many of these pests as they could. It didn't take long for the tactic to pay off.

Each patrol base posted a night security watch on the road on either side of the outpost. While pulling one of these static watches, Sergeant

Victor Chavez and Specialist Robert Pool were parked north of 152 facing toward Inchon observing through NVs when they spotted two figures slinking from the shadows. Apparently thinking themselves concealed by darkness, the mad bombers scurried onto the road and began digging. Sergeant Chavez radioed Delta for permission to engage.

Pool sat behind the two-forty in the turret. The M240B 7.62mm machine gun came equipped with laser target acquisition, which made for extremely accurate night firing. The range was about four hundred meters, visibility unobstructed through his NVs. Pool beaded in on the two men and felt a sudden attack of conscience at the prospect of drilling a couple of guys unarmed except for pick axes. Of actually killing another human being.

Then he thought of all the times he had been personally blown up by creeps like these, of American GIs like Pitcher who had been wounded or crippled by IEDs. That cleared his conscience.

"Permission granted to engage," Chavez tersely informed him. "Hammer the cocksuckers."

Pool did. Red tracers plunged up the center of the road and stitched the two diggers, bursting into a thousand fireflies from impact against bone and asphalt.

"I got 'em—at least one!" Pool reported excitedly.

When they rolled up to the scene, however, there was nothing left but blood trails. Insurgents were sneaky about policing up their dead and wounded. It was hard to get a decent body count where there were no bodies.

Something similar happened to Lieutenant Dudish and Sergeant Montgomery. About midnight, Dudish was at the wheel of their hummer while Montgomery sat in the turret observing the road through a CAS (Covered Acquisition System), a large camera-like device with a special thermal-sensitive laser capable of picking out the wink of a bird's eye a mile away in the middle of the night. So far, no birds were winking.

"I got movement," Montgomery suddenly whispered. "A bunch of guys underneath blankets. Goofy bastards. I guess they think we can't see 'em if they hide under the covers."

"Give them time to start digging."

"Roger that."

The saboteurs crawled up onto the road bed underneath their dark blankets, resembling giant slugs. Since First Platoon soldiers were guarding an IED crater downrange, Dudish raised them on the radio to give them a heads up.

"One-Six, this is Two-Six. We have a target. You guys hunker down in your trucks. Tracers are going to be zipping."

"Roger, Two-Six. Good luck and good shooting."

The range was less than a thousand meters, still a fairly long shot for the two-forty. Montgomery watched, finger on the trigger, eye against the laser sight. Two of the perps armed with shovels threw off their blankets and started digging at the edge of the asphalt. It wasn't like they were out farming in the moonlight.

The laser sight locked on the target; the machine gun locked on the laser. Montgomery took a deep breath, let half of it out, held the rest, and gently stroked the trigger. Every fifth bullet in a belt of 7.62 was a tracer. A stream of red arched through the night sky and plunged into the enemy demolitioneers. One of the men dropped. A woman lookout somewhere in the roadside foliage emitted such a blood-chilling scream that, even at this distance, Montgomery heard it above the deep-throated chugging of his weapon.

It was remarkable how quickly insurgents could bug out. Hajjis appeared from everywhere to drag away their dead and wounded, leaving nothing behind except some tools and blankets.

Damned frustrating—but the campaign seemed to be working. The number of IEDs on Malibu declined, at least somewhat. Subversives began to get in a hurry to accomplish their tasks, get on the road and get off again, which meant carelessness.

Toward evening of one approaching night, when the voices of children at play hung in the sunset of what might have been one of the most naturally peaceful places on earth, the concussive blast of an exploding IED shattered the tranquility. Sergeant Chris Messer and three other Second Platoon members—Specialist Jared Isbell, PFC Michael Pope, and PFC

Chiva Lares—were pulling static security for 151. Reverberations from explosions going off at all hours of the day or night left even those out of the blast radius momentarily stunned and breathless.

Recovering, Pope peeled rubber heading toward the explosion. Anytime an American might be in trouble, those nearest him were expected to respond as backup.

Sliding the hummer around the first S-curve, Pope and his squad confronted a plume of black smoke anchored to the side of the road. There were no American vehicles in sight. Instead, a trio of Baghdads wearing *shemaghs* and *disdashas*, the traditional robes of Arab men, were hotfooting it north down the middle of the road. One held his skirts bunched up around his knees and was really pumping. None were armed, none were carrying digging tools. From the looks of things, they were a bunch of amateurs who had inadvertently set off the bomb they were planting. Only luck kept it from blowing their heads off.

They looked back over their shoulders and saw the hummer bearing down on them. One of them carrying a burlap bag full of something hurled it into the bushes. All three tried to scatter. Not fast enough. Pope almost ran them down. Messer, Isbell, and Lares flung open their doors and bailed out.

"Hold it up, girls!"

Isbell and Lares collared their suspects without resistance. Messer's turned at bay and drew a knife. Sergeant Messer unsheathed his machete and brandished it. "Now, *this*," he said in his best Crocodile Dundee impersonation, "is a knife."

The guy's eyes bugged. He tossed the knife aside as though it had burned his hand, dropped to his knees and surrendered.

One captive was sixteen years old, the other nineteen, and the oldest twenty-four. The burlap bag contained wires, fuses, and timers for igniting IEDs. All three were flex-cuffed and transported to Battalion at Yusufiyah for questioning; soldiers in the field weren't authorized to interrogate prisoners. Messer and his squad became Heroes For A Day in Delta Company, as they were the first to capture insurgents in the act of setting an explosive device.

Second Platoon never heard what happened to their captives. In light of how many times his platoon had hit IEDs on Malibu, Lares secretly hoped they tried to escape and somebody shot them.

"If they had the balls to shed their dresses and come out and fight," Isbell chafed, "we would kick their butts and go home next week."

But, of course, they weren't going to come out and fight, not in the traditional manner. The next time Isbell spotted Crazy Legs T-Rex'ing down the road, he took aim with his M4 and pretended to pull the trigger.

"Bang!" he said. "You're dead."

TWENTY-SIX

Unlike previous wars in which ordinary dogfaces had virtually no access to news from the home front, soldiers in Iraq were as well informed of political and social events in Modesto, California, or Tahlequah, Oklahoma, as their parents, wives, and friends who lived there, thanks to the modern technology of the Internet and satellite phones. More so, in most instances, since they realized they were political pawns in an ongoing cultural war. The hypocrisy of politicians in the nation's capital clamoring from one side of their mouths about how they supported the troops, then referring to them from the other side of their mouths as "ill-educated" or "ignorant" was not lost in the clamor of battle. It produced anger and bitterness in every FOB, patrol base, and battle position in Iraq.

It damaged morale immeasurably when senators and congressmen asserted that American soldiers were "stuck in Iraq" because they were too stupid to get a better job, who, like Senator John Kerry, accused U.S. troops of "going into the homes of Iraqis in the dead of night, terrorizing kids and children and, you know, women . . . ," who lauded young people who went on to college instead of the armed forces as "students who think for themselves in contrast to C students with their stupid fingers on the trigger," who declared how soldiers were mostly from the under classes and enlisted in the army because they couldn't get a "real job" in the private sector.

"If you aren't smart enough to get into college," they said, "you'll end up in Iraq."

Since the end of the draft and the Vietnam War, fewer and fewer Americans served in the military. That was especially true of politicians; there was only a negligible number of veterans in either house. Knowing very little about the military, they failed to understand that the modern all-volunteer soldier was in every way the equal of his peers anywhere in the United States. Disparaging and belittling remarks by public servants who should know better profoundly insulted the patriotism and sense of duty of men like Chiva Lares, Robert Pool, James Cook, Sammy Rhodes, Mayhem Menahem, Brandon Gray, Victor Chavez, Jared Isbell, Joshua Parrish, Jenson Mariur, Will Hendrickson, and the other 90 percent of Delta Company who had all enlisted following the terrorist attacks of 11 September 2001, not because they couldn't get a "real job" or weren't smart enough to get into college but instead because they thought defending the nation was the right thing to do.

"Fuck 'em!" Men exclaimed in the vernacular of the battlefield. "We go off to die and lose our arms and legs for these cocksuckers while they stay at home like fat pigs and worship money and Sean Penn. While we're getting shot and blown up, they're looting America like a bunch of thieves and calling us stupid. Not a one of them has the balls it takes to drive Malibu even one time."

GIs in The Triangle of Death endured hit and run ambushes, heat, uncertainty, privation, fear and separation from home for about one thousand bucks a month, each day venturing from their forts expecting to kill or be killed, pondering when they would be allowed to go home, wondering if, when they finally made it home, folks would understand and appreciate the true meaning of sacrifice. Or would they have to sneak into the airport latrines to change out of uniform as returning Vietnam vets had had to do to avoid assault and insult?

Having little access to media, resentful GIs fought back in subtle ways. Whenever someone received a supportive letter or chain mail "support our troops" missive from back home, it ended up on the fort walls for everyone to read. There was hardly a dry eye when the following "Author Unknown" appeared posted in the common area at Inchon:

> You cell phone is in your pocket;
> He clutches the cross hanging on his chain next to his dog tags.
>
> You talk trash about your "buddies" that aren't with you;
> He knows he may not see some of his buddies again.

NONE LEFT BEHIND

You walk down the beach, staring at all the pretty girls;
He patrols the streets, searching for insurgents and terrorists.

You complain about how hot it is;
He wears his heavy gear, not daring to take off his helmet to wipe his brow.

You go out to lunch, and complain because the restaurant got your order wrong;
He doesn't get to eat today.

Your maid makes your bed and washes your clothes;
He wears the same things for weeks, but makes sure his weapons are clean.

You go to the mall and get your hair redone;
He doesn't have time to brush his teeth today.

You're angry because your class ran five minutes over;
He's told he will be held over an extra two months.

You call your girlfriend and set a date for tonight;
He waits for the mail to see if there is a letter from home.

You hug and kiss your girlfriend, like you do every day;
He holds his letter close and smells his love's perfume.

You roll your eyes as a baby cries;
He gets a letter with pictures of his new child, and wonders if they'll ever meet.

You criticize your government, and say that war never solves anything;
He sees the innocent tortured and killed by their own people and remembers
    why he is fighting.

You hear the jokes about the war, and make fun of men like him;
He hears the gunfire, bombs and screams of the wounded.

You see only what the media wants you to see;
He sees the broken bodies lying around him.

You are asked to go to the store by your parents. You don't;
He does exactly what he is told even if it puts his life in danger.

You stay at home and watch TV;
He takes whatever time he is given to call, write home, sleep, and eat.

You crawl into your soft bed, with down pillows, and get comfortable;
He tries to sleep but gets woken by mortars and helicopters all night long.

TWENTY-SEVEN

At twenty-eight years old, Sergeant Chris Messer was almost the "old man" of Second Platoon, younger than only a few others. After enlisting in the army in February 2003, he pulled a tour in Germany and another in Iraq with the 26th Infantry Regiment before his reassignment to Fort Drum came through in July 2005. When the 2nd BCT deployed to Iraq in late August 2006, he left behind his wife Amie and his one-year-old daughter Skyle. With him he carried a haunting premonition that he would never see either again.

No amount of gentle coaxing by Sergeant Montgomery or the other men of the platoon could knock that dark conviction from his mind. He seemed resigned to his inevitable fate. Although his turn toward fatalism left him stern and distant, prone to long talks with Chaplain Bryan and quiet time with his Prayer of Salvation card until the lettering was almost worn off, he remained the good soldier and NCO he had always been. Duty came first.

Messer was First Squad Leader. PFC Nathaniel Given was the squad's SAW gunner. Neither realized just how inextricably linked they were to become on the afternoon freckle-faced Given, nineteen, breezed into Inchon to the congratulations and good-natured ribbing of his fellow platoon members.

Back at Fort Drum, Given had been one of Sergeant Montgomery's "problem children." Since then, he had gone from one of the worst soldiers in Delta Company to one of its best. A three-star general visiting the war zone selected him out of the entire company as an example of what a good soldier should be and personally presented him the coveted unit coin, inscribed with the 10th Mountain Division logo. The tall young

Texan was walking on air when he returned to Inchon from the awards ceremony. Even stepping in a minefield pile of IA feces failed to dampen his spirit or trigger his quick temper. He wiped off his boot but not his grin.

Messer was sharpening his machete while seated on the ratty old sofa with Brenda the Bitch at the other end. He got up to shake the private's hand.

"Nate, you done good," he said.

"I have to thank you and Sergeant Montgomery," Given replied, proudly displaying the coin. "I must have been a real fuckup at first."

"You've made up for it, soldier."

"That means something coming from you, Sergeant."

Some of the other soldiers dragged him away laughing to play cards. Second Platoon was on downtime. Messer sat back down on the sofa with his machete. PFC Chiva Lares pushed Brenda out of the way and sprawled next to Messer to clean his rifle and talk about his girlfriend back home. The two soldiers had been tight since Delta formed at Fort Drum.

"Talked to Amie?" Lares asked as preamble to light conversation.

Messer concentrated on his big knife, not responding. His lean face looked lined and stiff, his eyes hard and focused.

"Chris . . . ?"

Messer looked up. "I had the nightmare again, Chiva."

"It doesn't mean anything, Chris."

"This time it was more real than ever. It was like I was outside myself. You know what I mean? I was here, right here, looking down at myself on the ground. Chiva, I didn't have my legs. Both of them were blown off and I was dying. I don't know what to do about it. I can't tell Amie, Chiva. I'm never going home again, but I can't tell her that."

Lares didn't know what to say. They had been through this together before—nights when Messer couldn't sleep because of nightmares and climbed up to the roof to sit, rub his Prayer card, and stare at snapshots of his wife and daughter in the starlight. Days when he didn't seem quite up to going on. Lares could always tell when his friend had had one of his dreams by the torment in his eyes.

None of his previous nightmares had been as graphic and specific as this one.

"Chiva," Messer said, "I have a feeling it's going to happen soon."

TWENTY-EIGHT

Surprise. It was not going to be a White Christmas in the Sandbox. Partly out of nostalgia, partly from an effort to capture a little bit of home and the Christmas spirit, the platoons on Malibu Road went all out for the holidays. Some of the guys put up Christmas trees fashioned from whatever they could find on hand. Empty cardboard boxes knifed into shape, then erected in three dimensions and covered with poncho liners, served as a fair approximation of the real thing, especially when decorated with garlands of 7.62mm machine gun ammo belts, colored-pencil cutouts of angels, Santa Claus, humvees pulled by camels, and Christmas cards from home.

Mayhem Menahem and his buddies in Fourth Platoon reported for a mission wearing red Santa Claus caps they picked up somewhere. Lieutenant Tomasello rolled his eyes. The mischievous miscreants threw their arms around each other's shoulders and harmonized a vulgar rendition of "Santa Claus Comes Tonight."

"You've had your fun," Tomasello scolded, laughing. "Now get with the program. The war didn't stop for Ramadan. I doubt it'll stop for Christmas."

"Even Mohammed wouldn't shoot Santa Claus," Joshua Parrish protested with feigned indignity.

Some of the Joes in Second Platoon planned to throw a big Christmas dance with Brenda the Bitch as guest of honor and invite any GI who could make it. Piled underneath the makeshift Christmas trees were little presents to each other dug out of care packages from home, boxes from Blue Star Mothers, and shipments from "Give a Soldier Christmas" benefactors; MRE packets: beef jerky, oatmeal cookies, hard candy; *feaky-feaky* magazines, paperback books, CD games and music . . .

Delta had the Christmas spirit. Guys were "ho ho'ing" each other all day Christmas Eve. An anonymous voice kept popping up over the company radio net to relay Santa's progress from the North Pole. Someone rendered his best Alvin the Chipmunk impersonation, and a duet sang *he knows if you've been naughty or nice, so be good for goodness sake* . . .

"Have you been a good boy, Mayhem?" James Cook teased.

"Ask my girlfriend."

"She's probably doing 'Silent Night' with some other dude by now."

Everyone looked forward to the Christmas Day feast Cookie Urbina promised. He started whipping it together the day before. The aroma of baking turkeys coming from Cookie's kitchen trailer drove the Joes crazy with anticipation. Lieutenant Tomasello's platoon made a quick trip to Battalion at Yusufiyah to pick up a resupply and the final Christmas mail run.

On the convoy's way back, the desert sun was lowering in the west above the Euphrates River and there was even a bit of December chill in the air. The four hummers traveled fast, trying to make it back to Inchon before dark. Other than necessary security details, all other missions had been suspended in order to allow the soldiers a brief holiday. Delta squads and platoons from outlying patrol bases would be rotating in and out of Inchon all day tomorrow to partake of Sergeant Urbina's masterpiece.

Joshua Parrish, James Cook, Doc Luke Bailey, and Michael Smith occupied the second humvee in the procession. Theirs was the vehicle whose entire cargo space was full of Christmas mail for the company—Christmas cards and photos, gaily wrapped packages, magazines . . . It would be delivered to Company HQ at Inchon, and from there separated and distributed to individual platoons.

It had been a good Christmas Eve. Nobody had been blown up or anything. Cook began singing off-key.

"Here comes Santa Claus, here comes Santa Claus, right down Santa Claus Lane . . ."

The convoy swung into the small S-curve approaching Inchon, in the bend of which crater watch was busier than anywhere else on Malibu Road due to the large number of IEDs that kept going off there. The trucks were almost through it when the "Christmas sleigh" with the goodies hit an IED.

It was a small charge, as IEDs went, but it was still a hell of a jolt that rung the ears of the four occupants and blew off the rear hatch. As per Company SOP, the convoy busted on through and out of the kill zone before pulling up to check on injuries and damage.

The Christmas sleigh made it past the explosion on momentum alone. The back of the truck was mangled and twisted like a stepped-on tin can. It was done for and would have to be towed. Joes who jumped out of their vehicles to establish security for the disabled hummer were astonished at the amazing sight that met their eyes.

The explosion had done more than damage the truck; it had also blown up the Christmas mail. A blizzard of Christmas cards and wrappings, *Playboy* magazines, candy, summer sausages, little stuffed love bears, fruitcake, and other presents all shredded into little sparkles of color swirled and drifted like a fractured rainbow in the red light of the setting sun.

"Merry Christmas from Mohammed and al-Qaeda in Iraq," Michael Smith groaned. "They know how to screw up a perfect day."

Parrish stared. "I never thought they'd blow up Santa Claus."

TWENTY-NINE

Delta Company tried everything to put a stop to IEDs—patrols, stake-outs, crater watches, static guards. No matter what pest control measures it initiated, the mice continued to plague the corn crib. It seemed impossible to eradicate them short of placing armed guards every ten feet along the road, an endeavor both impossible and impractical. It would have required almost unlimited manpower.

Business returned to business as usual right after Christmas dinner. Lieutenant Dudish and Sergeant Montgomery came up with the idea of clearing off the roadside undergrowth by burning it and thus eliminating hiding places for mice to collect and plot their mischief. They started at the S-curves where reeds and weed beds had overtaken many of the neglected fields and choked the bar ditches.

The best time to do it was after nightfall, when snipers would have more difficulty in selecting a target. Four Second Platoon trucks loaded with bear—Polar Bears—pulled up in the crooked road between Inchon and 152 and soldiers armed to the teeth piled out in the gathering darkness. The sun was setting inflamed and wonderful with scarlet and orange and streaks of violet and lavender, an evening so lovely and peaceful that it was inconceivable that evil could exist anywhere in the world.

But, of course, evil did exist and no one understood that better than the boys of Malibu Road. Spidery purple shadows deep in towering reeds lurked and slithered and made everything seem to come alive. In the soldiers' imagination, each bush, each blade of grass concealed a hostile waiting to jump out and drill a hole through the nearest GI. This truly was Indian Country. It was just that no one saw the Indians until they were ready to be seen. Maybe the platoons could burn them out.

While the rest of the platoon kept guard, Sergeant Montgomery and

Sergeant Chris Messer left the road and waded into the scrub, disappearing. They flicked their Bics to ignite a tangle of grass and brush alongside a canal that would act as a barrier against the fire running out of control. They could safely burn off only small sections at a time. What kind of community relations would it be if they accidentally torched a farmer's house or left his orchard in ashes?

As soon as the flames caught and began to spread, the two tall sergeants crashed back through to the road. Flames twenty feet tall were already licking at newly appeared stars and flickering across the front of a nearby house where a number of Iraqis gathered to watch. The soldiers kept an eye on them, nervously fingering their triggers and wondering how many Jihadists might be among them.

"Back home," Nathaniel Given said, "farmers sometimes burn off their fields in the winter to get rid of rats and snakes."

Jared Isbell responded with a grim little laugh. "Isn't that what we're doing?"

Heat from the blaze grew so intense that the platoon retreated to the other side of the road, behind the trucks, in order to escape it. That turned out to be a fortuitous move. Somewhere inside the inferno, the fire reached an enemy weapons cache and began to cook off explosives and rounds of ammunition, spewing smoke and tufts of flame high into the night. Ricochet bullets and green tracers spanged against asphalt and steel armor and rocketed wildly into the sky from all angles. Soldiers ducked for cover and waited for the fireworks to subside, laughing and hurling one-liners at the Iraqi spectators who took off in alarm.

It didn't take the fire long to consume the patch. The platoon loaded back up once the fire had burned down and returned to 152, where it was currently on rotation.

"We'll come back in the morning and check out that cache when things have cooled off," Lieutenant Dudish decided.

Later that night, Sergeant Messer pulled roof security with Specialist Robert Pool, who was temporarily attached to Second Platoon from Third. Pool was the tall, slender kid from California who wanted to be a psychiatrist. The two soldiers had a lot in common. Both were married, both were Christians, and both possessed that true passion for helping people that transcended the ambivalent love-hate relationship nurtured by most American GIs when it came to the Iraqis.

The fire up the road in the S-curve had burned down to glowing embers. Above, the night sky was full of stars like jewels spread from horizon to horizon. Messer and Pool discussed Scripture and human weaknesses in the privacy of the night high on the roof overlooking the date palm groves and the Euphrates River.

Specialist Dar-rell Whitney and Nathaniel Given relieved them after four hours. Given yawned and looked down the road.

"The fire's still burning," he observed.

"It's just coals," Messer said.

The four men stood and watched the glow for a moment, Messer and Given shoulder to shoulder as though unable to break some inextricable link that somehow bound them.

"Tomorrow's my wedding anniversary," Messer said, and his friends heard the ache and longing in his voice.

THIRTY

Second Platoon was gearing up for a patrol to check out the burn from last night where the weapons cache cooked off. Specialist Jared Isbell finished a shift of guard duty on the roof and entered the small common area at 152 just as Lieutenant Dudish completed his OpOrder.

"Hey, dude," Isbell called out to Nathan Given. "My buns are dragging and I'm starving my ass off. I didn't have any breakfast this morning. How about getting me a Gatorade and some food?"

"What do I look like, your *aide de camp?*"

Some of the platoon was scheduled to remain behind to provide post security. Given, Chiva Lares, and Mike Pope were supposed to run the security truck to overwatch the foot patrol from the road. However, there had been one of those serendipitous changes of plans that sometimes altered a man's destiny. Given volunteered to take Isbell's place on the dismount and relinquish his seat in the truck to Isbell, who had been up much of the night on watch.

"You're a real buddy, Nathan," Isbell said. "What do I owe you for this?"

"Your firstborn," Given joked. He thrust a Gatorade and sandwich at Isbell and snatched up his SAW to join Sergeant Messer's First Squad. "It looks like me and you are connected at the hip," he said to the sergeant.

Sergeant Montgomery was already outside in the yard getting the patrol organized. He was moving a little slow and should have stayed in his rack from an infection and a fever that had him on antibiotics. But he never copped out of a mission. The guys got a little nervous without him. Young soldiers looked to their leaders for guidance and motivation.

Accompanied by an IA interpreter, the dismount departed the fort into Indian Country on foot, crossed Malibu in a traveling overwatch and took to the fields on the other side to parallel the road toward the burn. Isbell,

Lares, and Pope kept pace on the road in a humvee. Now and then they caught sight of their platoon mates as the patrol wended its way through palms and across an open meadow nestled against a citrus orchard.

A traveling overwatch entailed two V-shaped wedges of men in tandem, the trailing wedge "overwatching" the point wedge. Lieutenant Dudish commanded the lead element, while Sergeant Montgomery took trail. Specialist Sidney Streibel had point with Joe Merchant. Nathan Given, Sergeant Messer, PFC Chris Christopher, and the rest of the section fanned out behind Streibel and Merchant at intervals. Lieutenant Dudish walked the command position between the two wedges with his RTO (radio telephone operator), interpreter, and medic. Sergeant Montgomery's element followed about twenty-five meters back with the rest of the platoon.

The mission was threefold: search for more caches in the vicinity; chat up local farmers and villagers through the interpreter in hopes of picking up information about anyone suspicious that might have been hanging around the area; and, three, possibly jump up an insurgent trying to get to the burn to scarf up anything left.

"Watch it, people," Sergeant Montgomery cautioned. "Don't let your guard down. We're heading into bad-guy territory."

It was about 1000 hours, the day was already heating off last night's winter chill, and it was slow and dangerous work. Children laughed, waved energetically and gave "thumbs-up" as the wedges crept through small settlements. Montgomery had heard somewhere that the "thumbs-up" sign carried an offensive connotation in the Arab world, almost as insulting as being hit with a shoe, but the kids employed it so enthusiastically and with such flashing white teeth that he figured they intended it in a friendly way.

On the other hand, old men and women and their adult families tending livestock and miniature gardens around their simple mud huts remained as closed-mouthed and standoffish as usual. The passage of soldiers through their homesteads elicited little visible reaction. Lieutenant Dudish halted the patrol a number of times while he and the terp questioned people. But, of course, few had anything to say. See no evil, hear no evil . . .

Sometimes Montgomery felt like a dirty secret smuggled into the country.

Signs of old violence marked some of the buildings nearest the road—walls scorched by explosives and pock-marked by gunfire and shrapnel. Tall marsh grass grew so thick along canals and irrigation ditches that anything could be hiding in it. An ambush threatened around every corner, at every turn.

A taxi unoccupied on a dirt road near some houses caught the patrol's attention. Lieutenant Dudish and the IA questioned Iraqis in the nearest residence. A couple of kids ran out and tossed a soccer ball back and forth with the soldiers. Some more kids rode by on rusty, big-tired bicycles. The patrol trudged on.

Lieutenant Dudish collapsed the formation into a "modified wedge," otherwise known as a file, in order to jump across the narrow point of an open sewer cutting across one end of a meadow, with a scattering of mud houses on the other side. A sickening odor rose from raw sewage.

Given took a short run when it came his turn to cross, his gear rattling and flopping. He sailed across the sewer, only to stumble and fall on the other side. He caught himself by thrusting out one arm elbow-deep into the filthy water. It seemed he could never go out without getting his feet tangled in something at least once and falling. Today was no exception.

He scrambled disgustedly to his feet, shaking his dripping arm and performing a credible impersonation of First Sergeant Galliano getting hit by an IED. "Damn this fucking place. I hate this fucking place. Everyplace you go there's all this fucking shit."

Someone shut him up with an amused, "Hey, Given. There's no crying allowed in baseball."

Streibel, on point, turned the wedges toward the burn by the side of the road at the little S-curve. A wire fence stretched loosely between crooked eucalyptus posts separated the burn from an ancient orchard grown up in weeds and the houses where the Iraqis had gathered last night to watch the fire. Streibel halted at a gap in the fence where the wire was broken.

"Hey, Sergeant Messer," he called out. "I'm not taking this. I'm making my own way."

Sergeant Messer to Streibel's left and rear walked forward. "Go on," he said. "I'm going this way. That cache should be right over there somewhere."

Streibel and Merchant off to his right both hesitated. This wasn't like Messer. He and Sergeant Montgomery used almost the same litany: Never take the easy road; the harder route is always safer; go around even if it takes more time; better caution over haste.

PFC Given shifted toward Messer in order to pass through the downed fence with him. Weapons and armor made crawling through fences a real bitch.

Sergeant Montgomery couldn't tell what was going on up front from his place in the trailing wedge. The first indication he had that something might not be right was when he spotted kids running toward their houses like the devil was pitch-forking their little bottoms. He grabbed his radio mike to broadcast a warning.

THIRTY-ONE

The first indication those in the security truck on the road had that something might be about to go horribly wrong was when Sergeant Montgomery's voice suddenly blurted over the air: *"L.T., something's going on!"*

That was as far as he got. The enormous *Thu-wump* of the explosion rattled the truck and the three men inside it. Out in the field, between the gnarled old orchard and the scattering of Iraqi houses, a plume of earth, black smoke and flame jetted fifty feet into the sky.

"My God!" Isbell cried, aghast at its size and power. Smoke and pulverized earth smudged out all view of any of the soldiers crossing the field toward the fence. One thing was obvious, though: the dismount had set off an IED. Who and how many were involved was impossible to determine.

Chiva Lares' first thought was that he had seen Crazy Legs walking down the road earlier that morning. Then, voices over the radio erased all rational thought and replaced it with panic and emotion. The net came alive with men yelling and screaming like Chewbacca in *Star Wars*, everybody trying to get his transmission heard at the same time. Company HQ was going apeshit. The beginning of what everyone hoped would be an unremarkable day had unexpectedly turned into a soup sandwich. As Mayhem Menahem liked to say, "It only takes one IED to screw up your whole day."

"Break! Break! Everybody clear the net . . ."

"Man down! Man down!"

That froze the blood of every soldier listening. Combined like that, in a combat zone, they were the two most chilling words in any dictionary.

"Two-Six, this is Delta . . . Two-Six, tell me what you got . . ."

". . . platoon caught . . ."

"*I need you to calm down. What is your grid, over?*"

"*Medic!*"

"*Say again. How many personnel are involved, over?*"

"*. . . need a medevac!*"

"*Delta X-Ray, this is Four-Six . . .*"

"*Four-Six, clear the net . . .*"

"*Four-Six, we have visual on possible enemy personnel trying to exfil along the river.*"

Lares, in the security truck, caught glimpses of his platoon mates running about in a whirlpool of black smoke, as though engulfed by mindless panic. Shrapnel chirping and whistling fell out of the sky to land all around the hummer.

A voice on the platoon net took over. In spite of all the chaos, Sergeant Montgomery sounded unruffled and in charge. *Circle up the wagons. Get out local security. Everybody, keep your heads down and get ready for an attack . . .*

Order returned, such as it was, although no one monitoring the radios knew what was going on. Conflicting reports continued. At first, it appeared one man was down. That was quickly amended to two men down, then *three*. It soon became clear that the IA terp was one of the injured. Minutes later, Lieutenant Dudish requested medevac for one IA and two U.S., their identities unknown since names of casualties were never broadcast in the clear, only their roster numbers followed by the last four of their social security numbers.

Second Platoon seemed to have stepped into some serious shit.

At 151, radio watch turned up the volume and put it on speaker box. Unable to leave the fort unsecured, Fourth Platoon gathered around to listen. Lieutenant Tomasello and Platoon Sergeant Garrett frantically shuffled through rosters and company manning tables, looking for SS numbers. Mayhem Menahem's heart pounded against his ribs. *Who are they? How badly are they wounded?*

He wouldn't let himself consider that one of his friends might have been killed. So far, Delta Company, unlike a couple of other companies in the battalion, had suffered not a single KIA.

A similar scene played itself out with First Platoon at FOB Inchon.

Gathered around chattering radios inside the Company TOC, Gray, Murphy, Anzak, Jimenez, Corny, Fouty, Schober, and all the other men lapsed into a grim, white-faced hush, their attention riveted on the radio and whatever news came out of it next, hoping for the best, fearing the worst.

"First Platoon!" Sergeant Burke ordered. "Get your battle rattle on . . . Just in case."

At the Battalion TOC in Yusufiyah, Colonel Michael Infanti and CSM Alexander Jimenez had just returned from battlefield circulation checking on 4/31st companies in the field when all the excitement began. Infanti's policy was to stand back and let subordinate commanders fight their own companies unless they started fucking up things. All hell was breaking loose at the scene of the attack, but Captain Jamoles and Second Platoon appeared to be getting control of things.

A chill crossed the Colonel's spine as he monitored the company net. All the shouting and crying broke his heart, the pleas for help growing louder and more frantic. He realized what he was hearing were the sounds of soldiers dying.

THIRTY-TWO

There is a technique of film making in which action slows down to almost stop time, then suddenly speeds up again to convey the confusion and fast pace of battle. That was the way it was with Sergeant Montgomery after the IED went off. The monster explosion all but obliterated sight of the platoon's leading wedge in a display of dirty gray and black smoke that began out of a red fire center and billowed upward and outward in agonizing slow motion. Shards of flying metal sliced the air into ribbons, whistling dangerously, but even they seemed sluggish enough to be plucked out of the air with a quick hand.

Then everything sped back up to double, even triple time, until things happened so fast it was like an old Charlie Chaplin movie fast-forwarded. Montgomery's wedge went to ground. The sergeant buried his face in the weeds and forced himself to take a deep breath to slow down. Always after initial contact came that period of damage assessment that required a cool and rational mind in order to reorganize an appropriate response.

The man who rose back to his knees to see what was going on was once more the total professional soldier, a sergeant who knew by heart the Infantryman's Bible, the Seven-Dash-Eight manual. The first thing he did was grab his nearest section leader, Sergeant Nathan Brooks.

"Set up security until we get this mess straightened out," he ordered. An IED often preceded an ambush.

The platoon's commo was going crazy. There was no small arms fire. That was a plus. Montgomery broke in on the net to initiate reorganization. "Get a head count going. Everybody okay?"

"All good to go," responded a team leader from up front. *"We're all up."*

"Man down! Man down!" came an interruption.

Montgomery rushed forward to link with Lieutenant Dudish, bent low and ducking and dodging to prevent making an easy target of himself, Sergeant John Herne right behind him. The lieutenant was already on his feet and on the radio trying to determine the extent of the hit. Nearby in the weeds lay the IA interpreter with a hot piece of metal sticking out of his arm. He was writhing on the ground and trying not to scream. Doc Bailey was bent over him with his aid bag open. He looked up.

"He'll be all right," he said. "It's not serious."

Smoke obscured everything forward from that point. Out of the swirl came the sound of men coughing and calling out to check on each other. Specialist Streibel, the point man, had pushed on through. He stood on Malibu Road next to the security truck, waving his arms to attract attention. From his elevated position, he commanded the patrol's only overall view.

"*Hey, Sarge! Sarge!*" he shouted over the platoon radio. "*They're down. Given and Messer. They're down!*"

He pointed, then bounded off the road toward them. Sergeants Montgomery and Herne ducked into the smoke toward where Messer and Given were last seen. Montgomery grabbed Doc Bailey on the way. Somebody else could look after the lightly wounded IA.

The smoke dissipated some to reveal a four-foot crater blown into the raw earth at the gap in the fence. The two Second Platoon soldiers appeared to have been picked up by the explosion and dumped out into the weeds, almost to where last night's burn began. They must have been standing on top of the mine when it went off. They lay twisted on the ground like a pair of broken mannequins. Streibel was already with them, kneeling at Messer's side, his rifle cast aside.

Montgomery took in the situation at a glance. Given lay quietly on his back with his shattered right leg bent sideways against his ribs at an impossible angle. His uniform, webgear, and boots were torn and scorched. The boy's eyes were closed. Not a drop of blood marred his face. Just freckles and a kind of at-peace expression.

Messer had fallen a few feet away, groaning and barely conscious but not otherwise moving. Montgomery couldn't believe what he was seeing. *Holy Christ!* The man's legs were blown off below the groin. Nothing remained except strings of torn flesh. Blood pumped from severed arteries. Streibel snatched a cravat from his first aid packet. He looked up helplessly as Doc Bailey dropped down next to him.

"What do you want me to do?" he pleaded, tears streaming down his cheeks. "He's bleeding, but I can't get on a tourniquet. He doesn't have any legs left."

"We gotta put pressure, pinch off the bleeding."

Doc went to work with Streibel on one side of the body, Herne on the other. They ripped open combat bandages and stuffed them into cavities where Messer's legs used to be. Shooting arteries sprayed their faces and uniforms and they were immediately soaked. The copperish smell of fresh blood mixed in the air with the pungent cordite whiff of smoke. Herne and Streibel kept talking to the wounded man at the rate of a mile a minute.

"Chris! Chris, you can't leave us, man. You hear me? Stay with us, buddy. Hear me, you can't go. Damn it, Chris, you can't leave us. We won't let you."

Horrified as they were by Messer's condition, they were equally stunned by the realization that everything was occurring almost exactly the way Messer's dream foretold it. More than once he had instructed teammates that *when* it happened he didn't want anyone trying to save him. He said he couldn't live without his legs.

"I'm not going back home half a man," he had said. "I couldn't stand the pity."

Streibel looked up, tear tracks on his face. "*Damn!* Damn it. He kept saying he was never going home again."

"We've not lost him yet, Streibel," Doc Bailey snapped.

In the meantime, Sergeant Montgomery was seeing what he could do for PFC Given. He took out his knife and cut off the soldier's gear to check for wounds. Given still hadn't moved. It was the strangest thing. There was almost no blood. A large hunk of shrapnel had pierced his side beneath one armpit and went all the way through, exiting below the other armpit and apparently sucking out all his blood with it.

PFC Nathaniel Given, former fuckup turned model soldier, was dead.

The sergeant rose wearily to his feet and looked around. Lieutenant Dudish had formed the platoon into a protective defensive perimeter around the wounded men. Soldiers glared at the little knots of Iraqis forming in front of houses down the road to watch.

"Sons-of-bitches!" someone carped bitterly. "They *knew*. Them fucking ragheads knew what was happening and they let it."

Time was critical if Messer was to survive. As Inchon afforded the nearest landing site for a Black Hawk medevac, heartsick GIs loaded their buddies onto stretchers and strapped the stretchers one to a hood on arriving humvees. The hummers scooted around the S-curve to Inchon, soldiers on either side jogging along with them, their rage and sense of loss almost palpable. It would not have been a good time for an Iraqi, *any* Iraqi, to show any kind of hostile intent. There was even another proposal to blow away Crazy Legs if he was stupid enough to present the opportunity.

Sergeant Montgomery stayed back with a few other soldiers to police up body parts and put them in a bag. The burn and weapons cache forgotten, he still reached Inchon ahead of the medevac. He rushed to the aid station to check on his men.

Messer was intubated because he couldn't breathe on his own. The blanket that covered him flattened out below his hips. Given lay on another stretcher next to him, his young face covered.

"Sarge, you can't be in here," Doc Bailey reminded him gently.

The rest of Second Platoon waited out in the yard in almost total silence. Jared Isbell looked up. Tears stained his pale face. He was twenty years old.

"Sarge," he said, choking up. "Today was Chris' third wedding anniversary. He was upset because he didn't get a chance to call his wife before we left on patrol."

THIRTY-THREE

Sergeant Ronnie Montgomery knew the score as soon as he spotted the short, square figure of Chaplain Jeff Bryan get out of a humvee at Inchon late the same afternoon of the explosion. The chaplain would be spending the night counseling with Second Platoon, which had been relieved of all duties because of the blow it suffered. The death of even a single soldier made a major impact in limited warfare, unlike at Gettysburg, Normandy, or Hamburger Hill where soldiers were so busy surviving they failed to immediately grasp the enormity of their losses. Casualty rates were so proportionately higher in previous wars because it took hours, days, sometimes weeks for a wounded soldier to reach a hospital. Part of the modern U.S. Army's creed that no soldier would be left behind included the promise that if you were wounded on the battlefield, the army would do everything it could to save your life and not let you die. A soldier who reached a hospital within thirty minutes of being wounded had a 99 percent chance of surviving.

Of course, there was always that one percent.

Chaplain Bryan took Montgomery and Lieutenant Dudish aside. "I'm sorry," he began. His eyes were red. Messer and he had been close. "Your boys didn't make it."

Montgomery stared back, feeling numb, dead. The platoon's losses were still sinking in.

"Damn it," he managed.

"You all right, Sergeant?"

"Yeah, yeah. I guess. I knew Given was . . . that he wouldn't make it. But Messer?"

"He died on the medevac. He was DOA when they took him off."

"This is so . . . Pardon me, Padre. This is so fucked up. Did you know about his nightmares? Is it possible that someone can predict his own dying?"

"I think it must be possible. Do you want me to tell the platoon?"

"We'll tell 'em," Lieutenant Dudish volunteered. "They're our boys."

Montgomery didn't know what to think, what to feel. But he knew he had to hold it together. He kept hearing Colonel Infanti's words: "How you react when you lose a soldier—and it *will* happen—sets the tone for the rest of your men for the remainder of the war. If they see you fall apart, they will fall apart."

Relaying bad news to the platoon without breaking down was the hardest thing either Lieutenant Dudish or Sergeant Montgomery had ever done. Sergeant Messer was liked and respected. So was Nathan Given once he got himself squared away and stopped playing the company shitbird. Now they were gone. They had people waiting for them at home, people who would now wait forever.

Delta Company took the deaths hard. Soldiers in the new company formed at Fort Drum only months before out of misfits and castoffs from other units had gotten tight. Emotions of bewilderment, survivor's guilt, rage, and despair painted themselves large on drawn faces filled with shock. There was a lot of quiet time, a lot of mourning. Many of the guys, like Specialist Brandon Gray, went off to themselves and wept, throwing themselves on their bunks or crouching with their faces in corners. Others sought each other out to talk, to be close, to touch each other.

"Messer *knew* it was coming. How can someone dream the future?" Sergeant Victor Chavez lamented.

"He *knew*."

Soldiers looked at each other as the fears crept in deep. Hadn't they all dreamed of dying in Iraq at one time or another? Which of the dreams might be considered precognitive?

Specialist Jared Isbell was particularly distraught, feeling like Given had died in his place.

"Nathan was supposed to be in the truck instead of me," he agonized. "He took *my* place on the ground."

"You can't blame yourself, Isbell. None of us could have known."

"Maybe this wouldn't have happened if we hadn't switched. That could have been me instead of him. Everything might have changed. He might still be alive!"

Sergeant Montgomery maintained his composure for the sake of the platoon. He walked among the mourners, attempting to engage them in conversation, to talk it out. Some were willing. Others were not. Hostile expressions implied that the platoon sergeant, Lieutenant Dudish, Captain Jamoles, Battalion, the army, America, or some other faceless and collective entity was to blame. That was understandable. They didn't want leaders comforting them as they grieved; they had each other for that.

Other officers and NCOs approached Lieutenant Dudish and Sergeant Montgomery to offer their condolences. The sympathetic looks on their faces communicated the same thought: these could have been their men.

The character of the platoon began to change from that day. Life was expendable. The Joes always told each other that, but now they were facing its reality. A certain grimness set in. It leached away the boyishness, the sense of adventure that had accompanied Delta Company to Malibu Road. Faces became harder, older. *Manticore* was no longer only a scifi movie, not in The Triangle of Death.

There was a lot of hatred. Sergeant John Herne called it a "hate fest." Guys wanted to go out and seek revenge by burning everything in the AO to the ground. Others plotted to start with Crazy Legs, especially after they learned he had been spotted nearby before Messer and Given triggered their IED. Hearts and minds, hell yes. But a bullet through the head and a stake through the heart. *Fuck these miserable, murdering ragheads!*

Men who had never had the habit took up smoking or chewing tobacco as part of the company's general sense of fatalism. After all, they had a better chance of dying here than from cancer or heart disease years from now. Life shifted into increments of one day at a time. The future no longer existed. Life was lived according to the next patrol, the next run on Malibu Road.

The Joes built a little memorial to the fallen warriors at Inchon. Above

Messer's photo on the wall hung the machete he always carried. Above Given's was the unit coin the general awarded him. Below on the floor, according to tradition, sat their boots and helmets.

"Soldiers die with honor," Chaplain Bryan eulogized. He swallowed the lump in his throat as he glanced at Messer's laminated prayer card he held in his hand. "Sergeant Messer and Specialist Given died on enemy soil here a long way from home. They died with honor and belief in America and its people. They died for a just cause to ensure freedom does not become lost in a world where evil attempts to conquer by force . . . They will not be forgotten. Not by their families, not by you, and they will not be forgotten by God . . ."

A tightness formed in Sergeant Montgomery's chest. The last thing he needed was a lecture about the sacrifices men make during war. He had a hollow feeling that his two soldiers would not be the last men in Delta to lose their lives in The Triangle of Death. Insurgents seemed to be cranking up the violence, as though desperate not to let the Americans reach that turning point in the war that Colonel Infanti was always talking about.

THIRTY-FOUR

In The Triangle of Death, the normal drama of Iraqi life continued to unfold on the periphery of the war: families working and growing; laughing students on their way to a recently reopened school; boys courting girls in a genteel manner reminiscent of eighteenth-century America; farmers bent over hoes and rakes and scythes in their tiny fields along the river; coy young women in black burkas slipping down their veils to reveal flashing smiles in brown faces; the rush of kids across a rubble-strewn lot toward a convoy passing through, most waving madly, some plucking up chunks of concrete to fling at the American soldiers.

Sometimes PFC William "Big Willy" Hendrickson of Bravo Company saw himself as more of an observer of the war than a participant, a small cog in a big machine creating one of history's turning points in Iraq's long and sometimes tragic saga. When other soldiers could be found in their off-time watching movies on their PCs or playing video games or cards, Hendrickson had his nose stuck deep in a book somewhere, generally a history. A budding intellectual at twenty years old, he envisioned himself in some future academic career where ivy replaced IEDs, and rational discourse took the place of violence. Service in the Cradle of Civilization, for him, was an opportunity to expand his knowledge about the oldest piece of continuously occupied real estate on earth.

If any soldier was out of place in the military, miscast as a grunt, it was Big Willy Hendrickson. He enlisted from curiosity and a deep sense of duty. After completing basic training, he was assigned to the 10th Mountain Division only weeks before the 2nd BCT deployed. Missing out on most of the unit's combat up-training left him nervous and apprehensive, worried that he wouldn't have any more knowledge about army stuff when he reached the war zone than when he got out of boot camp. He soon met another misfit after his arrival in Iraq—the chaplain.

He and another soldier were manning a security post at Battalion HQ in Yusufiyah when they saw two other soldiers walking around on the grounds, one of whom was short and rather stocky and unarmed.

"Look at that idiot," Hendrickson observed. "What the hell is with that retard, goofing around out here like that without a weapon?"

A few minutes later, the stocky soldier walked up to him. Hendrickson saw the crosses on the soldier's uniform. *Oh, crap! It's the chaplain!*

Hendrickson relished long intellectual discourse. So did Chaplain Jeff Bryan. On that basis, they developed a relationship and made a point of getting together whenever duty permitted. It was the chaplain who encouraged the private from Bravo to expand his knowledge not only into the secular history of the region but also into its historical period in the Bible.

During its five thousand years of hosting empires, of invading and being invaded, the fertile valley between the Tigris and Euphrates Rivers had suffered many tyrannical rulers—Sumerian, Assyrian, Persian, Greek, Roman, Mongol, Turk, British, and, more recently, Saddam Hussein. Between the seventh and thirteenth centuries when few in Europe could read, much less write, Baghdad was renowned for its scholars and artists.

In 1258, however, a Mongol invasion from the east cast the region back into the Dark Ages, a collapse from which it had never fully recovered. In more than a millennium of conflict between Christianity and Islam, Islam had been the aggressor most of the time. Scholars generally agreed that the problem of Islamic terrorism had its roots in the Mongol invasion and the fall of the Tigris-Euphrates River Valley. History was asking the Islamic world to adjust to modernity in less than a century, a condition it took the West nearly six centuries to achieve.

Hendrickson discovered the prominence of the River Euphrates in the Bible to be extraordinary. It was mentioned in Genesis, the first book of the Old Testament, and in Revelation, the last book of the New Testament—and twenty-five times in-between.

"Israel is mentioned more times in the Bible than any other nation,"

Chaplain Bryan pointed out. "But Iraq is a close second place, although that's not the name used in the Bible. It's called Babylon, Land of Shinar, and Mesopotamia."

"Mesopotamia" meant "between the two rivers." Its later name of Iraq meant "country with deep roots." Indeed, Iraq had deep roots. If the Bible was believed, mankind began in the region of Iraq—and mankind would end there.

Iraq was the approximate location of the Garden of Eden, where God created Adam and Eve in the beginning. The Greatest Story Ever Told unfolded from there step by step, event by event.

Satan made his first recorded appearance in Iraq. The Tower of Babel was built in Iraq, followed by the confusion of languages. Abraham hailed from a city in Iraq, as did Isaac's wife. Jacob spent twenty years between the two rivers. Iraq was the site of Persia, the world's first empire. The greatest Christian revival in history occurred in Nineveh, now the city of Mosul. The events in the book of Esther took place in Iraq. The book of Nahum prophesied against a city in Iraq. The Euphrates River was the far eastern border of the land God promised Abraham. Finally, the book of Revelation warned against the resurrection of Babylon.

The Euphrates River was 1,800 miles long. According to Revelation, it would dry up after a full-scale invasion of the West coming from the East. And blood would rise to the level of a horse's bridle.

"America has invaded the Garden of Eden," Hendrickson speculated. "Does that mean we are to be a part of the Battle of Armageddon in the end times?"

Chaplain Bryan looked up somberly and shrugged. "We may be in the right place at the right time," he said.

"Or in the wrong place at the right time."

THIRTY-FIVE

Command Sergeant Major (CSM) Alexander Jimenez, the highest-ranking NCO in 4th Battalion, was the enlisted equivalent of Lieutenant Colonel Infanti. He was a dark, solidly built Hispanic of forty-five with a professional bearing and a son and daughter back home, both of whom were in their twenties. Although he knew most of the more than eight hundred men in the battalion by sight and last name, knew all of their names on rosters and manning tables, he seldom got to know any of them well. There were three men in the battalion other than those occupying staff positions who stood out in his mind above others, each for a different reason.

It was obvious why the first should be Specialist Alexander Jimenez, the gunner in Delta Company's First Platoon. They shared the exact same name, even though they were not related. Both were career soldiers from similar working-class backgrounds. Their mothers even bore the same name: Maria.

Specialist Jimenez had a reputation for being a good machine gunner, a hard-charging soldier, and the only non-Arabian soldier in the battalion who spoke Arabic. Down in Delta, he took a great deal of good-natured ribbing about his "daddy," all of which he laughed off with his enormous sense of humor.

"Jimenez," CSM Jimenez once said to him, "I'm proud to lend you my name. Don't sully it."

The second soldier was a skinny little private named Harold Fields, who was only seventeen years old when he deployed to Iraq. U.S. law forbade any soldier under the age of eighteen from combat theater assignments. Fields somehow slipped through the cracks and wasn't discovered until he reached Baghdad. The CSM had to send him back to Fort Drum, even though his birthday was only a month away. Fields begged to stay.

"Sergeant Major, don't you understand? My outfit needs me. They're the only family I've ever really had."

"I have no choice, son. We'll send for you next month as soon as you turn eighteen."

"Promise, Sergeant Major?"

These kids were amazing people. They were asked to do things most civilians would never do. Not only that, they pleaded to be allowed to do them. The sergeant major kept his word and brought the private back to Iraq. Fields was now back with Bravo Company. Jimenez hoped he never regretted his decision. He would blame himself should anything happen to the kid.

The third man was Sergeant First Class James D. Connell from the same Tennessee hills that produced World War I's Sergeant Alvin York. Connell, the divorced father of three and, at forty, beginning to bald and build a thicker waist, had enlisted in the army in 1989 and spent much of his subsequent military career serving as a paratrooper with the 75th Ranger Division and the 101st Airborne Division. He received orders to the 10th Mountain in July 2004 and deployed with the 2nd BCT as assistant operations sergeant in Colonel Infanti's TOC.

CSM Jimenez knew Connell well, since they worked together almost daily. Connell chafed at the inaction of his desk job.

"I need to talk to you, Sergeant Major," Connell would say in his soft voice. "Working up here in staff, you get pulled away from the troops. I want to be assigned back to the field. I'd like to have a platoon."

The CSM kept putting him off, not because he thought Connell wasn't up to it but instead because he thought the senior sergeant might not be tough enough for day-to-day combat. Paradoxically enough, for an Airborne Ranger type whose job it was, in the words of the Joes, to break things and kill people, Connell was a gentle, compassionate man who honestly tried to see the better side of everyone and everything. From the perspective of many hardcore career infantrymen, this kind of mindset connoted a weakness. CSM Jimenez thought Connell might be better suited for Civil Affairs where he could actually employ his philosophy in helping Iraqi people rather than killing Iraqi insurgents.

Still, the man deserved a chance, had earned it. It was another decision CSM Jimenez hoped he never lived to regret.

"Sergeant Connell," he finally promised, "you'll be considered the next time a field opening comes up."

Delta Company's First Platoon needed a new platoon sergeant after an IED injured Platoon Sergeant Charles Burke and he had to be evacuated for recovery.

"You still want the job?" CSM Jimenez asked Connell.

"You bet."

In such ways are decisions made that alter lives and change the course of individual histories.

"I'll deliver a big howdy for you to your 'son' in first Platoon," Sergeant Connell joked, meaning Specialist Jimenez.

CSM Jimenez looked at him. "All those boys are my sons," he said.

THIRTY-SIX

Sergeant Ronnie Montgomery remembered well the chain of events that led him and many other soldiers like him to Iraq. In September 2001, Bravo/502nd (Bravo Company, 502nd Infantry) of the 101st Airborne Division was running patrols in another far-flung trouble spot of the world, interdicting weapons and drug smugglers down by Chicken Lake in the crossing point between Kosovo and Macedonia. It was tough and dangerous work, with the occasional firefight and a few artillery or mortar duels. One night while Montgomery and his platoon hid in the woods to catch a few well-needed winks of sleep, a barrage of artillery rounds sought them out, almost jarring him out of his sleeping bag.

The next morning, Bravo Company's CO got on the horn to inform his platoons that terrorists had flown hijacked airliners into New York's World Trade Center and the Pentagon. The loss of civilian lives was expected to top three thousand, perhaps as many as ten thousand. President George W. Bush had declared war on terrorism.

"The terrorists have been at war with us for ten years," a GI grumbled. "It's about time we went to war with them."

That was five years ago. Some of the guys in Second Platoon, like Jared Isbell, Chiva Lares, and Nathan Given, were only thirteen or fourteen years old when it happened and the War on Terror began. Now they were fighting it; Given had lost his life in it.

First came the Afghanistan campaign to destroy the Taliban and the terrorist training camps. Montgomery had missed out on that. But he knew he was going to war when he received PCS (permanent change of station) to the 10th Mountain Division, the most deployed outfit in the army. The U.S. had some unfinished business with Saddam Hussein and his support of terrorists.

Kosovo had been a piece of cake, a walk in the park, compared to The Triangle of Death. Although Delta Company had occupied its positions on Malibu Road for only four months or so, it seemed like forever since the 101st Airborne sergeant predicted that Polar Bear soldiers would never safely drive Malibu. Well, they *were* driving Malibu. Maybe not safely, but they were driving it. What's more, Delta Company had established battle positions the length of the road—and was holding them. Montgomery supposed that counted as progress toward Colonel Infanti's "turning point."

While the deaths of Messer and Given were not the first KIAs the 2nd BCT suffered, they were the first in Delta Company. The mental picture of Messer lying in the field with his legs blown off and Given with the blood all sucked out of his body would stay with Sergeant Montgomery for the rest of his life. Sure, guys had been blown up before all along the road and a few even shot by snipers, but Messer and Given seemed to jolt the soldiers into a new realization that the war had jacked up another level.

Each day, they still underwent the necessary routines of briefings, inspections, and rehearsals before they donned their heavy body armor, helmets, weapons, night-vision devices, rucks, and other implementa of modern warfare and moved out to do a job on the treacherous devil road where each and every one had a price on his head. Their faces reflected how they thought the odds were against them.

"We're dead. We're never going home."

"Yeah, but at least you'll die with your buddies."

"We'll deal with it," Sergeant Montgomery said. "We're all in the same shitty situation together. There's nothing we can do about it. We're soldiers and we're getting paid to clear this road."

It was up to leaders to project an image of confidence and optimism. They must not show disillusionment with the American mission. Whenever the men voiced their doubts, Montgomery staunchly defended the war and all its intricacies, waving his right hand in a shaking motion at shoulder level in the Iraqi gesture for "What the fuck you talking about?"

The soldiers of Second Platoon gradually reached a turning point of their own. Montgomery sensed a new, harder, more dangerous mood starting to develop to replace the fatalism that had infected the platoon since the day of the deaths in the field. The guys became anxious, angry, itching for payback. They weren't going to take this shit any longer.

"They're mindfucking us," they protested. "We need to start mindfucking *them*."

THIRTY-SEVEN

Malibu Road remained a lawless environment in spite of Delta Company's every effort to tame it. Since it sometimes took Rapid Road Repair crews days to get out and patch up holes in the roads left by IEDs, Joes charged with the additional duty of standing static crater watches became even more vulnerable to attention by local insurgents. Sergeant Montgomery looked at the watch as an engraved invitation to be attacked. Sitting in one place too long, especially at night, was like the tethered goat in the movie *Jurassic Park* waiting for T-Rex to come eat him. Sooner or later, the goat got eaten.

Prior to his enlisting in the army, Montgomery worked as a laborer with a concrete company where he learned how to mix cement and knead in steel rebar to make the mixture stronger—and, therefore, in the case of Malibu Road, more difficult for insurgents to dig down into it to plant their devices. He offered to speed up the road repair effort by taking over a share of it to limit the time his men spent as bait. Engineers agreed to provide the necessary materials to repair the blast holes if Montgomery's soldiers wanted to do the work themselves. It was worth a try.

Second Platoon's first and, as it turned out, last endeavor in road-building was the daunting task of filling in a five-feet-deep pit left in the blind S-curve south of Inchon. The platoon's "motor pool" of four humvees arrayed themselves in a perimeter on the road around the hole. Some of the guys pulled security in the hummers while the rest mixed and poured cement from utility trailers pulled onto the worksite. They found it a satisfying break from the daily grind of getting blown up. Their greatest handicap was working beneath the hot desert sun garbed out in all their battle rattle. Uniforms and faces were soon soaked in sweat, to which adhered a patina of gray concrete dust that lent the soldiers the appearance of a gathering of ghosts moving about on the road.

It was backbreaking work. Montgomery designated a long-abandoned mud hovel by the side of the road as a safe house in which his men could remove their suffocating armor for brief rest periods. After one break, he looked at his watch, drew a last puff from his cigarette, stomped out the butt on the bare dirt floor, and shrugged back into his gear.

"Time to get back to work, people."

"War's hell," Sergeant Herne said. "At least you Joes are learning a trade."

Lieutenant Dudish and Montgomery were removing lengths of steel rebar from one of the trailers when something caused the sergeant to suddenly pause and look around. The sun was high and bright, a couple of kids were herding sheep across a distant field, and there was the somnolent hum of normal daily activity in the air. Nothing extraordinary at all. Then why had the thought passed through his head that, *Oh, my God! We're going to get shot!*

He looked up and down the road and saw soldiers in the turrets of their humvees. Steffan in the nearest vehicle caught him looking and gave a thumbs-up. Montgomery dismissed his sudden premonition as part of the hyper-awareness that Second Platoon had experienced after Messer and Given died.

He turned to walk away from the trailer with an armload of steel. The thought struck him again—but it was too late to react. A sniper's bullet whapped him in the upper chest with the force of a big guy like Joe Anzak slugging him with a ten-pound sledge hammer. The blow staggered him and knocked the wind from his lungs. He somehow managed to stay on his feet. Realizing he was hit, but not knowing how badly, he ran in a lumbering, staggering gait toward the cover of the nearest hummer.

One of the guys on security heard the shot and spotted a muzzle flash from the window of a small house in a field about five hundred meters away. He opened fire with his .50-caliber and shouted the target location into his platoon band mike. Every soldier in the platoon able to reach his weapon in time opened up in a mad minute. Two-forties, .50-cals, SAWs, and M4s riddled the mud exterior of the house, nearly exploding it in a furious dust storm of hot lead and steel. Someone was yelling so loudly that his voice carried above the fierce rattle.

"Motherfuckers! Motherfuckers!"

Another soldier was even laughing demonically. The guys were pissed. Pissed on and pissed off. Working off their rage and frustration. It was good for their morale to get a chance at some payback after what happened to their dead platoon mates.

Montgomery was in such pain that he hardly dared breathe. He opened the door of the hummer in which Chiva Lares manned the turret and was hammering away with his .50-cal machine gun. He collapsed into the front seat. Lares glanced down and saw blood.

"Holy shit! The Sarge is hit!"

"Don't worry about me," Montgomery managed.

"I'll call Doc Bailey."

"Everybody—" He coughed, but there was no blood in it. Probably not a sucking chest wound then. "Everybody keep what you got," he wheezed, "until we know what's going on."

He hunkered down below window level to check himself out, shrugging out of his FLK to get to his shirt and armor. His Kevlar chest plate was shattered. He reached a hand underneath it and it came back bloody. He took some deep breaths to double check whether the bullet had penetrated his lungs. It hurt like hell, but there was no lung congestion so far.

When he got down to bare skin, he saw that his chest was bloody and turning black and bruised from the collar bone down to the bottom of his rib cage. He felt for an entrance wound and found where a piece of the broken vest had gouged out a superficial but bloody laceration just below his heart. The slug that did it was still lodged in the Kevlar. But for the vest, he would have been a goner sure. He could have almost wept from relief.

"Sarge? Sarge?"

"I'm good to go, Chiva."

Lieutenant Dudish ran by. "Ronnie?"

"I'm all right, L.T."

Dudish kept going. Montgomery lay back on the seat and closed his eyes. His head was spinning. He heard the lieutenant restoring order. "Cease fire! Cease fire!"

The somnolent hum of a normal day returned. The hajji who fired the shot was no doubt long gone by now, scooting down weeded irrigation ditches to get out of the AO and collect his bounty for having shot at and nailed an American. Chances of apprehending him were slightly less than that of winning the New York lottery. The QRF would try, but none of the locals were likely to snitch on him.

Doc Bailey crowded into the front seat with Montgomery to check out his injuries. Top Sergeant Galliano came up on the company freq wondering what the hell was going on.

"I'm good, Top," Montgomery reassured him. "But the plate in my vest is bent to shit."

"You need to come in for a checkup."

Montgomery was wired, now that he knew he wasn't going to die. "Can't do that right now, Top. I'm not getting on no damned truck and running. We're going to check out this house."

"Let me speak to the medic."

Bailey took the mike. Galliano's voice was as hard as turpentine, like he was the one getting shot at and about to kick a few tires. *"Medic, you tell that stubborn, pigheaded sergeant to get his ass in here or I'm coming out to get him—and it won't be pretty."*

"He's right, Sergeant Montgomery," Doc Bailey said. "There could be complications. All the bruising might cause a blood clot to the brain or to the heart."

Montgomery relented. It still hurt to breathe and his entire chest was the color of rotting grapes.

Within the hour he was at the CASH in the Green Zone. After being examined and assured that he would survive, he went outside to smoke a cigarette. Company and Battalion TOC, he subsequently learned, were already on the hook with each other about the road repairs. Rifle platoons would no longer serve as road engineers; that wasn't their job.

A physician's assistant came out. He was a thin guy with thin white hands, his gentlemanly appearance all the more contrasted by the big, grimy sergeant in the bloody ACU jacket.

"You're a lucky man, Sergeant Montgomery," the PA said. "Two inches higher and the bullet would have got you instead of your vest. My guess is the sniper was aiming for your face and missed. What's going on down there on the Euphrates? It seems we get two or three of you up here every week."

"It's called war, sir," Montgomery said. "We're winning, I think."

THIRTY-EIGHT

Few people, even in the military and certainly almost none in civilian power in the United States, understood a guerrilla war as complicated and involved as that being waged in Iraq. It was a formidable and burdensome job for field commanders to maintain a balance between what the soldier was trained to do—break things and kill people to win battles—and at the same time interact with locals to win hearts and minds. In many ways, straight combat would have been less stressful.

The ordinary U.S. soldier rarely saw all the behind-the-scenes maneuvering for advantage and intelligence. As it was the job of Battalion XO Major Mark Manns, Colonel Infanti's second-in-command, to oversee with the Colonel the "Big Picture" of the war, to help implement the grand strategy of reaching a "turning point," he sometimes felt apart from the real action, stuck as he was in the TOC with other rear-echelon types. This in spite of the fact that there was no rear in this kind of war; he had been blown up twice so far during battlefield circulation, neither time suffering serious injuries.

In his behind-the-scenes capacity, Manns often ventured into the various communities with a PSD and Civil Affairs officers to have a cigarette and tea with Iraqi counterparts and cultivate local sheikhs and community leaders with incentives like building schools and power plants. Colonel Infanti did likewise, except they never went together in order to prevent a single ambush from wiping out the battalion leadership all at once. Gradually, they began to form not only a picture of the structure of resistance within The Triangle but also of a developing rift between insurgents that might be exploited to the Americans' advantage.

Intelligence suggested that at least three insurgent groups controlled the network of power and influence in the AO: The Islamic State of

Iraq; al-Qaeda in Iraq; and the 1920s Revolutionary Brigade, which was the Big Momma and genesis of the al-Qaeda movement in-country. Neither of these groups was all that powerful in numbers, but since money was the basis of power in The Triangle, and money talked, dark organizations used money to recruit insurgents and amplify its potency by bribing any number of chauvinistic, bigoted locals devoted to a perverted interpretation of Jihad. Most were thugs and bullies who thought of themselves as brave because they planted an IED in the middle of the night, took a long-distance shot at an American soldier before running away, or conned a delusional or stupid teenager with a death wish into driving a car loaded with explosives into a crowded market. The insurgents' complete lack of respect for life was heartbreaking.

Money was also how U.S. forces countered terrorist and insurgent activity. Battalion commanders and even company COs were allowed to deal out cash to buy information. They had to use caution, however. What with sheikhs and everybody else in the AO struggling for influence, it was sometimes difficult to determine motive. If a snitch sold information that Fadoul Sharif over in Kharghouli was in bed with al-Qaeda, was he squealing out of moral outrage and a desire to serve his country, or was his motive revenge, greed, or power?

Some motives were clear-cut. It was a swindle pure and simple when old Farmer Mustafa attempted to sell a cache site containing nothing more than a few rusted non-usable weapons—an AK-47 that hadn't been fired since the first Iraqi war in 1991; some shotguns with the barrels eaten out; maybe a bag or two of ammonia nitrate fertilizer. Major Manns soon distinguished between three different categories of informants: First, and so far a minority, the good, ordinary Iraqi citizens no longer comfortable sitting by while terrorists and thugs ran their communities; second, people offering to exchange information for cash or for a new life in America, unreliable in either case; and third, those seeking vengeance over a bad business deal or a dispute with a neighbor.

The important thing was that money allowed the Americans to compete with the insurgents. It wasn't long before sound intelligence resulted in more important apprehensions and the recovery of more and better-quality weapons and bomb-making materials. A side benefit was how active and accurate intelligence used by the Americans to exploit the situation led to the sowing of discord and suspicion among individual insurgents and between the major organizations. Dissent in insurgent ranks became apparent when one group would attack an American patrol, then run into an opposing neighborhood in hopes of provoking U.S. soldiers into attacking its rivals.

This struggle for power among the factions promised to be a very good thing for the Americans and the emerging Iraqi government if properly exploited. Iraqis were already beginning to take sides, preferring the less fanatical 1920s Brigade over the rabid al-Qaeda branches. It was that dissension between factions that had produced the severed sheikh's head dangling from a tree near the 109 Mosque.

The next step was to win the people entirely away from the insurgents and bring them over in support of Americans and the Iraqi Army.

THIRTY-NINE

One evening, just after nightfall and before the onset of curfew, Specialist Dean Fetheringill on roof watch for Second Platoon at 152 observed an Iraqi walking by on the road in front of the compound. He watched the man through his NVs. He was a chubbo with a dark beard and a dirty white shawl over his head and shoulders, either to ward off the night chill or disguise his appearance. Fetheringill had seen him around before—one of the farmers from down past the S-curves. The guy was acting as hinky as a pregnant camel.

It got even hinkier. He walked slowly past the outpost, stopped in the dark, then walked back again. Fetheringill keyed his mike and gave Joe Merchant at the gate a heads up when the hajji started toward him. Merchant drew down on him with his M-4.

"What do you want?"

"I will speak with commander."

Lieutenant Dudish and the entire platoon were at home for the evening, having been out since before dawn helping some SpecOps people run hits on high value targets. Summoned to the gate, Dudish and Montgomery patted the guy down for weapons or a martyr's belt and invited him into the compound. They didn't feel comfortable standing around in the dark outside the walls. He didn't feel comfortable going inside, preferring instead to remain concealed in the shadows. A man suspected of collaborating with the Americans could end up without his head.

"Go find the terp and bring him out," Dudish told Merchant.

The visitor understood. "No!" he said. "I am speaking the English. Little so."

"All right. I'm the commander."

The man glanced nervously about. He seemed to be controlling his breathing. "Al-Qaeda will attack here soon," he said.

"How do you know this?" Sergeant Montgomery asked.

"I am sheikh," the Iraqi said in his broken English, as though that were sufficient explanation.

So was every other clodhopper. Sometimes it seemed there were more sheikhs than Indians. Still, the guy *had* come forward of his own volition to issue the warning. Montgomery supposed that meant Delta was making progress with the people, considering the largely unfriendly climate along Malibu Road.

"When is this going to happen?" Lieutenant Dudish asked.

A shrug. "Soon, I am thinking. They are plan to murder you all here. I know nothing more."

"Why are you telling us this? For money?" Montgomery asked. The sergeant had learned to trust no one; his chest was still sore from the bullet he took.

"I am . . . How you say? I am ally. I want nothing."

Right. In Iraq, as in Washington politics, you bought a dog if you wanted a steadfast ally.

Second platoon passed the tip on up to higher headquarters without specifically identifying the source. No need to have S-2 (Intelligence) snooping around the guy's house, tagging him as an informant. Not only would that get him killed, it would also dry up other future sources. Who would dare come forth if doing so got him waxed?

Rumors were always circulating in the AO about some "big" operation or another the insurgents were planning. So far, they hadn't had the balls, or perhaps the numbers, to seriously assault one of the fortresses. They should know by now that it would take more than a few threats to drive out the Americans.

Even so, 152 *was* the most vulnerable of the three battle positions on Malibu. S-curves in the road blinded the base to approach from either direction. Woodlands and swamp clotted the rear of the compound all the way to the river, providing sufficient cover and concealment for an entire battalion to sneak up to the walls unobserved, even through night vision devices.

Activity picked up at the patrol base immediately after the sheikh's nocturnal visit, seeming to validate his warning. It appeared the bad guys might be probing and testing the compound's defenses. Mortar rounds were lobbed over the walls on two or three occasions. Shooters on the other side of the Euphrates returned to take potshots at sentries.

One sultry afternoon, Specialist Jonathan Watts and Dar-rell Whitney on the roof spotted a Toyota nosing along the road beyond the river. The car stopped. A man with a rifle jumped out. Watts and Whitney lit him up, Whitney with particular fervor because of the shot he had taken to the head from these guys. The hajji jumped back in the car and it took off.

The sentries were calling in to report the contact, though any good it would do was doubtful since these guys were like Mao's fish in the sea, when a crashing boom rent the air. It came from the direction of Inchon. The house shook to its foundations from the power and proximity of the detonation. A giant column of smoke erupted in the nearest S-curve. Gravel, asphalt, and other debris rained out of the sky.

Sergeant Montgomery whipped together a foot patrol and cautiously approached the site through the trees. He couldn't believe the size of the bomb crater. A section of the road had been obliterated from drainage ditch to ditch so that even a mule would have had trouble passing through. He doubted this was another thousand-pound bomb exploding spontaneously like the one at 151. There was a purpose behind it.

With one boom, Patrol Base 152 had been isolated from Inchon. Blow up the other end of the road toward 151 and Second Platoon would find itself on its own against an attack for up to an hour or more. Montgomery thought of the sheikh's warning.

Company jumped right on the radio. "*Two-Six, what the hell is going on down there?*"

Montgomery gave his SITREP. Company didn't believe him.

"*Two-Six, put your actual on the radio.*"

Lieutenant Dudish was monitoring everything from the compound's radio room. *"If my people tell me this, sir, then it's so,"* he said.

Company sent down a patrol of its own from Inchon to confirm the size and location of the detonation. Sergeant James Connell led it. The patrol stopped at the crater. It was still smoking.

"Holy shit!" Specialist Alex Jimenez marveled.

Maybe the insurgents *were* trying to start some shit. First Cav dispatched a Bradley fighting vehicle as support while Company and Battalion decided what to do about 152's vulnerability. Finally, orders came down that Delta Company platoons should vacate the current 152 and occupy another that provided better defenses. It wasn't like they were running from a fight; they were simply going to even up the odds.

About one hundred meters down the road and on the opposite side sat a rundown mud-and-concrete shack that had at some point served as a barbershop, now converted to a residence. Not only would its occupation provide better fields of fire across farmland and meadow to the rear, it also opened up the S-curves to better observation. Dudish and Montgomery explained the decision to the owner, a farmer with his hair matted and dirty and in need of being cut. Yellow teeth broke up the gaps in his mouth.

He protested very little. The U.S. Government would compensate him generously. Besides, he said, he wanted to move his family somewhere farther away from the road. Both his little daughters were playing outside when the IED went off, peppering them with debris and breaking out a front window in the house. Many of the locals were starting to get fed up with the constant boom-boom up and down the road and the threat insurgent activity posed to their wives and children. That was a good sign.

Montgomery tried to persuade him to tell who set the bomb, but he was too afraid.

"I have a wife and two babies," he explained through a terp. "They will kill my children if I talk."

In spite of the fact that the new position was smaller and down-scaled into the slums compared to the original 152, having only four rooms, moving day was a day of excitement, a break in the routine. The owner of the old 152 got his house back, the family of the new 152 moved out, and Delta Company's Second Platoon moved into the renovated barbershop.

"Get this place cleaned out. Load all the ammo and gear in the vehicles. Assholes and elbows, okay? Make it happen."

"Oooo-rah! Let's do it."

"You dumb motherfucker, get that cigarette away from the ammo."

"Fucking boot. Kiss my ass."

"Go back to Drum, amateur."

The larger of the four rooms became the main platoon bunkroom. In it, the men built wooden bunks three tiers high in order to accommodate everyone. The platoon leader, platoon sergeant, and section and squad leaders occupied the other bunkroom. The remaining two rooms served as a CP/radio station and common area where Brenda the Bitch might feel comfortable coming for a visit.

The Bradley remained on station until battalion engineers helped sandbag the house, put up blast barriers, string razor wire, and erect three protected fighting positions on the roof. Chiva Lares looked around when it was done.

"Be it ever so humble . . ." he commented drily.

It was a true fort in every sense of the word, standing as a challenge against insurgents to give it their best shot.

FORTY

Humvees and utility trucks with their lights off idled deep-throated in the middle of the night on Malibu Road, the beds of the utilities filled with rolls of tough concertina wire delivered from Battalion and Brigade. Second Platoon's concrete-pouring, brush-burning, wire-laying infantrymen labored in the ditches on either side of the road, unraveling concertina into Slinky-like coils and filling ditches all the way up to the edge of the road so that even a mouse would have a hard time getting through without cutting himself to death. They wondered what they would have to do next to win this strangest war of all.

Battalion had come up with the bright idea of using wire to restrict access. Delta Company had tried everything else in its ongoing struggle with IED artists. Why not just fence the monsters out? If saboteurs couldn't sneak up to the blacktop, they couldn't plant their fireworks.

Being nothing but neighborly invaders, of course, the Joes weren't allowed to wire across side roads and private driveways. The reasoning went something like this: You wouldn't want to piss off more people, as there already seemed to be a surplus of pissed-off people in the AO. The Americans were even pissed off, and getting more so.

"Check this out," Specialist Jared Isbell sourly invited. "We fence them out, but we leave them gates so they can still get in."

"That's because we're a considerate, fair-minded people," Chiva Lares explained. "We wouldn't want to violate the rules of the IBTU."

"IBTU?"

"International Bomb Throwers Union."

Second Platoon Joes bitched about how they seemed to get assigned every shit detail that came down the chain. Everyone knew how all the others had turned out. Brush burning got Messer and Given killed; road repair ended up with Sergeant Montgomery shot. Laying wire was bound to go the same way. Why not just line up the 130,000 American soldiers in-country shoulder-to-shoulder and march through Iraq like green grass through a goose, leaving nothing behind standing except one sign saying USA THIS WAY?

The wire project would take months to complete since the plan was to lay wire from the JSB all the way down Malibu through the S-curves. Theoretically, each new roll of wire unstrung in the ditches left the Jihadists less access to the road and therefore fewer places for the platoons to cover. But just because the platoon toiled each night with wire didn't exempt it from its other duties. It still had patrols to run, raids to execute, craters to guard.

At first, Command wanted the assignment carried out during daylight hours. Lieutenant Dudish argued that working in the sun would subject his men to being picked off by snipers. He used Sergeant Montgomery's incident as an example.

"You tell me what to do," he said. "I'll come up with the plan."

That was how Second Platoon's Joes began moonlighting. Wearing night vision goggles, they resembled a voracious swarm of giant bug-eyed insects. It was tough laboring like that in the dark, even with NVs, but it was better than working exposed to the world and every Ali Baba with an urge to shoot Americans and access to a rifle. Security could see bad guys sneaking up, but the bad guys couldn't see them. Hopefully.

"Maybe if we're lucky," someone suggested, "Crazy Legs will come along, stumble over his feet, fall into the wire and bleed to death."

"Better yet. We could rig up a grenade booby trap and give the asshole a little thrill of his own medicine."

The Joes were always devising new schemes to get rid of him, each more outlandish than the last.

"That's fine, if you want to spend the rest of your life in Leavenworth for murdering civilians," Montgomery cautioned.

"Hell, Sarge. Ain't they *all* civilians?"

"Better take a look at what's happening to the Marines at Haditha."

"This, Sarge, is one fucked-up war."

"It's not much of a war, but it's the only one we got."

Sergeant John Herne blamed concertina for finally ending his long streak of luck as the only member of Second Platoon not to have been blown up by an IED. According to the way he told it, what the openings in the wire did was channel the saboteurs into placing more IEDs in fewer places, therefore increasing his chances of hitting one.

One night after the beds of the utility trucks were empty, Second Platoon headed toward Company HQ at Inchon to pull a rotation with Lieutenant Vargo's First Platoon. Except for sentries, most of First Platoon was on downtime. An explosion down the road jarred everyone awake. Joe Anzak, Brandon Gray, and a few other guys jumped out of their bunks to follow the new platoon sergeant, SFC James Connell, outside to see what was going on.

Assured by radio that everyone in Second Platoon was all right, Lieutenant Vargo's boys were smoking, joking, grabassing and teasing Brenda the Bitch when Lieutenant Dudish's convoy swept through the gates and unassed their vehicles at the motor pool. John Herne, Chiva Lares, and Dar-rell Whitney staggered through the door into the common area with their faces powder-stained and their hair all frizzed out like they had stuck their collective fingers into an electrical outlet. Their ears were still ringing and they were seeing white flashes before their eyes.

Big Anzak, who was gabbing with some of the others about their favorite subject, *feaky-feaky*, and the girls they had seduced, each of whom became hotter and wilder with each retelling, looked up and couldn't help bursting into laughter. He ran over to encircle the three unfortunates in his big arms.

"Let ol' Joe kiss your boo-boos and make them better," he offered.

That night forever ended Sergeant Herne's standing in the community of charmed lives and initiated him into The Malibu IED Club. Everyone wanted to hear the story, which the little sergeant was obliged to tell with suitable exaggerations.

Lares had been behind the wheel, Whitney in the turret with his head stuck up, and Sergeant Herne in the TC seat on the right dismount when Lares spotted a suspicious freshly dug spot in the road. He swerved to avoid it. Too late. The blast blew off the rear axle, one rear door, and sent Whitney's nitch flying out the top of the turret and all the way across the road.

"Anzak, you light off one of your farts in a helmet," Herne challenged, "and I'll bet it goes further than Dar-rell's helmet."

"Put your money where your mouth is, Sar-jent."

That prompted a round of laughing speculation about which was more powerful—an Anzak fart or a medium IED. No longer feeling blessed, Herne let out a deep, weary sigh. Sanchez offered him a canteen cup of coffee and an MRE cake. Cookie Urbina came in, trailed by the ugly brown dog that the Joes had taken in and started feeding scraps. He offered to serve up soup. Captain Jamoles stood back and let his young soldiers burn off their energy and relief, thankful not to have lost another man.

Herne pushed Brenda out of the way and plopped down on the sofa. "We're gonna need more wire," he said.

FORTY-ONE

What most civilians failed to realize when they thought of soldiers was that many of them were kids only a year or two out of high school. High-spirited, rowdy, energetic, optimistic, with all the quirks and charms of eighteen- or nineteen-year-old boys all over America. Downtime members of First and Fourth Platoons not on patrol, security, or crater watch were having a Saturday night dance at Inchon. Brenda the Bitch was the guest of honor. The Joes would have preferred *real* girls, but an Iraqi female caught so much as smiling at an American ruined her reputation for life. Besides, as far as the GIs could tell, Iraqi women didn't dance or do much of anything else except take care of the men and children.

Someone mysteriously produced a stylish black burka for Brenda to wear to the dance. She quickly shed it in favor of a pair of lace panties open at the crotch. Hard rock music blasted from a CD player. The Joes were having a hell of a good time forgetting about the war. Dancing exaggeratedly and obscenely with the blow-up doll, passing her around, tossing her, jerking her about until it seemed she must surely burst at the seams or rupture like a balloon and fly all over the common room before landing deflated and spent in the coffee.

PFC Byron Fouty, nineteen, smiling bashfully the way he did, watched from a corner of the room where he had retreated with a copy of Stephen King's *It*. A sensitive, introspective kid who liked Jolly Rancher candy, Stephen King, and W. E. B. Griffin novels, he had impressed teachers in high school with his acting and improvisation talents, the one area where he seemed to overcome his innate shyness. A troubled home life, his parents' divorce, and being kicked out of the house by his father had left him rootless. He dropped out of school to get his GED and enlist in the army.

Almost the first thing he discovered about himself in the army was that he didn't belong there either. The army was such a testosterone-driven organization. Some of the other guys in First Platoon, such as Alex Jimenez and Joe Anzak, were true warriors who thrived in a combat environment. In contrast, Fouty seemed to fade into the background most of the time, like now, the kind of kid who just went along to get along, never saying much, scared to death most of the time, a kid who should not have gone to war.

Sometimes he thought that the politician's quote about "C students with their stupid finger on the trigger in Iraq" applied to him. Except he wasn't even a C student. He was a dropout with a GED.

"How did you end up in the army?" Sergeant James Connell asked when he took over as platoon sergeant.

"I didn't have anywhere else to go."

Sergeant Connell was the decided opposite of hard-nosed Sergeant Burke, the previous platoon daddy. If possible, Connell seemed even more unsuited to warfare than Fouty. He was a gentle man with a kind voice who treated all the Joes in the platoon as though they were his sons. When they went out on patrols, Connell always carried a pocket full of candy for the local kids, his honest contention being that extending kindness to people paid off in the long run. He never referred to the Iraqis as hajjis or Baghdads or dune coons or ragheads as most of the other soldiers did. He truly embraced the view that Americans were here to win friends and influence people. That was how to win the war.

Fouty found it easy to talk to Sergeant Connell. He was almost like having a real father.

The dance was becoming a bit too loud. Captain Jamoles would be shutting it down soon. Fouty closed his book and slipped out to go to the roof. No one noticed when he left.

The night guards were in the watch towers, which left the roof to him. He leaned both elbows on the lip of the roof and gazed reflectively out above the date palms toward the Euphrates River, catching only a glimpse of silver moon on water through the trees. There was something romantically soothing and deceptively peaceful about the Iraqi countryside under a full moon. Something out of *Arabian Nights* or *Lawrence of Arabia*.

Nights on the roof this time of year were cold, as most desert nights were. He pulled his neck gaiter up over his ears. He liked it up here alone, working through his thoughts and feelings.

The people here, the Iraqis, both confused and annoyed him. First of all, he had never seen such poverty. Being poor, however, didn't mean they couldn't at least pick up their own garbage. It didn't cost anything and it would improve their lives overnight. You would think that cell phones spreading all over the country and satellite dishes sprouting from even the most humble mud hovel would bring improvements to their wretched lives. Sergeant Connell said they lived this way because they didn't know how to do things for themselves, having existed for so long under a tyranny that told them what to do and when to do it.

They were so *damned* demanding.

"How soon are you going to repair my house?"

"We need more money."

"Are you going to build us a school?"

"Who will pay for my wheat field that the soldiers crossed?"

"Our roads must be repaired."

Yeah! Then why do you keep blowing 'em up?

Iraqis swarmed humvees begging for food or attempting to peddle Blue Death cigarettes at five bucks a pack. Knots of young children ran out and pleaded for new soccer balls in front of a house where there were two craters left by previous roadside bombs. Is that why the Americans were here, to be ripped off by the people during the day and shot at by wacko Jihadists night and day?

Fouty's nerves were always strung to the snapping point. He had been startled more than once by automatic weapons fire outside a mosque, only to realize that it was a wedding celebration and not an attack. Now *this* was a gun culture. Every once in awhile some hajji guzzled too much Turkish whiskey and worked up the courage to show up in front of a U.S. battle position somewhere in the AO to shoot at it. "Fuck you, America!"

Sometimes the Americans shot back and killed him—after which the U.S. Government paid reparations to his family.

None of it made sense. Couldn't these people understand that Americans were here to bring democracy, freedom, and peace? Why were they so ungrateful?

A U.S. soldier was ambushed and killed while trying to do good in delivering a donation of classroom supplies to a school. Sergeant Messer and PFC Given were murdered, and for what? These people would never appreciate the sacrifices American soldiers were making for them.

Shops in the villages sold fruit and kabobs of goat, peppers, and only God knew what else. Jewelry, fans, satellite dishes, live chickens, and dead goats were on display next to large posters of masked Muslim Jihadists and racks of anti-American, anti-Western CDs with titles like *Heroes of Chechnya, Jihad Warriors, Fallujah Resistance,* and *Allah Will Destroy the Jews.*

Fouty stirred, startled, when somebody walked up beside him. Sergeant Connell leaned on the roof lip next to him.

"You seem tired, Sergeant," Fouty said.

"All the patrols day and night are beating us to death. I'm due for leave in April. When I get home, I'm going to sleep for days. When's the last time you were home, son?"

"I think my dad's in Mississippi. Mom's in Texas. I haven't seen them for a while."

"Your folks know you're in Iraq?"

"I guess they do, I don't know."

He knew the sound of an AK-47 bullet when it zipped past his head, the deafening blasts of exploding IEDs and mortar shells—but he hardly knew where his home was. He knew the screams of the wounded and had seen the tears of soldiers grieving over their dead—but he wasn't sure he remembered his father's face.

A chill breeze gusting up from fog along the river made him shiver. The awful truth he had discovered in Iraq was that war was horrible and to be avoided. Yet, if you were a soldier, the only way you could measure your worth, test it, was by going through it. Soldiers left their families, those who had families, and rushed off to war because *that was what they were supposed to do.*

He doubted he would ever measure up as a soldier.

FORTY-TWO

The deaths of Messer and Given had rocked Delta Company to the core. Rather than making the infantrymen timid and fearful, however, it turned them hard-core and more aggressive. The change became apparent the same day they died. Delta Company and a QRF from Alpha Company kicked in a score of doors and rounded up some dozen men with control or influence in the area for questioning. Intelligence acquired from these detainees led to a series of midnight-to-dawn raids that netted two important insurgents implicated in the bombing.

The aggressiveness continued under Delta's new young company commander, Captain John Gilbreath, who relieved Captain Jamoles. Hard-charging and as stubborn as a pit bull terrier, he was determined that when the enemy struck his men he was going to strike back. What followed were 24/7 days of ceaseless, nerve-wracking patrolling of streets and roads; hunting, fighting, and sometimes killing insurgents; making a presence and demonstrating a willingness to maintain order.

In Iraq and other Arab cultures, men derived respect through displays of powers and sometimes violence, a concept foreign to most Western countries but one the common Iraqis understood at a fundamental gut level. Anything less was interpreted as weakness—and weakness, even perceived weakness, could never hope to secure and stabilize the country. Pacifying Iraq without shedding blood was virtually impossible. The trick came in maintaining the delicate balance between protecting the population from the insurgents and showing over-aggressiveness that might drive traditional Muslim families into the radical camp.

The more Delta Company pressed the outlaws, the more they pressed back, as though desperate to stop American influence and maintain and increase their own. Insurgent mortar fire that had slacked off some began once more to rain down on all three Malibu battle positions on a regular basis. Typically, they came in just before daylight or just after dark. Three or four rounds, then the shooters hauled ass under cover of darkness and before battalion mortars or 105mm howitzers could home in on them.

No attack, however ineffective, was left unanswered. Delta's QRF responded by searching homes, corralling likely suspects, and questioning witnesses with a new no-bullshit intensity. Locals gradually began to accord the American soldiers more respect.

"Winning hearts and minds means never having to say you're sorry," Specialist Jimenez joked.

War was always chaotic, unpredictable, and in many ways incomprehensible, even to those involved. Crank it all up a few notches and what you had was guerrilla warfare. The enemy's presence in The Triangle was all around, always there, but blending into the surroundings and rarely recognized until it was too late. Infantrymen became people-watchers as a matter of self-defense and survival. They could generally tell if it was going to be a good day or a bad day by observing the behavior of the people.

Things were probably going to be all right if the kids came out chattering and waving and running alongside, and if the adults were going about their normal business. But watch out if the adults slipped furtively into their houses and the kids started throwing rocks and running away.

As a general rule, women were more opposed to war and disorder than men, thus more receptive to efforts to restore peace to the land and save their teenagers from being conscripted into the ranks of the fanatics. This didn't mean they were used as sources or even that they were the objects of any direct psychological operations to win them over. To do so would be against the culture's moral code. Besides, no Arab woman would dare speak out against her men. Daughters, sisters, and wives had been "honor killed" for less. Bringing in a woman for interrogation or using her to obtain information would have sparked an international incident.

Women in Iraq had few rights and even fewer privileges. They served specific purposes as cooks, cleaners, and breeders. Otherwise, they seemed to have less value than goats or sheep. November through January were raw winter months in Iraq, with lots of rain and wind. Often on a winter's day, the Joes marveled at seeing an old truck rumbling through with the women and girls in the back of the truck exposed to the elements, and the men and boys crowded into the cab.

While the Americans watched the people, the insurgents watched them back. All the observers were not as obvious as Crazy Legs, whom the GIs permitted to continue about because he could be useful to them as a barometer—and because he would be replaced by someone less visible and therefore more harmful. And so in the winter when many of the dusty roads of summer that intersected with Malibu became muddy trails and travel became treacherous, hostile eyes watched and waited and charted the Americans' habits—when they ate, slept, patrolled; when re-supply trucks arrived and departed; when the soldiers were at their peak and when they were ebbing. The U.S. Army was good at forming patterns and establishing predictable routines. That made life more comfortable for everyone involved. Including the enemy.

Rumors persisted about something "big" the insurgents might be planning. Things apparently hadn't panned out so well for them in their attempt to cut the road at 152 and leave the outpost isolated and vulnerable. That didn't mean they had given up.

Lieutenant Joe Tomasello's Fourth Platoon was patrolling on a cloudy, rain-spitting morning through a nameless settlement not far from al Taqa. A group of young men loitering in front of a market glared at the convoy. One of them drew a knife hand across his throat, as if to indicate an impending beheading.

FORTY-THREE

It was well into mid-morning when Fourth Platoon's trucks rumbled back through the gate at Inchon. Gloomy overcast concealed the sun. The platoon had been out on an area patrol since 0500 after spending most of the night on a raid over near Latifiyah. Cookie Urbina had breakfast chow waiting for them in the trailer. The troops were worn out.

Joshua Parrish stopped to scratch Brown Dog's ears. The friendly pooch wagged his tail and begged in his special way for the soldier to bring him a treat when he came back out. Mayhem, Fletcher, Sergeant Tony Smith, Private Michael Smith, and all the others piled on through the door to the rich aroma of scrambled powdered eggs, butter biscuits, and hot coffee. Nothing was too good for the troops.

They shucked their battle rattle, stacked arms, and were just settling down at the long table when Lieutenant Tomasello and Platoon Sergeant Garrett rushed in after having presented their After Action to the commander. The look on their faces said everything. No rest for the weary. James Cook scalded his tongue trying to get down a cup of coffee before the boot slammed.

"Get your shit back on," Sergeant Garrett said. "We're heading back out."

Bitch all they wanted, it did no good. Fourth Platoon was the day's QRF.

A Raven UAV (unmanned aerial vehicle) had gone down and had to be retrieved. It was a small surveillance aircraft with a four-foot wingspan and a body a little larger than a remote-controlled model plane. An operator on the ground flew it through a visor he wore that displayed images from a small video camera mounted in the aircraft's nose. The plane was crash-landing somewhere near Malibu Road between 152 and 153 when the camera went out; it continued to send its emergency locator signal. The pilot, Sergeant Dorr, thought it had been shot down.

The trucks roared out of Inchon with Tomasello's vehicle in the lead. Specialist Michael Smith drove. James Cook occupied the gunner's turret hatch while the Raven pilot took the back seat behind the lieutenant.

Specialist Edwin Caldero drove the second truck, with gunner-medic Bryan Brown in the hatch, Sergeant Joshua Parrish in the TC slot, and an IA interpreter named Izzat holding down the back seat.

The third truck was Sergeant Garrett's, being driven by a new kid named Wilson. Sergeant Tony Smith, the chunky Italian from somewhere in New England, rode behind the machine gun in the turret.

Corporal Mayhem Menahem TC'd from the front dismount seat of the fourth truck, with PFC Justin Fletcher at the wheel and Scribner in the hatch.

All the soldiers had the same thought in mind: this could be a trap using the Raven as bait. They kept particularly alert as the trucks sped through the curves toward the aircraft's last-plotted location. There was the feel of spitting rain and a taste of danger in the air.

The trucks failed to make it through the curves. A carefully concealed IED erupted beneath the wheels of Corporal Mayhem's fourth truck with a deafening, heart-stopping roar that picked the hummer off the road and flipped it through the air like a child's toy. Mayhem glimpsed ground and sky exchanging places. The truck landed back on its wheels on the embankment, doors and hatch ripped off and occupants flung out into the roadside ditch near the concertina Second Platoon had been laying in recent weeks.

Mayhem blacked out when his body struck the ground.

The attack was choreographed for maximum effect, and well-coordinated to stop the trucks and trap the soldiers in a kill zone. Command-detonated explosions in a daisy chain disabled trucks two and three almost at the same instant. Sergeant Garrett's number three lurched off the ground in a burst of smoke and went dead in place. Caldero, driving number two, fought his hummer on through the smoke of the explosion until he lost inertia on four blown tires and a busted axle and came to a stop.

Only Tomasello's lead vehicle survived the bomb meant for it and escaped the kill zone, driver Mike Smith twisting the wheel and jamming his foot hard against the accelerator just in time. The bomb went off to one side instead of underneath. Smith gunned on through the danger per SOP before braking for a SITREP and a possible fight.

Up in the turret with the two-forty, James Cook saw smoke boiling like a forest fire engulfing the road and cutting off sight of Mayhem's fourth truck. The other two hummers were dead in the water with more smoke seeping all around them, some from fires in their engines.

"Turn around! Go back!" Tomasello ordered.

Mike Smith cut a sharp donut and headed back into the maelstrom, Cook hanging on in the turret and searching for targets. Smoke burned his eyes and brought tears.

The attackers weren't through yet. Hardly had Tomasello's truck re-entered the curve than a waiting IED nailed it. Tomasello, in the front passenger's seat, was holding on against the acceleration, braced back into his seat with his legs spread. The IED blasted a hole through the floor-board directly between his knees, filling the compartment with smoke and eardrum-bursting energy. He would have lost both legs and perhaps his life but for the coincidence of having had his legs spread.

The truck was still running. "Keep going!" Tomasello shouted. "I'm good, I'm good. I just can't hear a fucking word."

Neither could anyone else. They were yelling at each other as loud as they could to compensate for ruptured eardrums.

Nearer now, through the twisting whirlpools of smoke, Cook picked up a visual of Mayhem's truck wrecked at the side of the road with its doors and rear hatch missing. Two of the Joes lay sprawled not far from the humvee, whether dead or not Cook couldn't tell. They weren't moving.

The third crewman, Justin Fletcher, was up on the road staggering around in a daze, like he had no idea where he was. His helmet was missing and his ACUs were scorched and torn.

The orchestra was just warming up. The chorus chimed in suddenly. Mortar tubes hidden in brush on the river side of the road and from a scattering of houses in the farmland began *thu-wumping* shells at the convoy.

They were small 60mm foot tubes, but their shells packed a wallop against troops in the open.

Geysers vented in a series of thundering booms, stomping around among the disabled trucks and filling the air with the burr of shrapnel. The ground shook so hard that Sergeant Parrish had the impression of T-Rex's first appearance in *Jurassic Park*.

Now for the symphony's main score. From out in the reeds and among the palms appeared a swarm of black-garbed fedayeen advancing toward the trucks at a lurching run, firing AK-47s and shooting rockets with the RPG's double-explosion signature—once when the rocket was unleashed, the second when the grenade struck its target. The concertina wire in the ditch wouldn't stop them; mortars were blowing gaps through it.

Every GI still cognizant of his surroundings and not addled by all the detonations understood that the attackers had the platoon trapped and intended to wipe it out to the last man. Fourth Platoon was in a fight for its life.

FORTY-FOUR

The experience of combat took a more or less predictable pattern. First came the shock of being under attack; followed by acceptance; then by trained, instinctive responses to it. In the beginning, the Joes would be so scared when something happened that they thought their hearts would stop beating. Once they had been through it a couple of times, however, they learned to depend upon their training, react to it, and almost subconsciously do what a soldier must. It never ceased to be terrifying, but it did become less daunting.

When Corporal Mayhem regained consciousness and his eyes focused, he saw brown blades of grass directly in front of his face. Drops of black water were on them, and he didn't understand. There was a roar in his ears, a tremendous pounding that at first sounded a long way off, then grew louder and louder as it threatened to swallow him into it. He gave a start as he remembered tumbling through the air in the hummer with the other guys, like so many pebbles in a tin can, then being ejected from it and falling some more by himself. The raindrops were black because of black powder from the explosion.

He passed out again, revived, and this time he gingerly moved his head to look back toward the road. That was when, still only half-conscious, he accepted his platoon was under full attack and about to be overrun. He was lying in a ditch. Nearby, his truck looked as though it had been stripped for the salvage yard. Mortar rounds burst blossoms of red and black. The smoke trail of a rocket streaked through the maelstrom. Green tracers zipped from various angles.

Instinctively, he reached for his M-4, surprised that it had landed with him, probably because the platoon was tense with apprehension and he had been gripping his weapon tightly when IEDs started going off. He turned his head again, this time toward the direction of rifle fire. Black-masked figures advancing through the reeds next to a canal sent him into shock all over again. The muzzles of their assault rifles winked and flashed and spat tracers.

More mortar shells walked along the ditch toward him, roaring like an approaching tornado, filling the air with shrapnel-length pieces of shredded concertina wire. The enemy combatants were coming to an opening in the wire that would allow them through in numbers not experienced in this AO before.

He figured he was done for—but not without a fight. His left arm felt numb and unresponsive. He returned fire, lying on his belly in the grass and shooting one-handed, uncertain whether he was scoring or not because of his blurred vision and the handicap of his arm. The ground underneath him shook like a wet dog trying to shake fleas off its back.

From out of nowhere, it seemed, out of the smoke and confusion, suddenly appeared two soldiers. Both were injured, confused and disoriented in the blaze of the developing fight. Scribner was dragging one leg. Fletcher reeled drunkenly back and forth. Both had lost their weapons when the truck flipped.

They were rushing to Mayhem's aid, risking their own lives after having discerned their buddy down in the ditch and apparently unable to adequately defend himself. Floods of gratitude, pride, and love swept through Mayhem. Now he knew how Pitcher must have felt when Mayhem went to his rescue that first time Fourth Platoon got mortared during the occupation of 151.

The two soldiers threw their own bodies over Mayhem's, hugging him close to shield him from gunfire, shrapnel, and bits of flying wire.

"Are you okay, man?" Scribner asked.

"I think so. I can't move my arm."

They hugged the ground together as shells roared and exploded around them, gripping each other to prevent being thrown off the face of the earth. Scribner suddenly grunted and his body stiffened into a spasm as he took either a bullet or a piece of shrapnel meant for Mayhem.

"I can't feel my back!" he cried.

They had one rifle for the three of them. Still one-handed, Mayhem threw a few more rounds at Fedayeen running across the fields and toward the opening in the wire. They just kept coming and coming. But they were no longer unopposed. Mayhem heard Fourth Platoon responding with return fire out of the smoke on the road.

"We gotta get out of here!" he yelled. "Move back to the trucks."

Further down the road sat what had previously been Sergeant Parrish's second vehicle in the caravan. Although the truck was inoperable on four flats and a busted engine, the men inside were still functioning. Medic-turned-machine-gunner Bryan Brown's African-dark face became a fierce mask as he turned his .50-cal in the turret on the insurgents threatening Mayhem, Scribner, and Fletcher. His big dog of a gun began barking rhythmically as it delivered two-inch-long bullets into the foliage through which the main enemy body was ducking and dodging toward the ripped-apart concertina.

"Is this a private fight?" Parrish yelled at Brown. "Or can anybody get in on it?"

"Help yourself," Brown encouraged. "Fuck 'em up!"

His .50-cal kept chugging. Parrish and the IA Izzat jumped out on the road. Crouching behind the humvee for cover, they engaged several riflemen on the flat top of a house. The shooters sailed off the roof when the 5.56mm high-velocity rounds began chipping at them. Parrish held down his trigger on full automatic and nailed at least one of the shooters in midair. He crumpled like a game bird shotgunned in flight. The man's scream of pain rose above the crackle of the developing battle before he vanished from sight.

Lieutenant Tomasello's men from the three disabled trucks were accounting for themselves in a valiant effort, even though most were either injured or in shock from all the falling ordnance. It was clear to Tomasello as Mike Smith roared their truck back into the fury of the kill zone that they were in a desperate fix and couldn't hold out much longer. They were outgunned, outmaneuvered, outnumbered, and about to be overrun. The only chance the platoon had was to withdraw in a hurry. Problem was, only one truck remained operable.

Withering return fire temporarily stalled the attacking insurgents just on the other side of the road's drainage ditch, no more than one hundred yards to the front of Mayhem, Scribner, and Fletcher, whose more exposed position remained to the rear of the other trucks.

"Pick everybody up on the way through," Tomasello instructed Smith.

Smith didn't question how they were going to load fourteen GIs into a humvee designed for no more than six or seven. All he knew was that it had to be done. After all, back at Drum, he had once crammed two squads into a Saturn.

He was a demon behind the wheel. Whip-thin James Cook braced against anything he could find in the hatch in order to free both hands to keep the mounted two-forty talking. From the sound of things, the Raven pilot might have been praying as insurgents spotted the returning vehicle and lay down on it with everything they had. Bullet-resistant glass on the truck's downrange side spidered from the sheer volume of fire. Bullets clicked and nipped at the armor. Cook kept his head as low as he could without slacking up on his trigger.

Parrish, Brown, Caldero, and the IA were first in line. Smith whipped the hummer through the smoke and turmoil and skidded to a stop between the four men and the incoming fire. Blood stained the Iraqi interpreter's trousers. The back protected door flew open for a flying pickup.

"Get in! Get in!"

Nobody questioned it. Truck two's crew piled into the back seat, tumbling over each other. Tomasello flung open his front door and blazed away with his carbine over the hood until he heard the back door slam. They were on their way again within seconds after having set a new world's record for loading a hummer.

Next in line were Sergeant Garrett, Wilson, and Tony Smith. They also piled in. Wilson was hurt. Doc Brown reverted back to medic, even though the truck was getting so crowded with a tangle of arms and legs and weapons and shouting, cursing men that it was hard to breathe, much less administer first aid.

One of the "bullet proof" windows finally shattered and fell out. Everybody tried to stay below window level. Parrish lay across their bodies to shoot out the open window as Mike Smith gunned the vehicle toward Mayhem, Fletcher, and Scribner, whose circumstances could best be described as untenable.

"Cover fire!" Tomasello yelled. "Give 'em hell!"

Sergeant Garrett joined Parrish at the open window. They went on full automatic to lay down fire on the insurgents and keep them ducking. Everybody else passed up weapons as best they could from the dog pile. Tomasello cowboy'd it by holding on with one hand and leaning out his open door to fire across the hood of the wildly careening hummer with the other hand.

Mayhem, Fletcher, and Scribner came running and shambling up to the road to meet the truck, Mayhem and Fletcher supporting Scribner between them. But for the heavy fire coming from Tomasello's truck and the partial concealment provided by smoke, all three would surely have been mowed down.

Tomasello dragged Scribner into the front seat with him. Mayhem and Fletcher scrambled over all the bodies and tumbled into the rear hatch on top of other bodies. Helping arms reached to pull and drag them out of harm's way.

Everything was utterly insane—Scribner in severe pain screaming about his back; James Cook in the turret swearing at the top of his lungs as he picked out and engaged targets; Tomasello shouting for help over the radio; Mike Smith trying to find room to drive and keep the truck running long enough to get them out of the kill zone. Everyone was scared to death, knowing they were all going to die here in this miserable, shitty land.

Doors slammed. The hummer's tires dug into the blacktop and squealed off rubber. Smith swung into the S-curves toward Inchon. A cheer of premature relief went up from the mass of bloody, frightened soldiers.

Mortar fire had blown rolled lengths of concertina into the middle of the road. Smith swerved to miss them. Too late. Stout razor wire entangled itself in the front wheels and brought the truck to an unscheduled halt so abruptly that it may as well have run into a wall. The shifting of the load propelled Parrish and Sergeant Garrett into the front seat on top of Tomasello, Scribner, and Smith. Scribner bellowed in agony.

Smith gunned the engine in a desperate attempt to break free. Back tires boiled smoke and pivoted the vehicle on its frozen front wheels until it fronted back into the kill zone and the charging mob of masked insurgents now running up onto the road. Cook found himself and his two-forty in a target-rich environment.

Mayhem thought it was all over for Fourth Platoon. It was Custer's Last Stand all over again.

FORTY-FIVE

While IEDs were common (but not so common as they were at the beginning) ambushes employing insurgents of the numbers that had apparently downed a Raven to lure Tomasello's ass into a crack were not. At least a platoon-sized element was apparently intent on wiping out Fourth Platoon to prove the point that the insurgency had teeth and was not afraid to use them.

Sergeant Montgomery out on the yard at 152 heard the ambush triggered. A sudden *Boom! Boom! Boom!* that shook the dust from the old converted barbershop-turned-fortress, followed by mortar and RPG explosions and the deep-throated coughing of heavy machine guns and the cacophony of rifle fire.

Jesus Christ!

He broke into a run for the platoon CP/radio room. Lieutenant Dudish was back in the States on a short leave, which left Montgomery in charge. Second Platoon had been out all morning stopping vehicles at checkpoints, dismounting through villages, confabbing with local sheikhs, checking out a suspected weapons cache . . . There had been no indication something this big was coming down in 152's own backyard today.

Specialist Joe Merchant was on roof watch. He heard and felt the explosions, followed by the sight of black funnels of smoke gusting up against a cloudy backdrop. As usual when something happened, the radio nets came alive with men yelling and screaming. Merchant sprang down the roof stairs to meet Montgomery as he burst through the front door.

"IEDs, Sarge!" he shouted. "Right down the road. It sounds like some of our trucks are bad hit. One of 'em might have flipped into the ditch."

Messer and Given had been killed near the same spot. Weeds hadn't yet overtaken the burn.

"Get back on the roof and keep your eyes open," Montgomery ordered. Merchant hustled to obey.

The crackling of gunfire and the rattling of bullets against metal and asphalt provided an urgent background to stressed-out voices over the radio. It didn't take Montgomery more than a few seconds to ascertain that something had to be done fast or Fourth Platoon was history.

"Delta X-Ray, we have contact. My platoon in the S-curves . . . between Inchon and 152 . . . My God, I'm the only truck left!"

"We got mortars. Mortars! Small arms, mortars, RPGs . . ."

"We got men down. Repeat. We got men down!"

". . . fire from the buildings. I see them moving on top . . ."

"Fire them fuckers up!"

"For God's sake, hurry up. We got to get the hell out of here!"

Sergeant Montgomery jumped on the radio to Delta X-Ray Six, Captain Gilbreath at Company. "Delta-Two is enroute" was all he said. Any unit in the vicinity of another in distress was expected to respond immediately.

Montgomery called in his two outriding security trucks. Reinforcements would meet them at the gate of 152. Then he threw down the mike and tasked one of his squad leaders with rounding up every Second Platoon soldier he could, on the fly, no time to lose. Montgomery would have to stay behind on the radio to monitor the fight as it developed and keep control over his part of it.

Sergeant Jeremy Miller leading a group of soldiers that included Nathan Brooks, John Herne, and Specialist Jared Isbell busted out the front door and rushed out to the road. Montgomery sent everyone else to the roof, all armed to the teeth in the event this was some kind of Vietnam-style Tet Offensive, the something "big" long rumored to be in the mill.

Specialists Robert Pool and Dar-rell Whitney were manning the security truck south of 152 in the direction of 151. They caught up to Miller's bunch hotfooting it up the road, slid to a stop, picked up the soldiers, and headed on north at full speed toward the sounds of combat.

Steffan and Streibel had the other truck, the one north of 152 in the direction of Inchon and the S-curve and therefore almost within sight of the action. They didn't bother with returning to 152; they bore down upon the curve, Streibel in the turret and eager to throw his two-forty into the melee. From the sound of things on the radio, Fourth Platoon survivors were trapped inside a single stalled vehicle.

Montgomery kept radio contact with his trucks. *"Delta-Twos, don't go into the curves. Stay back from the KZ and engage the enemy on both sides of the road. Roger that?"*

It would do no one any good to feed more trucks and soldiers into the grinder.

Pool had the 7.62mm two-forty machine gun in his truck's turret. Whitney swerved into the start of the curve. Pool caught his first sight of the scene. Men dressed mostly in black civilian clothing were running up to three heavily damaged and abandoned humvees on the road, their AK-47s hammering not at these trucks but at a fourth alone in the middle of the road nearest arriving reinforcements from 152.

Lieutenant Tomasello's men seemed to be holding their own. Whoever was behind the two-forty in the turret was giving the enemy all kinds of hell, slugging it out with a half-dozen or so insurgents in the palm groves off to his left. The rest of Fourth Platoon, at least those still able, had piled out of the vehicle and were all around the lee side of it, using it for cover as they pounded back with everything they had.

All these guys had been in a single truck?

The vehicle occupied by Steffan and Strebel stopped short of Tomasello's. Streibel crouched on the roadway behind the front fender, shooting down the road, laying down a wall of suppressive fire along with Steffan's two-forty in the turret.

Whitney braked and skidded his hummer sideways in the road behind and to the left of the other Second Platoon truck. Reinforcements jumped out onto the road from the back-facing protected doors. Using the truck as a shield, they opened up with SAWs, M-4s and 203s. Miller's M203 grenade launcher attached to his M-4 began seeding a barrier of fire and protective steel in front of Tomasello's stalled truck.

Pool's two-forty was an awesome weapon. He raked a web of red tracers down the center of the road, scattering a group of enemy combatants.

He must have nailed at least three of them. The others headed for the woods, dragging their wounded or dead comrades. They seemed to have the same creed as the U.S. Army: leave no man behind.

The insurgents had lost their momentum and their element of surprise. Second Platoon gunfire continued to shred foliage after the last of the attackers vanished into it.

Back at 152, Sergeant Montgomery sweated out an interminable four or five minutes before the word he awaited came over the air. Lieutenant Tomasello sounded a lot calmer.

"This is Delta Four-Six. They're falling back into the treeline and some houses ahead of us . . ."

The cavalry had arrived just in the nick of time.

FORTY-SIX

If the insurgents could get away with an action like this, it only made them stronger and more aggressive. Alpha Company acting as a Battalion QRF arrived in force. Soldiers from Second Platoon and those still able from Fourth Platoon took over the house at the side of the road where Sergeant Parrish winged some of the enemy jumping off the roof. Blood trails all around led off across fields and into brush bordering canals and drainage ditches.

Occupants of the house had vacated it either before or during the ambush. Alpha Company used it as a command post; whoever lived there didn't return until several days afterwards. From its hub, Alpha and some members of Delta supplemented by a platoon of IA divided their forces into two elements and methodically moved through neighboring villages and countryside questioning witnesses, searching homes, confiscating weapons, and rounding up the usual suspects. These were brought cuffed to a collection point in an alley behind the CP house where they could be hauled to Baghdad for more extensive interrogation.

In short, the Americans ruined everybody's day in order to send the message that Delta didn't appreciate its troops being attacked.

Raiders and interrogators dug up the names of several believed to have participated in the attack. Most of them were now on the run and wouldn't be captured for weeks or months down the road. Others drifted back into The Triangle to hide out and continue their villainy. One thing seemed certain, however. Insurgents along Malibu were no longer satisfied merely to plant IEDs and ambush in small numbers. This wasn't exactly the turning point Colonel Infanti anticipated.

Miraculously, none of Lieutenant Tomasello's soldiers were killed that day. A few suffered minor shrapnel wounds and concussions, including

Mayhem Menahem. A bullet grazed one soldier, and others were shook up pretty good. Only Specialist Scribner had to be medevac'd, due to his back. Platoon medics treated everyone else.

The Black Hawk medevac came in so quickly to whisk Scribner away to Baghdad that Mayhem didn't get a chance to thank him for possibly saving his life. That was a drawback of having a tight outfit. You got extraordinarily close to each other, and then when one was wounded there was seldom a farewell. He was simply gone, medevac'd immediately. Most injured soldiers were back in the United States recuperating at Walter Reed Hospital within a couple of days, after which they were often medically discharged from the army.

And the war went on in their absence.

FORTY-SEVEN

There has always existed a certain friction between the soldier on the front line and his counterpart in support, between the grunt who fires the bullets and the supply personnel who provides the bullets. For these rear-echelon types not involved in the actual fighting, perhaps ensconced at a cush desk job back in the Green Zone, life was usually no more exciting or risky than at Fort Drum or any other army base stateside. Vietnam-era GIs coined phrases and terms such as "Remington Raiders" or REMF (rear-echelon motherfucker) to express their contempt for—and perhaps envy of—the soldier who slept under clean sheets every night and whose greatest danger lay in breaking a fingernail on his typewriter.

As for the REMFs, while thankful not to be in the thick of battle, they were also a little resentful and jealous of the "real" soldier. They often got back at the dirty, scroungy, war-fighting infantrymen every chance they got through rules and regulations more applicable to the peacetime military than to a combat environment. All too often, it was also the rear echelon in their clean uniforms and striking military appearance who defined the soldier and set the army's image, for better or worse.

As a result, the army sometimes suffered from poor image modeling and indecisive leadership—high-ranking officers who sent men into harm's way while they remained safely behind in the comfort of their air-conditioned offices; grossly overweight commanders who bragged about how their units were secure behind walls and were going to stay that way; pogue-bait NCOs riding out their combat tours in the relative safety of the rear; Pentagon-level generals on "fact-finding" missions who breezed in and out of the war zone, experienced it superficially, then returned to report to politicians . . .

Like most combat leaders, Colonel Infanti expressed little more than contempt for such men and was quick to defend his soldiers against them.

"Before you lay crap on my men," he warned, "you need to get on the ground and get some American blood on your hands. Fight your way out of a couple of ambushes, hold a buddy's hand while he dies, then come back and talk to me."

It seemed to him that many high-ranking brass and civilian leaders back in the States relied on the mainstream media for most of their information about the war. A dangerous habit, in his opinion, since he regarded the media as biased and quick to present a prejudiced, superficial, and downright fraudulent version of events occurring in Iraq. It seemed reporters were always present to televise clips of American "atrocities" or to imply that American was losing the war by showing Iraqis celebrating U.S. casualties by jumping around and waving frantically while American Army vehicles burned in the background.

Precious few journalists dared stay long enough in-country, or delve deeply enough, to get the story right. They arrived in Iraq with skeptical my-mind-is-made-up-don't-confuse-me-with-the-facts attitudes. Politicians and, too frequently, high-ranking, rear-echelon military officers ignorant of what was really going on played right into their hands.

A Pentagon-level general officer accompanied by some politicians and TV and print reporters showed up one morning at Yusufiyah to tour Colonel Infanti's Delta patrol bases on Malibu Road. The transport into the zone was twice as large as usual and heavily armed; heaven help the commander who let a politician get hurt.

Although Battalion provided what amenities it could to make life easier for the dogfaces in the outposts, life remained nonetheless Spartan. There was, after all, a war going on. Several reporters expressed dismay about how soldiers could live like this for long periods of time. The general either revealed his complete ignorance of what combat was like in Iraq, or he was attempting to create a more palatable image for public consumption back home.

"Oh," said the general, "they don't live out here all the time. They come out for a week at a time, then go back to the rear to rest up."

Infanti couldn't let that pass, even though protocol dictated that a colonel never publically contradict a general. He stepped forward.

"That's not exactly accurate, sir," he said. "My men are out here *all* the time. This *is* rest for them."

Friction existed between the front lines and the rear at all levels. And at all levels, leaders were willing to speak out to protect their men from the "chickenshit" REMFs attempted to dump on them.

It sometimes took months for Delta Company soldiers to escape Malibu Road for a quick "refit" in the rear. When they got there, they were in no mood to take crap from the pogues.

Near the end of the winter rains, Sergeant Victor Chavez took his squad to Camp Liberty in Baghdad for its very first refit. He had been here in 2004-2005 when Camp Liberty was still called Camp Victory. This was the twenty-five-year-old's third combat tour—once in Afghanistan, now twice in Iraq. The members of his squad were excited at the prospect of a fairyland in the middle of the desert where they could acquire a Big Mac with a double order of fries, a Burrito Supreme, or a Whopper with an ice-cream shake.

The Post Exchange was huge and stocked like a Super Wal-Mart back in Kansas or Texas. The men parked their two humvees in the big lot, secured their weapons, posted a guard, and headed off in high spirits to the PX. They had arrived in Iraq some six months ago wearing crisp new ACUs. They were now stained and frayed; their helmet covers and gloves worn as threadbare as their nerves; their vehicles dented and twisted, dimpled, chipped, and pock-marked from battle. They wore unshorn mops of hair, and their uniforms were rancid from poor hygiene and the normal grind of battle. They looked what they were: combat-hardened warriors.

Chavez looked around at all the other neat, Army-Regulation-type soldiers. Then he looked at his Joes. *Man, we're a mess. Somebody is going to say something.*

Sure enough, a bright and shiny captain from the 3rd ID blocked the entrance to the PX. Chavez, who had lagged behind, walked up to ask him what the problem was.

"Are these your guys, sergeant?"

"Yes, sir."

"Your uniforms and hair are not within army standards. You're not allowed to use the facilities until you make corrections."

Chavez had to muster restraint to keep from bum-rushing this pompous, overbearing asshole across the lot and ramming his to-army-standards crew cut into the side of one of the hummers. He took a step into the captain's space and locked his eyes on the officer's. He spoke in a low growl so no other passing officer would overhear.

"Sir, this is the first time in months we've been to a place with something other than MREs and army chow to eat and water or coffee to drink. I can see that's not true for you, sir. You get this shit all the time. I want you to listen to me carefully, sir. My men and I *are* going in there to refit. Then we'll go back to fighting the war to which you'll never get any closer than you are now. So unless you want to take this further, you'll get your soft white ass out of the way of real soldiers. And we know where the barbershop is, too."

Obviously, the captain hadn't been around too many combat soldiers. Chavez and his squad pushed past him and entered the PX while he stood there, speechless.

"I wanna be a rear pogue just like him when I grow up," Matt Moran jeered. "How about you, Sergeant Reevers? What do you want to be when you grow up?"

Deadpan, Reevers replied, "Alive."

FORTY-EIGHT

Personal dishonesty and corruption were virtually a way of life with Iraqis. The Saddam regime had been an extreme plutocracy in which everyone stole from everyone else as a matter of survival. In the rural areas and in the small towns and villages, extended families consisted of parents, grandparents, great grandparents, aunts, uncles, and cousins of various degrees all living in the same area and farming the same land while they pilfered from each other, their neighbors, and the Americans whenever they could. The only persons considered even moderately incorruptible were Iraqi Christians, whose honesty was the main reason they exerted influence in professional fields far out of proportion to their numbers. Even Saddam used to say that the Christians didn't steal.

Since Christians were such a tiny minority, and since there was no tradition of selfless national patriotism in the country, the Americans dared not assume people would do the right thing. The safest approach was to trust no one and view everyone with suspicion.

Delta Company raided a house near JSB after alert patrols spotted people sneaking in and out at night. Caught red-handed, the man of the house grinned sheepishly and shrugged. He had built a general store in his back room to service his neighbors with stolen goods. In the room were cases of such items as Pampers, Johnson & Johnson foot powder, Colgate toothpaste, Barbasol shaving cream, jeans and other Western apparel, all apparently stolen from American PX warehouses or hijacked from cargo trucks on their way to the PX. As the guy explained, he wasn't an insurgent, simply an honest thief making a living. People seen creeping around the house were consumers coming for Winstons and Aqua Velva and not bombs and fuses.

Patrols and recons served the dual purpose of disrupting enemy activity in the AO while at the same time building relationships with residents and communities. It had been repeatedly demonstrated that security had to be imposed upon an area before anything else could be accomplished. Chaos and lawlessness inevitably reigned where units attempted to appease rather than fight; they were cut to pieces and chased off their bases with their tails between their legs.

In contrast, in those AOs where battalions were determined to hunt down, kill, and capture insurgent cells, the higher level of security provided the necessary conditions for legitimate economic, civil, and political reconstruction. Many of the insurgent cells took the path of least resistance and moved into AOs where they were not so rigorously challenged.

Colonel Infanti agreed with a statement made by British Prime Minister Tony Blair: "One thing is for sure: the extremists have faith in our weakness just as they have faith in their own religious fanaticism. And the weaker we are, the more they will come after us."

Plenty of bad guys were still hanging around in The Triangle plotting and scheming. As part of an aggressive strategy, Colonel Infanti's 4th Battalion cut them no slack. Companies and platoons were always out hunting.

Delta Company troops poured out of their trucks and stretched into a line across a neglected field where scrawny weeds spurted up after the last rain. Curfews kept most Iraqis indoors after nightfall, all except those attached to the insurgency. There had been a lot of after-midnight activity in this region lately. Delta Company decided to conduct a nighttime sweep to see what it could jump up.

Troops began to walk forward, weapons at the ready. They passed around a local cemetery in pitch darkness, the only sound coming from the electricity-producing generator in a nearby house. In a more built-up community, dogs barking from every house and alley marked their progress. If it weren't for the dogs, nobody would know they were coming. Now, everyone knew.

"Keep alert," sergeants cautioned. "If you don't keep your eyes open, you're as good as dead."

Without a night vision device, a hajji walking along a narrow road failed to see the soldiers until they were almost upon him. He ditched a bag he was carrying and bolted.

"Catch that motherfucker!"

A couple of soldiers took off after him in what would have been a futile effort, laden as they were with armor and equipment, except the guy hit a fence in the darkness that shot him back into the road like an arrow from a bow. The soldiers tackled him. The bag he discarded contained thousands of Iraqi dinars.

"That's a shitpot full of loot."

The guy was barefooted and clad in baggy pants and a filthy t-shirt. He sat silent and unmoving on the ground with his head hanging and his hands flex-cuffed behind him. He looked like he was scared shitless. Someone offered him a cigarette. He sat smoking silently, eyes downcast. Not making a sound.

An IA interrogation team arrived. Everybody figured the guy was a courier delivering cash or else he had just been paid a bounty for planting an IED or taking shots at Americans. The IAs threw him face down on the road. He began to shake violently. He thought they were going to put a bullet through his head. After all, that was what he would have done had their roles been reversed.

Delta continued to sweep, crossing into a farmer's backfield to gather around a mound of freshly turned earth next to a shallow irrigation channel. Excavating it, soldiers removed several plastic sacks containing AK-47 ammunition. They approached the nearest house and brought the man to the mound.

"Where did this come from?" an Intel officer asked the farmer.

"I don't know. Maybe my neighbor, who has a hate for me."

"You have a dog. This is almost in your back yard."

"Maybe the dog was sleeping."

"I think you're lying. Cuff him."

The IA added him to the courier and the sweep moved on. At each house, a squad circled, looking, before banging on the door to enter and search for weapons. Soldiers calmly and politely searched houses from which Jihadists might have launched actions to kill or maim Americans just days before, demonstrating restraint that would have astonished anyone not familiar with the American soldier. Some of the young GIs felt guilty and conflicted about the casual rifling through private residences.

Each household was allowed one AK-47 and one magazine of rounds. Anything more than that was confiscated and the owner arrested, depending on how much more. Iraqi families stood nervously, fidgeting, looking at each other.

Battle-weary, hard-core and hard-bitten, often cynical, and certainly capable of violence when necessary, the American soldier nonetheless possessed a basic decency that was the main reason the U.S. military was succeeding in the same kind of war at which the Soviet Red Army had failed in Afghanistan. The GI might not be perfect, but he managed to largely avoid graft, cruelty, revenge-seeking, and advantage-taking under difficult circumstances that provided both opportunity and temptation.

Officers asked the women and children about water, electricity, and sewer service.

"No water. No sewer. Electricity come on sometimes at night."

The Iraqis had been completely dependent upon government for the past thirty-five years to take care of their needs, solve their problems, and dictate every decision. As a result, they never learned to take charge of their own lives. They expected Americans to come in and take up where Saddam left off, a dependency culture comparable to the welfare enclaves in many inner cities in the United States.

Delta Company moved on.

A lone streetlight down at the end of an alley provided the only illumination. Three young hajji males were gathered around a rusty four-door compact. They spotted the Americans too late to flee. When asked to produce IDs and questioned about what they were doing out after curfew, one of them repeated, "Bee-bee. Bee-bee."

"Baby?"

"Yes. Yes. Bee-bee. Wife he have bee-bee. I can go to hospital. Car she not start."

"You speak English."

The man pinched his fingers together. "A few."

"Don't lie to me. You speak more than a few."

The men were too hyper to be entirely innocent. In the trunk of the old car were two howitzer rounds, each pre-rigged with detonation cord and prepped with fuses to be employed as IEDs. The IAs added them to their retinue of captives. It was turning out to be a remarkable night. And it wasn't over yet.

There were times when the troops needed to be open and friendly, other times when necessity prescribed the destruction or detention of the enemy and those who sheltered or protected him. A psychological struggle was underway, with the Iraqi people as the prize. On the one side were American forces who demonstrated remarkable gentleness and forbearance. On the other side, the remnants of Saddam's regime reinforced by foreign Jihadists using fear and terror to further their goals. The trick to operating in such a delicate, schizophrenic climate was in determining what was required by any particular situation, whether open and friendly or suspicious and prepared for destruction.

Several men had built a small fire in an alley, around which they gathered with a number of boys to visit and play dominoes. It was after curfew, but the little congregation appeared harmless, just hanging out. The Americans were invited to have chai tea and naan bread just for passing through and keeping things safe. It would have been rude to refuse. As strange as it seemed, a representation of GIs sat down in the fire-lit alley with a group of strangers in the middle of a war to share tea.

Some of the Joes kicked a soccer ball a few times with the boys before a platoon leader advised the Iraqis they should go home. They were violating curfew.

"Lieutenant?" a soldier said.

He had investigated a pile of old blankets bundled up against a nearby wall. Wrapped inside the blankets was paraphernalia that included steel pipes cut to length for use as improvised mortar-firing tubes and a pile of al-Qaeda literature with titles such as *What is al-Qaeda?; Why Osama bin Laden Went to Afghanistan; The Glorious Explosions in America; Why God Chooses Martyrs . . .*

Scars from the ongoing war were everywhere—on the road with its holes, craters, and patched-up places from IEDs; on a house smeared with graffiti and forlorn with blown-out widows and piled-up trash; on the face of an old man sitting outside staring at it and looking as though he remembered other times. It was Colonel Infanti's hope that, with enough pressure, there would be fewer weapons in the hands of guerrillas, less money for them to spend on recruiting and insurgency, and not so many old men with that heartbreaking look on their faces.

There were encouraging signs the more it became clear that the 10th Mountain was not going to cut and run. Locals got to know some of the soldiers and greeted them with smiles, waves, friendly faces, and shouted greetings rather than turning away with stone-cold faces. More children crowded around and asked for anything and everything they could think of, especially treats, and not so many of them hurled stones at the trucks when they passed by.

At a market, a middle-aged man sidled up to Sergeant Montgomery and cautiously observed in poor but practiced English how the presence of the Americans was making him and his family feel safer. Farmers near where Sergeant Messer and PFC Given were killed cleared some of the surrounding fields of reeds and growth to make it harder for insurgents to hide there. People in one village established a democratic town council to make the community more livable by instigating "beautification" projects to clean up the trash. A sheikh with a small militia used it to enforce curfew.

American soldiers did their part. They were active and visible in the villages distributing food, school supplies, building materials, and other goods. Wherever some of the soldiers like Sergeant James Connell went, they were recognized for their kindness and their affection for children. Kids followed them like they were Pied Pipers. "Polar Bears! Polar Bears!" they chorused.

Company and platoon medics made a point of taking into the field with them little things to make the people's lives more comfortable— lotion for a child's dry skin; painkillers for a woman in the terminal stages of cancer; antibiotics for a farmer's infection.

A little boy of about seven, dirty and unshorn with eyes darker than the Euphrates River, tapped an American soldier on the arm.

"Mister, what is your name?" he asked in surprisingly good English.

"Brandon Gray," the soldier said.

"It is nice to meet you, Brandon Gray," the boy replied. "My name is Qassim. I hope you will stay."

FORTY-NINE

It required about six months for an outfit in combat to reach its peak. Efficiency and morale started to go downhill after that. Soldiers complained about why they were in Iraq and wondered when they would be allowed to go home. Conditions were even more frustrating because of the nature of the war and its rules of engagement. It sometimes seemed they were fighting merely to avoid losing, fighting for the sake of fighting rather than trying to win and go home. No wonder the Joes were schizophrenic. Making nicey-nice one moment, kill or be killed the next; laughing children here, around the next bend in the road a sniper waiting; deliver some schoolbooks, find the pages later tamped into the end of a 155mm homemade explosive to hold the powder in.

Tempers sometimes flared. Soldiers' anger and resentment built up as casualties mounted.

Some of the senior NCOs and officers in Delta Company got wind of a conspiracy by soldiers to assassinate Crazy Legs. Although the cripple had been rendered virtually impotent, was even an asset in a rather curious way as defined by Sergeant Montgomery, his mere continuing presence was a thorn in the side, an insult. At first, he proved to be a source of amusement and entertainment as Joes made a game of devising schemes to get rid of the most conspicuous spy in their midst. Apparently, however, a few of the soldiers had turned the game serious.

NCOs nipped the conspiracy at the roots before it had a chance to get out of hand. Afterwards, Joes received little impromptu lectures on how you couldn't frag somebody simply because you *knew* him to be the enemy. GIs had ROEs, the enemy didn't. Besides, U.S. soldiers could be charged with "war crimes." It seemed that certain politicians and the antiwar crowd back home, while clamoring their support for the troops, were all too eager to second-guess soldiers from the comfort of their safe air-conditioned offices with a warm cup of coffee in one hand, an intern's ass in the other, and no fear whatsoever of getting killed in the next ten minutes. With this bunch, who to many soldiers seemed to constitute almost a second enemy front behind lines, even righteous combat could be considered a war crime; an assassination would most certainly bring down their ire like the wrath of God.

The Haditha incident seemed to prove to the soldier in Iraq that he would automatically be presumed guilty until proven innocent.

In 2005, a roadside IED hit a U.S. Marine convoy in the little town of Haditha, wounding several Marines and killing a humvee driver, Lance Corporal Miguel Terrazas, twenty. Staff Sergeant Frank Wuterich and his men cleared several nearby houses from which they received hostile fire. Unfortunately, unarmed civilians were sometimes slain in the heat of combat. Insurgents often claimed "victims" were both unarmed and civilians, whether that was the case or not; it produced good psychological warfare and even better press. Sergeant Wuterich, three other enlisted men, and four officers were later charged in the killing of twenty-four Iraqis.

Whether they were guilty or not (they were later exonerated) wasn't the initial issue. The baying began even before the Marine Corps completed its investigation. Antiwar politicians and an unfriendly press convicted the Marines in advance. Newspapers began comparing Haditha to My Lai in Vietnam. Congressmen from the House floor commenced howling about how Haditha was "worse than Abu Ghraib"; the Marines had committed war crimes "in cold blood."

"I will not excuse murder and that's what happened . . . ," U.S. Representative John Murtha proclaimed. "I hear one (of the victims) was even in English asking for mercy . . . We cannot allow something like this to fester . . . We've already lost the direction of this war . . . These kinds of things have to be brought out immediately, because if these Marines get away with it, other Marines might think it's okay . . ."

To the Joes in The Triangle of Death, fighting a war unlike any other in U.S. history, the episode illustrated how they would be thrown to the hyenas if it would score a political point. It sometimes seemed the American GI had as much to fear from his own country as from IEDs and bullets.

Not that atrocities weren't committed, in Iraq as in every other war. In July 2006, one month before the 2nd BCT arrived in Iraq to take over The Triangle of Death AO, five soldiers of the 101st Airborne Division were charged with murdering an entire family in Mahmudiyah, including a five-year-old girl, and raping a fifteen-year-old. The news was hot in the Iraqi streets, sowing distrust and suspicion among citizens and making it more difficult than ever to win them over. It also provided insurgents a justification for their resistance.

The 10th Mountain Division had a lot to overcome. A single outrage painted everyone subsequently with the same brush. Colonel Infanti and his staff constantly reminded officers and noncoms that nothing like this must ever happen in 4th Battalion.

It appeared the 101st Division in The Triangle had reached the same breaking point that now threatened the 10th Mountain. Bravo Company 1/502nd (1st Battalion, 502nd Infantry) of the 101st was being worn ragged by shadowy insurgents who seldom engaged in face-to-face combat. Instead, sniper fire, IEDs, and RPG attacks occurred almost daily, claiming at least one Screaming Eagle soldier every week. Bravo Company alone suffered eight KIAs.

PFC Steven D. Green witnessed two of these casualties. He and five other airborne soldiers were manning a checkpoint when an Iraqi civilian approached them. The troops knew him because of his status as an informant. He greeted the soldiers warmly, then suddenly pulled a pistol and shot two of them at point-blank range. Green was never entirely "right" afterwards.

Three months later, in March 2006, Green's platoon manned another checkpoint in Mahmudiyah, through which pretty 15-year-old Abeer Hamza had to pass almost daily. She complained to her mother that U.S. soldiers were hitting on her, making suggestive remarks. Her mother Fakhriyah was afraid the soldiers would come for her.

"The Americans would not do such a thing," a neighbor reassured her.

Steven Green was a bony-faced twenty-year-old from Texas, a cocky loner who had been allowed to enlist in the army despite a petty criminal record and a history of drug, alcohol, and emotional problems. On the afternoon of 12 March 2006, after drinking bootleg Iraqi whiskey, Green rounded up some buddies and talked up the idea of raping Abeer, who lived about 300 meters from the checkpoint.

Green, Sergeant Paul Cortez, Specialist James P. Barker, PFC Jesse V. Spielman, and PFC Bryan L. Howard set out, in Green's words, "to kill and hurt a lot of Iraqis." At Abeer's house, they herded her father, mother and five-year-old sister into one bedroom and forced Abeer into another. Green shot the father in the head several times with a legally owned AK-47 found in the house. Then he riddled the mother and her five-year-old daughter with gunfire, killing them instantly.

He came out of the room and proudly announced to his buddies, "I just killed them. All are dead."

In the other bedroom, Green and two of the soldiers ripped off Abeer's clothing and took turns raping her. Afterwards, Green shot her two or three times with the AK-47, threw a blanket over her body, then set the house afire in a crude effort to cover up the crime. He returned to the checkpoint, buried his blood-drenched clothing, and swore everyone to secrecy.

Eventually the secret leaked out, and the five soldiers were arrested and charged.

"I came over here because I wanted to kill people," Green admitted with casual indifference. "The truth is, it wasn't all I thought it was cracked up to be. I thought killing somebody would be a life-changing experience. And then I did it, and it was like 'All right, whatever . . .' Over here, killing people is like squashing an ant. I mean, you kill somebody and it's like, 'All right, let's go get some pizza.'"

Green's crimes (for which he was later convicted) constituted the most horrific instance of criminal behavior by American troops during the four-year-old war, a worst-case scenario of mentally and emotionally unfit soldiers slipping through the army's pre-enlistment screening to end up on the killing fields in Iraq where their maladjustments might be triggered under stress.

Even normally adjusted soldiers could crack under the pressure, as the Crazy Legs incident proved. They sometimes thought they were damned either way, whether guilty or innocent.

FIFTY

In previous wars, "Go tell it to the chaplain" was the mantra served to disturbed or "shell-shocked" soldiers. Chaplains were counselors of choice for no matter what ailed the soldier psychologically or emotionally, whether a marital crisis back home or adjustment problems on the front. Psychiatrists to help soldiers deal with combat stress entered the military picture as early as the Vietnam War, but they were never in great numbers. The commencement of *Iraqi Freedom* in 2003 changed all that. The army began sending military mental-health teams to Iraq's most intense combat zones to keep an eye on soldiers and pull them from their units for therapy.

Almost immediately after PFC Stephen Green witnessed the shooting of his two friends at the roadblock and still three months before the rape-murders in Mahmudiyah, an Army Combat Stress Team found that he had "homicidal ideation" and diagnosed him as a homicidal threat. Reports said he was angry about the war and desperate to avenge the deaths of his comrades. Treatment consisted of a prescription for a mood-regulating drug and orders to get some sleep before returning to duty the next day.

After his arrest, the army launched the most aggressive campaign in history to deal with hidden scars like Green's and with soldiers suffering from PTSD (post-traumatic stress disorder) that might cause them to flip out. Exposure over long periods of time to suicide bombers, roadside mines, and the constant threat of attack posed a unique challenge to the mental health of American soldiers.

"When you're in a combat theater dealing with enemy combatants who don't abide by the laws of war and do acts of indecency, soldiers become stressed," Army Brigadier General Donald Campbell told a Pentagon briefing. "They see their buddies getting blown up, and they could snap."

The Iraq War had so far produced more cases of PTSD than any conflict in decades. A study published by the New England Journal of Medicine estimated that one out of six of the more than 300,000 soldiers who had served in Iraq to date may have been struggling with PTSD. Fully 40 percent of the soldiers fighting in The Triangle of Death were treated at one time or another during their tours for mental and emotional anxiety.

The aim of the "shrink campaign" was to treat soldiers as close to the front lines as possible.

"Every time you evacuate the soldier further from where they work, your chances of getting that soldier back to full duty decrease," explained Lieutenant Colonel Elizabeth Bowler, an army psychiatrist. "The closer we can treat to the front, the better our chances."

What they army was trying to avoid, she said, was "a whole generation of veterans sitting by the side of the road with a cardboard sign saying WILL WORK FOR FOOD."

Soldiers often resisted seeking psychological help because of the "loser" stigma attached to it. It seemed to the troops of Delta Company on Malibu Road that shrinks were always sniffing and snooping about, trying to "catch" them and send them up to Brigade to be checked out.

FIFTY-ONE

Signs of progress in The Triangle didn't mean the war was over. There were lulls in the action, then hot spots again, the ebb and flow of a stubborn insurgency. Within Delta Company and within the platoons, things seemed to be breaking down. Every day GIs went down that damnable road and got blown up for doing a good job.

Sergeant Rashid Reevers' truck was hit three times by IEDs in a single day. He kept towing and switching trucks and getting blown up. "Lucky child" Sergeant John Herne, who had gone months without striking an IED, was hit twice in one week in front of the 109 Mosque.

He wasn't the only one to take it in the shorts at the mosque. Located at the beginning of the S-curves, it was a typical dome-shaped, sand-colored building with a big loudspeaker on top that played the muezzin calls for prayer five times a day while a vendor down the road sold dried goat heads. One afternoon as Second Platoon went roaring by, a freshly patched spot in the road caught Jonathan Watts' attention. He yelled for driver Dean Fetheringill to slow down. Fetheringill hit his brakes, almost throwing Chiva Lares through the windshield.

The truck stopped just in time to avoid being blown to Kingdom Come. A big IED erupted directly in front of the truck, bending its grill and front bumper. It would have been a lot worse but for Watts' sharp eye and Fetheringill's quick reflexes.

Specialist Brandon Gray, the kid from Oklahoma who wanted to be a cop, was driving for First Platoon's Sergeant James Connell when his vehicle struck a mine in the road that blew open his door and spurted blood from his ears. He maintained consciousness long enough to bring the truck to a stop without crashing it into the roadside ditch. When he regained awareness, it was 0400 the next morning and he was lying in the first aid station at Inchon being treated by a doctor helicoptered in from the Green Zone.

An explosion right in front of Specialist Alex Jimenez' truck burst a front tire. As the vehicle veered toward its flat, heavy machine guns opened up from the flat roofs of nearby houses. TC Sergeant Anthony Schober heard slugs ricocheting off Jimenez' turret. Jimenez ducked.

"Holy shit! That was close!"

Then Jimenez popped up again. He had two or three spare cans of 7.62 ammo for his two-forty. He burned it up shooting at anything that moved within range, pinning down a bunch of Iraqis in their houses. Battalion QRF rounded them up and marched them to 152. IA and Brigade interrogators came down and hauled them away. Schober and Jimenez couldn't care what happened to them. It would have suited them just fine if the IA had taken them out back, lined them up against the blast wall, and shot them. Enough of this shit already!

Corporal Mayhem Menahem, second only to First Sergeant Galliano as the company's "IED magnet," was hit so many times that none of the other guys wanted to ride with him. The day of the "daisy chain" when Fletcher and Scribner threw their bodies over his proved the final straw. After that, every time he heard a crashing boom rippling through the air, whether he was wide awake or fast asleep, he jumped up automatically to throw on his body armor, grab his weapons, and rush off to defend the perimeter.

He wasn't particularly superstitious about being a magnet. It was just that he was scared to death all the time, particularly when he had to go out on the road. Like most good infantrymen, however, he tended to ignore his aches and pains and phobias. To admit to them and seek help was tantamount to admitting a weakness.

His nerves finally got so bad that Lieutenant Tomasello and First Sergeant Galliano sent him to Brigade to see a shrink. The psychiatrist was a colonel sent down from the Green Zone by the Army Combat Stress Team. He reminded Mayhem of TV's Doctor Phil.

"How do you feel about your friends Sergeant Messer and Private Given dying?" the shrink asked in his best you're-lying-on-a-couch manner.

"How am I supposed to feel, sir? I don't know how to feel. I go back and forth in my mind over and over again. It could have been me—or any of the other guys. I feel guilty about it, but I'm glad it wasn't me if it had to be somebody."

"Are you afraid, Corporal?"

"All the time, sir. I guess that's why I'm here. I've started having nightmares, sir, like Messer had—that I'm going to be blown up and killed. I've been blown up so many times that my string's got to run out sooner or later. Have I become a coward? What kind of person does that make me?"

The doctor gave him a kindly pat on the shoulder. "It makes you normal, Corporal," he said. "I've spoke with a lot of soldiers since we've been in Iraq. Some of them have long roads ahead. You're struggling with what's happening to you, and that is a struggle to retain your humanity. You've seen things no human should have to see, done things people shouldn't have to do. Combat is contrary to all that we've been taught. It's not a black and white world over here. Some of us move too far to the dark side. Corporal Menahem, I don't believe you will be one of them."

As treatment, the doctor prescribed "three hots and a cot": burgers and fries, conversation in air conditioning, a movie, and a good night's sleep in a real bed. It helped Mayhem forget the war. He was still afraid when he returned to Malibu Road, but at least he could sleep.

Platoon leaders and sergeants were reminded that it was up to them to hold things together while the pressure continued to build.

"Are your soldiers out of their fucking minds?" officers raged. "What the fuck are they thinking?"

"We'll fix it, sir."

"Unfuck them, or I'll unfuck you."

The Joes tried. Anzak and Murphy and Chavez and some of the others sometimes got together with Brenda the blow-up to put on a little strip show, anything to pass the time and distract from where they were. Somebody might sneak in a jug of Iraqi black market rotgut. Everybody had a few shots, stuck dinar bills down Brenda's panties and whooped it up. What it did mostly, however, was remind them of home and *real* girls.

Guys like Sergeant Jeremy Miller, Specialist Joe Merchant, and Mayhem had all served previous combat tours in Iraq. They thought they had done their share and would be discharged and allowed to go home. Stop-Loss extended them in the army and sent them back to Iraq one more time. It was harder on them in many ways than on first-timers. They had already survived one tour. Now, they had to survive another one. Double jeopardy.

One morning, Second Platoon prepared for a mission over toward JSB and the Russian power plant. Lieutenant Dudish issued the OpOrder before breakfast. The sun was up, it was a warm day for January, the flies were not biting, there had been no incidents the previous night, and everything appeared all quiet along the Euphrates. However, a murmur of discontent started over breakfast when somebody bitched about rubber eggs and refused to eat. Several other Joes tossed their plates in a gesture of solidarity that had nothing to do with Cookie Urbina and his kitchen. Eating or not eating, unlike the IEDs along Malibu, was something over which the soldiers had control.

Sergeants John Herne and Nate Brooks were in an intense discussion with Miller, Merchant, and a couple of other guys out where the trucks were lining up in front of 152 when Sergeant Montgomery exited the old barbershop with his rifle slung over one shoulder and carrying his nitch by its strap. Lieutenant Dudish was still inside taking care of a last-minute commo problem.

"They won't get in the trucks," Sergeant Herne said, indicating Miller and the others.

Montgomery's drill sergeant hackles bristled. "What do you mean, they won't get in the trucks?"

"They say they're not going back out."

Miller had been behaving edgy lately, nervous, chain-smoking, and not sleeping much. Montgomery got in his face. Miller was senior man of the "revolt" and therefore its leader.

"Get your ass in that truck," Montgomery ordered.

"Sergeant, I'm tired of this shit," Miller said. "We're getting hit all the time while we have to grin and bear it. We've all had enough. It feels like we're taking crazy pills. So I quit. I'm walking back to Yusufiyah and going home."

He threw his rifle down, turned abruptly and started toward the compound gate that opened onto Malibu Road. An American soldier alone wouldn't make it three hundred meters before some sneaky asshole nailed him. Merchant and the others looked uncomfortable, but they remained in-place.

"Sergeant Miller, I'm giving you a direct order. Get back here now or face charges."

Miller kept walking. It seemed he was desperate enough not to give a damn what happened to him.

"Sergeant Miller, this will land you in Leavenworth. You still have a chance to reconsider. Either way, I'm going to stop you before you get to the gate."

The previous year, two soldiers from the 4th Infantry Division had hijacked an Iraqi and his personally owned vehicle and ordered him to drive them to Kuwait. They were stopped, given a summary court martial, and sentenced to serve long terms in the federal prison at Fort Leavenworth. It had been a big joke among the Joes all over Iraq.

Miller hesitated. Reluctantly, he turned around and came back.

That was his last day in The Triangle of Death. Company shipped him off to Brigade to see a shrink. Montgomery never learned what happened to him, whether he was punished for mutiny or whether he was diagnosed with PTSD and sent back to the States upon the recommendation of the Army Combat Stress Team.

The soldiers behind on Malibu Road laughed. Hell, PTSD for them was *normal*.

FIFTY-TWO

The inability to suppress the insurgency in Iraq prompted President George W. Bush to revise the war's strategy. On 20 January 2007, he held a press conference to announce "the Surge." Another 30,000 troops in five brigade combat teams would be infused into the nearly 140,000 already in-country. He named General David Petraeus to command the Multi-National Force.

Petraeus, along with his executive officer, Colonel Peter Mansoor, and General Ray Odierno, the new commanding general of Multi-National Corps—Iraq, had published Army Field Manual 3-24 the previous month outlining their new philosophy for counterinsurgency operations in Iraq. Although Petraeus was the primary architect of the new strategy, a number of combat military commanders had gradually come to realize that what they were doing was not working and was not going to work in a war unlike any ever fought by the United States. No one would get hurt if the Americans remained forted up in their major bases. Nothing would be accomplished, either.

Petraeus based his new approach upon Vietnam-era programs such as General Creighton Abrams' PROVN (Provincial Reconstruction of Vietnam) Report. Abrams advocated spreading U.S. platoons into villages and communities to work with local residents in "community policing" designed to pacify immediate regions while developing allegiances and collecting intelligence that would help the wider prosecution of the war. As Mansoor noted, "We needed infantry in patrol bases spread among the population. A military force must live with the people it would defend."

In Petraeus' opinion, securing the population was the key to effective counterinsurgency. He penned a detailed explanation of his "clear-hold-build" philosophy that he circulated among all troops in the war zone.

"Improving [the] security of Iraq's population is the overriding objective of our strategy," he wrote. "Accomplishing the mission requires carrying out complex military operations and convincing the Iraqi people that we will not just 'clear' their neighborhoods of enemy, we will also stay and help 'hold' the neighborhoods so that the 'build' phase can go forward."

Rather than undertaking large sweeps, small units would push out into communities to establish security stations and combat outposts that allowed them to live and fight among the population. Determined to minimize harm to civilians, he asked that commanders consider one simple question before they approved any operation: Would it take more bad guys off the streets than it created by the way it was conducted?

At the same time, the Surge called for pounding hell out of the enemy.

"The reality is that there is a hard-core minority who cannot be won over by any reasonable effort; they can only be incapacitated," Petraeus noted. "We have a pretty clear message. If you shoot at us, we will do our damnedest to kill you . . . and if you live in a neighborhood and you know there are bad people and you don't want Americans to return fire, endangering your families, you need to turn in the bad guys . . . It's great to be nice, but we've found that if you let up for one second against the bad guys, they're right back at your throats."

The larger point of the Surge was to create a breathing space in the violence during which political reconstruction and rebuilding efforts could take place.

The Surge validated operations already being conducted by Colonel Mike Kershaw and his battalion commanders like Lieutenant Colonel Mike Infanti in The Triangle of Death. It also provided a common blueprint for the conduct of the war rather than leaving it to the discretion of individual commanders. Everyone would now be working together toward a common goal.

It would have been easy for Petraeus to say this is how you're going to fight, this is what you're going to do, then step back out of the picture and let the outfits root hog or die. That was not what he did. Not only were more troops sent into battle, but he also spread them out and got the entire country to fighting. He made sure BCTs had everything they needed to fight with.

Whereas 4th Battalion had previously been chronically short of certain supplies, it never lacked for wire, ammo, food, water, or anything else from then on. Infanti asked for hand-cranked washing machines so his soldiers could wash their uniforms. He got them.

Iraq's year of torment began to change with the Surge. Maybe Colonel Infanti hadn't reached that turning point of his yet. But he thought he could see it just around the bend.

FIFTY-THREE

Winter in Iraq arrived late that year and departed early. With a laugh, the jolly big workhorse of First Platoon, Joe Anzak, called it "The Winter of Our Discontent." Most of the rains were over for the year. Biting flies were back again in force. Foliage along the fertile Euphrates looked fresher and greener in the spring sunshine. Temperatures were reaching triple digits by the end of March, and people were once more taking to their open roofs to sleep. Even with the war, the normal cycle of life in the Tigris-Euphrates River Valley continued the way it had since the beginning of time in the Garden of Eden.

The Joes on Malibu Road thought they detected some decrease in violence after the start of General Petraeus' Surge. Their outfits seemed as chronically undermanned as ever, what with only twenty or so men available to a platoon at any one time when there should have been thirty or more. But they kept hearing about an infusion of new brigades, none of which, as far as they knew, had reached The Triangle of Death. And they kept hearing about how they were winning, and how more and more of the Iraqi police, military, and political classes were stepping up to the plate to take a swing at the insurgents. There weren't any home runs yet, but the soldiers were more optimistic when Colonel Infanti assured them they were reaching a turning point.

Life in wartime, as the soldiers of Delta Company were constantly rediscovering, was full of irony and grim humor. Often, however, irony wasn't recognized until long after its introduction.

Lieutenant Morgan Springlace relieved Lieutenant Vargo as platoon leader of First Platoon. Young officers were rotated in and out of combat to give them command experience. Whether true or not, rumor had it that Springlace was from an Old Blood military family and that he was a top graduate of the West Point Military Academy. He started out strict, but then relaxed under the rigors of war's reality.

One afternoon, First Platoon set out to check reports of suspicious activity near the old Russian power plant. Halfway there, Lieutenant Springlace received a radio message that Joe Anzak was needed at Company HQ immediately. It sounded urgent. Generally that meant some kind of crisis in a soldier's family. Captain Gilbreath ordered Second Platoon to take over the mission while First returned to Inchon.

Captain Gilbreath and Brown Dog met the platoon. Anzak was frantic with worry.

"Calm down, son," Gilbreath said. "Everything's okay. Just call your dad right away. He thinks you're dead."

It seemed that messages on the MySpace website appeared that morning stating that PFC Joe Anzak had been killed in battle. Anzak's hometown high school, South High in Torrance, California, a Los Angeles suburb, picked up on it and posted Anzak's obituary outside on the school's marquee: IN LOVING MEMORY, JOSEPH ANZAK, CLASS OF 2005.

Hearing of it, Joseph Anzak Senior contacted the Red Cross, who cut through red tape and military channels to connect him to Delta 4/31st in Iraq. Even though Captain Gilbreath assured him that his son was very much alive and well, and that the family would have been notified first in the event of bad news, the distraught father refused to believe him until he spoke directly to his son.

"Dad. It's me. Joe."

"Is that really you, son? Are you sure you're okay? There's a big sign at school that says you were . . ."

"Yeah, Dad. Everything's cool."

"We . . . We were so afraid we would never see you again."

Anzak batted back tears. It took him a few minutes to regain his usual composure after he got off the satellite phone with his father.

"Reports of my death have been highly exaggerated," he finally joked.

Specialist Chris Murphy had known Anzak since Delta Company stood up at Fort Drum and Anzak reported to the company for deployment. He didn't think cracks about dying were funny. Sergeant Messer's nightmares had been premonitions of things to come. He shuddered. Who knew but what this wouldn't turn out to be another premonition of sorts?

FIFTY-FOUR

The army had been good to SFC James C. Connell. Born in Lake City, Tennessee, he enlisted in the army in 1989 and since then had been to forty-two different states in the U.S. and thirteen different countries around the world. His son Nick once asked him why he stayed in the army.

"It's always what I wanted to do—so no one else has to do it."

At first after CSM Alex Jimenez gave him a platoon, Connell seemed happy to be back in the field with Delta Company and his "boys" in First Platoon. That was where he belonged, in the middle of the action where he really contributed to the American effort rather than riding out the war in a relatively safe zone behind a desk. It was his first combat leadership assignment. He remained a contradiction—a former Ranger running a rifle platoon, carrying weapons, and at the same time carrying a heart full of compassion for the Iraqi people and love for the Iraqi children.

"I have kids," he explained. "But for the grace of God they might have been born in a place like this. The children are innocent of what happened here. We have to give them a chance at a better life."

For some of the soldiers in First Platoon, he provided the only true father figure they had ever known. Byron Fouty sought him out frequently for advice and reassurance, as he might have from a real father. Connell was never too busy to sit down with a soldier and talk out a home problem or other concern. He was always *there* for them. Often, even in the middle of his sleep time, he would get up to take a hot cup of coffee or a sandwich to a Joe on roof guard or crater watch. For reasons he never explained, his friends and relatives back home had nicknamed him "Tiger." To First Platoon, he became known as Daddy Connell.

A few weeks after he was transferred to First Platoon, an IED blew up underneath his vehicle, puncturing the floorboard and salting his leg with shrapnel. It wasn't much of an injury. Doc Michael Morse, the platoon medic, patched him up. He recovered almost literally over a cup of coffee.

Afterwards, those closest to him detected a subtle, almost imperceptible difference in his demeanor. First off, he grew increasingly cautious, watchful, protective of his boys. The second difference was more difficult to pin down.

"Do you believe in predestination?" he once asked another platoon sergeant. "I need to go home and see my family while I have a chance."

Captain Gilbreath approved leave for the forty-year-old. Connell caught the next Freedom Bird to Tennessee where his mother and father were looking after his two sons and daughter while he was overseas. Nick was sixteen, Bryan twelve, and Courtney fourteen.

Lake City was Norman Rockwell Middle America. Mom and Pop, apple pie, Fourth of July celebrations, baby Jesus in the Christmas manger, sitting on the front porch watching lightning bugs, chatting over the yard fence with the neighbor, strolling the sidewalks where people smiled and called out greetings. "Good to see you, Tiger." That kind of America.

James had played Little League baseball in elementary school and first-string football for Anderson County High School before he graduated in 1984. James Senior always showed people photographs of his son in uniform.

"He's just a real good son," he said. "We're all so proud of him."

Connell's parents still lived in the same comfortable old porched house where he grew up. He arrived home just in time for Sunday dinner after church, a family tradition attended by his parents, three brothers, one sister, and their respective broods. There was laughter and hugs, and James seemed loose and happy. He avoided most questions about the war with a terse, "It's hard. Mostly it's hard on my boys."

He ran at full speed the entire time he was on leave. Catching up on old friendships, visiting and chatting with chums from high school, having dinner with relatives. Soldiers on leave were always on the go, but James seemed to bring a certain urgency to it. Someone observed that it was almost like he was trying to live an entire lifetime, make every minute count, in the couple of weeks before he returned to Iraq and The Triangle of Death. Those closest to him detected a sense of melancholy poking out through his normal cheerfulness and optimism.

He spent much of his time with Nick, Bryan, and Courtney. He wore the uniform in which he so proudly served and spoke to Bryan's and Courtney's classes at Lake City Middle School. The newspaper ran his picture in the paper. Father, two sons, and daughter took an all-day outing to Dollywood where they rode all the rides and stuffed themselves with hot dogs and cotton candy. Everybody took lots of snapshots. One showed him standing on a trampoline with the two younger children. In another he was sitting in uniform on a sofa with both sons.

Each of his kids was allowed to skip school for one day in order to do something special one on one with their father. Courtney wanted to go to West Town Mall to get a pedicure; father and daughter, laughing uproariously, took off their shoes together. Bryan chose Knoxville Center and a movie. Nick decided to go horseback riding in the Smoky Mountains.

James' melancholy appeared to build as his time at home came to an end. One morning he was standing at the kitchen window drinking coffee and watching the sunrise. When he turned back around, his eyes were moist.

That afternoon while the family was sitting around laughing and talking in the living room, James got up and returned a few minutes later carrying the uniform he wore home. He presented it to his Uncle Charles.

"To remember me by," he explained.

"You'll be home in another few months," he was reminded. "You'll soon have your twenty years in. What are you going to do?"

"I'm never getting out of the army. I don't know anything else."

The day before he returned to Iraq, he took his brother Jeff aside for a confidential talk. He watched Bryan and Nick working on a bicycle in the front yard. He looked up at the clear bright sky. America was such a wonderful, safe place to live. No one was afraid here. Any time he felt the urge, he could jump in a car and drive down to the local convenience store for a Coke without having to worry about snipers and IEDs.

"Jeff," he said, "some of my soldiers are not much older than Nick.

They're just kids. I don't want Nick or Bryan to ever have to be one of them."

"You're their hero. They're like you. They're following in your footsteps."

James nodded. He continued to watch the sky. Then he turned to his brother.

"I need you to make me a promise, Jeff. Look after my kids. I probably won't be coming back."

FIFTY-FIVE

A pair of First Platoon hummers sat parked in the night at the S-curve between Inchon and Battle Position 152, the darkest and most treacherous stretch of Malibu Road. Sergeant James Connell's platoon had drawn the midnight-to-0600 crater watch over the IED pit that took up most of the road. The explosion there that day had destroyed a Fourth Platoon truck and sent one of its occupants to the CASH in Baghdad. It would take the Rapid Road Repair crew a few days to get out and patch up the hole. In the meantime, somebody had to keep the cockroaches back.

The trucks, fronting opposite directions, were boxy silhouettes planted in the center of the road about 150 meters apart with the crater between them. Concertina in the bar ditches lined both sides of the road, except for the accesses left open to several nearby houses. Second Platoon had been busy most of the winter laying wire until it now stretched almost the entire length of the road between Inchon and 151.

It was a long, boring job on a hot, windy night in mid-May nearly four months after the start of the Surge. The wind blowing like that made the Joes uneasy. Foliage grew thick on either side of the road between the Iraqi houses—big date palms and eucalyptus that resembled twisted pines. Palm fronds rattled like old bones in the wind; the sorry excuse for a moon helped shadows creep and skulk about.

PFC Joe Anzak, PFC Chris Murphy, PFC Dan "Corny" Courneya, and Buck Sergeant E-5 Anthony Schober occupied the north truck facing toward FOB Inchon. Big Anzak was in the hatch manning the .50-caliber machine gun. NVs lent him that singular appearance of a goggle-eyed insect with its head stuck out of a hole, wary of intruders. He kept a particularly keen eye on the openings in the wire at the residence access points. That would be where the bad guys came through if and when they made an appearance.

He kept hearing movement, seeing things. He swiveled the snout of his machine gun a full three-sixty, back and forth and around in constant movement, scanning through his NVs. The NVs turned everything liquid green and surreal.

Damn that wind! It kept rattling things, creating furtive sounds, moans and creaking and low shrieks. Shadows stacked and unstacked so that you saw things in them that you knew weren't really there. Anzak hadn't uttered a single wisecrack in more than an hour.

"See something?" Sergeant Schober asked from below in the driver's seat. He felt Anzak's tension.

From Reno, Nevada, Schober, twenty-three, was lanky and intense. One of the more experienced soldiers in Delta Company, he had enlisted at seventeen to make the army his career and was currently on his third combat tour of duty in Iraq. His buds sometimes called him "The Gambler," due more to his origins in Reno than his skill with cards. He seemed to lose more than he won.

Anzak was still looking.

"In *Manticore*, you never saw the monster until the last minute," Corny commented bravely, trying to shore up his own nerves by making light of things. It was a sorry excuse for a wisecrack on a night like this and he dropped it.

"It's just shadows, I guess," Anzak said finally.

Everywhere, everywhere, they're everywhere, Corporal Mayhem sometimes joked in high-pitched imitation of comedian Ray Stevens. It wouldn't have been amusing tonight.

Anzak was sweating. It wasn't just from the heat and humidity. Soldiers in combat developed a kind of sixth sense after awhile. Something other than the wind was making the big gunner uneasy. Iraq could be a very scary place.

Nights like this was when Battalion's big guns received their most frequent workouts. From up toward Rushdi Mulla came the wind-muted *whumpft-whumpft-whumpft* of 105mm howitzers landing rounds in response to a call for a fire mission. Anzak suppressed a cheer. He felt like calling in a mission of his own, blowing up some of the shadows that kept moving around in the woods.

"Fuck 'em up good," Corny said from next to Schober.

"Some asshole out there with an iron pipe and two or three rockets," Schober commented drily, "and so we pound him with a quarter-million dollars worth of artillery."

"So long as it gets the job done," PFC Murphy said from the back seat.

On the opposite side of the IED crater, the second hummer faced south toward 152. Three U.S. soldiers and one IA interpreter manned it. Sergeant Connell, having recently returned from leave, volunteered to take the watch to help spell his men. Platoon sergeants weren't required to stand guard duty, but the platoons were short-handed, Surge or not. He sat in the front passenger's seat.

Specialist Alex Jimenez was in the machine-gun hatch. As with Anzak in the other truck, the wind kept him nervous and alert.

PFC Byron Fouty in the back seat was always scared, wind or not. He had one of his precious books in his pocket and stared out the windows at the constant interchange of moonlight and shadow. A month ago in his MySpace entry, he called his time in Iraq "a messed-up year . . . coated with nothing but bad news, very little good news showing through." Having recently learned that the 2nd BCT was being extended in-country for an additional three months did nothing for his mood, which he described as "aggravated."

The fourth man at the steering wheel was the thinly built Shiite interpreter named Sabah Barak, who looked to be about thirty or so. Having been detached from the 6th Iraqi Army to share room and board with the Americans at Inchon, he possessed a self-deprecating sense of humor and an open honesty that made him generally well liked and trusted by the soldiers of Delta Company. He was one of the few Iraqis who had adapted to going to the toilet in the latrine rather than on the ground, which made him even better-liked.

Wearing NVs, Sergeant Connell and Fouty climbed out of their truck and negotiated around the IED crater to approach the north humvee. Joe

Anzak spotted them coming through his NVs. He gave the others heads-up so they wouldn't startle. Schober offered to move over from behind the wheel to let the sergeant and Fouty inside behind the hummer's steel plates.

"We're just checking, taking a look-see," Sergeant Connell said.

Fouty flattened his back against the truck door, facing outboard with his M-4 at the ready, seemingly in a hurry to finish whatever business brought them here so they could return to the relative safety of their own truck. Snipers loved to catch soldiers out of their vehicles walking around.

"We're good to go, Sergeant," Schober said.

"I brought an extra thermos of coffee."

"Sounds good, Sergeant. Thanks."

"Make sure nobody sleeps."

Sergeant Connell had seemed on edge, not quite himself, ever since he returned from leave. More careful, cautious. He had confided in no one about the conversation he had had with his brother in Tennessee.

"It's been quiet," Schober said, then chuckled. He knew the trite old movie line was bound to elicit a response from Anzak in the turret. Anzak obliged him.

"Yeah. Too quiet."

Connell and Fouty visited a few more minutes before they departed for their own vehicle, talking softly while their eyes constantly probed roadside ditches and the foliage beyond the concertina.

"It's creepy out here tonight," Fouty said as they headed back.

The sorry excuse for a moon slowly arced westward. Anzak scanned roadside shadows through his NVs. Palm fronds chattered in the dark like conspirators.

From the corner of his eye he detected a sudden movement—a shadow detaching itself from deeper shadows. He shouted a warning and swung his machine gun. By that time the road was overrun with shadows, all sprinting toward the two American HMMWVs.

FIFTY-SIX

Blood-chilling whoops of *"Allahu Akbar!"* suppressed the keening of the wind as masked men in black swarmed onto Malibu Road, their forms blending with the darkness in the wan light from the partial moon. Insurgents could not have selected a better night, what with the wind covering any noise they made and shifting confusing shadows among the restless trees. They hadn't been detected even when some of them crept up through the weeds to cut passages through the concertina to allow the main assault party to rush the trucks, catching the Americans by total surprise.

Attackers sprang like big cats onto the sloped rear hatches of both trucks and slammed grenades down through the turrets, past the helmeted heads of astonished machine gunners. Detonating grenades lit up the insides of the trucks, flashing and flickering in the windows like photo flashbulbs going off. The trucks shuddered on their wheels, convulsing from inner turmoil. Screams of pain and panic tore from the interiors.

Having stunned their prey with grenades, the aggressors returned like lions on mortally wounded prey. Several Jihadists yanked Alex Jimenez out of his turret seat. He attempted to fight back, but he was dazed and bleeding from shrapnel having ripped into the flesh of his lower body. The insurgents overpowered him by sheer numbers, threw him down on the road, and dragged him away.

Armored humvees were double-edged swords in that while they protected occupants, they could also turn and become traps. Men surprised inside at close quarters found themselves at a supreme disadvantage in which they had to either shoot through open windows or leave the vehicle in order to engage. Sergeant Connell and Sabah Barak in the front seat had no chance to do either. Both were either dead or near death from the grenades landing on the seat between them.

The backs of the front seats partly shielded the back seat from the explosions, but the confined concussion knocked Byron Fouty to the floorboard. Through a slow motion haze of pain, confusion, and terror, he saw the back doors flung open. Dark forms glared at him. Monsters! He screamed as rough hands reached in. Live Americans were of far greater propaganda value than dead ones.

Through opened doors, automatic rifle fire riddled the two soldiers in the front seat, splashing blood and flesh, making sure they were dead. As an added insult, some of the hostiles turned the interpreter's body upside down in his seat as an expression of contempt. Others torched the truck. It burst into flames that lit up the road and exposed frenetic shadows dragging two comatose GIs toward a nearby house.

In the meantime, a similar scene was playing itself out around the other humvee. As with Sergeant Connell and Sabah Barak, Schober and Courneya in the front seat were either killed outright by grenade explosions or knocked unconscious, to be finished off with bullets. PFC Murphy somehow broke free from the back seat. Terrified and suffering from concussion and shrapnel injuries, he bolted up the road toward Inchon, shedding his armor and helmet as he ran in order to run faster.

Jeering insurgents shouting their "God is great!" war cry picked off the former high school football star with a barrage of rifle fire. He fell hard, his legs shot out from underneath him, flesh shredded and bones shattered. Paralyzed from the waist down, he rolled off the macadam into the ditch, desperately trying to get away. He continued to pull himself across the grass and weeds with his hands until he became entangled in concertina.

Behind him, a fireball engulfed his truck as insurgents set it afire. Both hummers were now blazing. Flames whipped by the savage wind leaped and danced against the black sky. Murphy might still have managed to hide in the darkness and escape except for the firelight. Masked Jihadists stalking up the road after him spotted him struggling in the wire. They yelled. Murphy rolled over, covering his face with his hands.

The last sounds he heard were the mocking laughter of his enemy and the cracking of their rifles.

That left big Joe Anzak. A skilled martial artist, he wasn't going down easy. Having been extracted from the turret of his hummer, he was giving a good accounting of himself in a hand-to-hand fight with a pair of Jihad-ists on the road. A mighty American right hook busted one hajji's jaw and put him momentarily out of commission. He was working on the other, getting the better of it, when a third man ran up and rifle-stroked him in the back of the head below his helmet.

Anzak crumpled. Even though only semiconscious, he continued to resist. All three Jihadists jumped on him, kicking and pummeling him into submission.

The attack lasted less than five minutes from start to finish. A flat-bedded bongo truck, lights out, pulled up on the dirt road in front of the residence to which Fouty and Jimenez had been dragged. There were no lights on inside the house. Having completed their mission, insurgents rushed to-ward the getaway truck. Incredibly enough, Anzak revived enough to re-sume his struggles, albeit feebly, until his captors threw him up onto the truck bed and somebody slugged him again with a rifle. Other insurgents tossed up the limp bodies of Jimenez and Fouty like so many bags of wheat.

Loaded with twenty or so enemy fighters and three unconscious Amer-ican prisoners, the bongo truck turned around at the house and took off along the dirt road, vanishing into the night. Twin bonfires consuming the bodies of three GIs and one IA interpreter marked its departure.

"Allahu Akbar! Allahu Akbar!" floated back on the wind.

FIFTY-SEVEN

Staff Sergeant Alan Ecle, forty, of mixed Guamanian-Filipino ancestry, had been transferred out of Bravo Company to Delta only a week before. Originally from Guam, he had enlisted in the army in 1983 while living in the Philippines. His father was in the U.S. Navy. Going airborne, he served in Germany, Fort Hood, Texas, and then in Panama during Operation *Just Cause* against Manuel Noriega in 1989. He accepted a discharge in 1995 to enter the Army Reserve program in Guam, but requested active duty again in 2006. He deployed straight to Iraq with the 10th Mountain Division's 2nd BCT.

As First Platoon's newest section sergeant, he awoke at midnight when Sergeant Connell and the other Joes of the platoon were preparing to leave Inchon to relieve crater watch in the S-curves. A cautious man who fretted over the younger soldiers, Ecle warned them in his clear, precise English to stay awake and not let down their guard. "Use your night-vision devices."

"Yes, Mommy Dearest," Anzak joked. "Have some warm milk for me when I come in?"

"I have some warm milk for you." Jimenez caught him in a headlock, and they wrestled and sparred their way toward the waiting trucks.

Sergeant Connell, the Iraqi interpreter, and six members of First Platoon left Inchon. Everybody expected to see them again the next morning.

Like most soldiers on Malibu Road, Ecle slept fitfully in stretches of three or four hours at a time. His eyes sprang open at 0400. It was still dark in the bunkroom. He heard snoring. Specialist Dan Seitz and Shaun Gopaul, and sometimes others, occasionally talked in their sleep. Someone was mumbling now, thrashing about on his bunk.

The little sergeant glanced at his watch and made his way downstairs to get a bottle of water from the cooler. Brenda the Bitch lay indecently sprawled half-dressed on the old sofa.

He got his water. Then—*Boom! Boom! Boom!* Like that. Muffled, thudding explosions in quick sequence, followed immediately by the unmistakable, deep-throated chuckle of AK-47 assault rifles. His first thought was of the crater watch. He ran toward the radio room. Sergeant Allen Wilson, the company RTO on radio watch, was already on his feet.

As with all bad news, word spread rapidly throughout the FOBs and patrol bases whenever anything happened in the AO. Radios were already starting to heat up from Yusufiyah to Rushdi Mulla to Mahmudiyah. First to break on the air were Specialist James Cook and Sergeant Tony Smith, who were pulling road security south of Inchon toward the S-curves. Sitting in the dark in their hummer, watching, they heard three or four grenades go off almost in sync, followed by automatic rifle fire. It came from further south.

Fire broke out almost immediately, casting an ugly orange glow against the dark sky that whipped back and forth in the wind. It had to be the crater watch. Cook keyed his mike.

"Delta X-Ray, something's going on down there. I'm pretty sure it's our trucks. Something's not right."

"Do you have a visual?"

"Negative. But there's a lot of shooting."

"Stand by for Delta X-Ray-Six."

Delta X-Ray-Six was Captain Gilbreath, the company commander. Sergeant Wilson left one of the other soldiers on the radio and ran to the CO's room. Captain Gilbreath was already up, having heard the sounds of contact. Only half-dressed, he ordered Wilson to spread the alert. By the time Gilbreath reached his CP/radio room, still only half-dressed, trucks and battle positions all along Malibu were chattering excitedly.

Wilson hit the lights in the enlisted bunkrooms. First and Fourth Platoons were currently manning Inchon, along with Company HQ.

"We got to go," Wilson exclaimed. "We got to go right now."

Fourth Platoon Section Leader Chris Kunert threw himself out of his bunk and started lacing on his boots while Wilson explained, pale-faced, that 152 and road security were reporting loud blasts and gunfire from the area of the crater watch. Nobody could make commo with Sergeant Connell.

"Maybe they dropped a cell," Wilson added hopefully.

Every soldier at Inchon was up and pulling on boots and armor. Nobody knew what the hell was going on. Everything was confused. Joes crowded the radio room or they ran upstairs and out onto the roof to stare down toward the glow of burning trucks. Wilson kept trying to raise somebody at the crater, but nothing came back except dead air. The distant *pop-pop-pop* of rifle fire subsided quickly.

Lieutenant Tomasello rounded up everyone in Fourth Platoon not on watch and set out from Inchon with Mayhem, Sergeant Parrish, and six or seven others in a shuffling, anxious trot down the road. Threatening shadows closed in with the black of the night all around and only the pale moon and the glow of fire to guide by. Mayhem's guts tied in a knot. They could all be walking into a trap, another ambush, lured into a kill zone as they had that time with the downed Raven. But they had no other choice but to rush to their soldiers' aid. Maybe it was already too late.

Down past the crater at 152, Lieutenant Dudish's Second Platoon was dressed, armed, and ready to go. Dudish ordered trucks brought out of the motor pool and lined up at the gate to be ready for when they were needed. Sergeant Montgomery stood on the roof and watched the distant flicker of fire. Position 152 was twice the distance from the scene of the attack as soldiers at Inchon.

Lieutenant Darrell Fawley's Third Platoon was even further away, having been temporarily chopped over to work with the 3rd Infantry Division over toward Anbar Province. Sergeant Victor Chavez was just being relieved from stationary guard duty on the roof of 3rd ID's battle position 132 when he heard distant detonations. Faraway and indistinct, they sounded like they came from Malibu Road. Chavez thought one of the other platoons had called in Battalion mortars on an enemy target, or that a weapons cache might be blowing in-place. It never occurred to him from such a brief contact sound that some outfit might be in deep shit.

Exhausted, he made his way downstairs and, fully clothed except for boots, helmet, and armor, crawled into an empty bunk. He dozed off immediately. The next thing he knew, somebody was shaking him.

"Sergeant Chavez! Sergeant Chavez, you got to get up, man."

Chavez opened his eyes. PFC Matt Moran continued to shake him.

"What the fuck, over?" Chavez grumbled.

"Get up," Moran insisted. "First Platoon is gone."

"Whattya mean, they're gone?"

"I don't know. They're just gone. They're gone."

In Yusufiyah at the Battalion TOC, Lieutenant Colonel Infanti still suffered from his undiagnosed fractured spine, which meant he slept little. He had retired to his quarters inside the old shipping container at midnight, just about the time Sergeant Connell's crater detail relieved the previous watch. He awoke before 0400.

He dressed and stepped from the shipping container directly into the tent that served as his TOC. Desert winds moaned around the steel box he called home and flapped the tent's loose folds. He poured himself a cup of coffee, black, and settled down with his XO, Major Mark Manns, to be briefed by Operations Officer Major Bob Griggs, who would now try to get some sleep.

The night had been uneventful, so far, Major Griggs reported. That was just about to change.

Captain John Gilbreath's voice suddenly burst from the radio monitoring Delta Company's net, asking for the Battalion Six. That was Infanti. Something big must be going down. Tersely, Gilbreath explained that explosions and gunfire had erupted at one of his observation posts on Malibu. The OP had gone off the radio.

"Delta X-Ray, start moving," Colonel Infanti decided.

"I have troops on the way to investigate."

"Roger. We'll get air and a QRF on the way. Keep me posted."

A TOC can get hectic during an action, what with radios blaring in stacks, sergeants and officers trying to keep up with movements on maps and charts, and everybody trying to coordinate responses. That was when a commander earned his pay. Although still in the dark about what had happened, Infanti placed 4th Battalion on full alert; it was obvious by this time that *something* big was going on. He began moving elements of his three other companies toward Malibu Road to block off enemy escape routes. Helicopters were grounded because of high winds, but it didn't take long to get a UAV in the air and flying over the site.

First images from the unmanned aircraft's nose camera weren't very encouraging. Two HMMWVs on Malibu Road were fully ablaze. Flames whipped by wind leaped twenty to thirty feet into the air and played shadows off against roadside palms and underbrush. The UAV's camera picked up no other movement.

FIFTY-EIGHT

Lieutenant Morgan Springlace and what was left of First Platoon, about seven soldiers, crammed into a single hummer and headed for the curve, all anxious, on the prod, and fearing the worst. As soon as the truck exited the walls of Inchon, PFC Sammy Rhodes in the turret spotted the flickering glow of fire, twin match flames in the black night. The truck passed Lieutenant Tomasello and his bunch running on the road toward the scene and reached the curve first, slowing down cautiously as it approached.

The fight was over, had been over for long minutes. Spare ammo in the two trucks was starting to cook off. Machine-gun tracers speared the darkness in all directions, streaking harmlessly toward the stars, bouncing off the road, or ripping through palms and eucalyptus. M19 grenades detonated in showers of sparks that turned the burning hummers into a great big pair of Fourth of July Roman candles.

"Jesus!"

No one could be sure whether it was a prayer or a curse.

The sickening stench of burnt flesh mixed with the odor of burning wires, battery acid, gas, and oil to make the air toxic. In the north truck facing them, platoon members saw two human forms in what had once been the front seat. They were blackened and shriveled and reminded Rhodes of candle wicks in the center of a flame. None caught inside the conflagration could have survived it. There was no way to tell from this distance if any of the occupants had survived and managed to escape. Trying to get too much closer was out of the question. It was too hazardous, what with all the fireworks.

The truck inched a bit closer. A cooked-off bullet ricocheted off the hood. Rhodes ducked.

"Look out!" he shouted.

From the turret, he spotted a 155mm howitzer shell casing illuminated by the fires. It lay on top of the asphalt directly in the middle of the road. Crush wire running off either end toward the ditches identified it as an IED. To the right of it lay another homemade IED constructed from a length of pipe. Tomasello guessed they were either timer explosives or pressure-activated rather than command-detonated. Either way, venturing any nearer from this direction was not only foolhardy, it could be suicidal.

At a safe distance from the cook off and the IEDs, soldiers piled out of the vehicle to set up a hasty perimeter, using the hummer as cover. Lieutenant Springlace kept in constant running radio contact with Battalion, Company HQ, and other platoons. Sergeant Ronnie Montgomery reported that Second Platoon coming north from 152 had reached the south truck, only to be stopped by another pair of IEDs lying on the road. There appeared to be other bodies burning inside this truck, but he couldn't tell how many.

The attack on the crater watch had obviously been well planned and executed, the IEDs laid out well to isolate the targets in the kill zone and prevent reinforcements from reaching them.

"L.T., we can't just stand here with our thumbs up our asses," Springlace's soldiers raged. "They're burning alive!"

"Calm down. It's too late. There's nothing we can do for them."

"Some of them might have got away and are hiding."

No one sounded too hopeful.

"Our orders are to get to them," Springlace said. "That's what we're going to do."

Soldiers were direct action types, like cops and firefighters and others of the breed who ran toward danger while others ran away. They were also riled up, some near to tears from shock, grief, and frustration. *Patience, hell! Let's go kill something.*

Firelight reflected from the front of a house a short distance off the road. Otherwise, it lay in darkness. If one or more of the crater watch, God willing, had survived, the most logical place they would seek to fort up was at the house. With the road blocked, the only way to reach it was to take to the bush on foot. That entailed a huge risk from other IEDs, snipers, or possibly an ambush.

PFC Rhodes had already discerned the option. "Sir, point me in the direction and I'll go."

Springlace and his men were interested in only one thing—finding their platoon mates if any were still alive and rescuing them from the bad guys. The Joes were in a killing mood, and in a hurry. Rhodes took point as the patrol abandoned its truck and skirted off the road toward the north and east through the shape-shifting woodlands and reeds. He almost hoped somebody, *anybody*, popped up and offered resistance. There wouldn't be enough left of the son-of-a-bitch to bury.

The patrol's goal, the house nearest the site, appeared deserted. It was a typical one-story, flat-roofed, adobe-type structure, small and compact and square. Rhodes glanced back through his NVs and received a signal from Springlace to go ahead. Soldiers warily approached, crossing the front yard to the door in practiced overwatch, half of the patrol kneeling with weapons ready, the other half rushing.

Rhodes and Brandon Gray flattened themselves against the walls to either side of the closed door. Sergeant Alan Ecle, Shaun Gopaul, and several others crouched behind the L.T., waiting for the word to stack and go. Springlace called out a warning to any civilian residents, which also served to identify themselves as GIs in the event Americans *were* hiding inside.

There was no response. The lieutenant nodded at Gray, who sprang back and stiff-legged the door, banging it open. That was the critical moment when entering the houses of suspected Jihadists. First guys in were the most vulnerable.

GIs in a stack cleared the house room by room, laser sights dancing erratic dots all over the blacked-out interior. Dinner dishes were washed and on a counter. Beds had been slept in and were unmade, as though the occupants had been jolted awake in the middle of the night and fled as fast as they could. People all seemed to have a way of knowing when something was about to come down so they could haul ass out of the AO.

"Hey, L.T.?" Specialist Timothy Grom removed his NVs and flicked a light on a stain next to the front door. The smear of fresh blood gave soldiers hope that at least one of their buddies from the crater watch may have been through here alive.

As Springlace's soldiers finished securing the house to use as a CP for a wider search, Lieutenant Tomasello's Fourth Platoon jogging down from Inchon reached First Platoon's truck, left in the road with its engine running and the radio chattering up a storm from all the activity on the net. Corporal Mayhem called out a warning, thinking the occupants may have been overrun and the truck booby-trapped.

He walked around it at a safe distance, keeping low from the cook-off in the burning trucks, exploring the interior with a flashlight beam. The turret gun was missing. Other than that, everything looked okay. First Platoon would likely have taken the machine gun on a dismount.

Lieutenant Tomasello raised First Platoon on his radio. "Delta One-Six, this is Four-Six. You copy?"

"*Affirmative, Four-Six. Can you see the house? We've taken it.*"

"Roger, One. Stand by ten mikes [minutes]."

Tomasello left James Cook and Michael Smith behind to guard the truck. The rest of the platoon located the cut gaps in the concertina and in less than ten minutes linked up at the house with First. After a discussion between the two leaders, they left a couple of Joes at the house to keep it secure while the reinforced patrol set out once more with Rhodes on point to look for survivors. Hope was rapidly dwindling. Wind whipped smoke and the stench of burning flesh through the trees and across the fields.

The patrol took a side road through a little cluster of houses, all of which were abandoned with no sign of the soldiers from crater watch. Rhodes came to the T of another dirt road that headed west to intersect with Malibu. A broken thermal scope from a GI's rifle lay in the dust next to fresh truck tracks, more evidence that all the watch may not have perished at the scene of the attack. Someone could have escaped.

The other possibility was too awful to contemplate—that GIs had been seized by insurgents to be used later in ritual beheadings for Arab Al Jazeera TV.

The twin flames on Malibu were starting to burn down. Only an isolated shot rang out from the cook-off, most of the ammo having already been consumed. At Lieutenant Springlace's direction, Rhodes selected the dirt road back toward the light. Platoon members from First and Fourth followed in tactical formation, feeling safe enough now to loudly call out the names of the missing, in fading anticipation of a response.

FIFTY-NINE

About forty minutes had passed since First Platoon dismounted and took over the abandoned house as a search CP. The patrol led by Lieutenants Springlace and Tomasello followed the dirt road back to Malibu where drag marks, blood trails, footprints, and tire marks signaled two things: First, that this had been the escape route; second, that prisoners had been taken; but who and how many could not be ascertained without further investigation.

Dawn was rapidly approaching, brightening the flatlands and chasing shadows out of the palms. The upper rim of the red sun slipped into view to take a look at the still-smoldering trucks, the worst devastation and loss of life experienced by 4th Battalion since it pushed into The Triangle of Death over nine months ago. The fires burned down and most of the ordnance cooked off, leaving only the hissing of errant blazes as they gutted the blackened truck hulls and worked on the charred stumps of corpses now clearly visible inside the hummers. Most of the guys were too shocked to speak. They stared numbly until a sergeant from another company finally spoke for all of them.

"Nobody should ever have to see something like this."

Daylight revealed a scene buzzing with activity. Company elements and QRFs dispatched by 2nd BCT and 3rd ID, by 1st Cav and the 6th IA, were perimetering off the road to search for evidence and organize a sweep in force across the nearby countryside. EOD arrived on the scene, quickly defused and dismantled IEDs left in the road, and began a mine check of the rest of the area. Tracking dogs were on the way. Black Hawk helicopters and Apache gunships buzzed low overhead now that the wind was laying, circling, looking, their rockets and guns armed and ready.

Sammy Rhodes and Specialist Chris York volunteered to go up to the trucks to count bodies and see if enough remained to make a visual identification. Two corpses in the front seat of the south truck were seared beyond recognition. They were still steaming. One of the bodies was upside down with what was left of its head stuck in the sizzling springs of the seat, its feet and arms having been mostly consumed by the blaze. The stench of charred flesh stuck to the inside of Rhodes' nostrils; he was afraid it would be with him for the rest of his life. He figured he had attended his last backyard barbecue.

Two more sets of remains, likewise unrecognizable, occupied the front seat of the other blackened truck. An unexploded enemy grenade lay in the road at the front of the vehicle. Blood and footprints around the hummer and in the ditch indicated what must have been a brief but fierce hand-to-hand combat.

"They wouldn't have taken Anzak unless they killed him first," York said.

That accounted for four of the eight soldiers on the crater watch. The morning light soon disclosed a fifth caught in concertina wire at the side of the road about fifty meters away. PFC Chris Murphy lay face down on the ground, his IBA and helmet cast aside as though he had shed them to lighten his load in his desperation to get away. Bullet holes stitched his back from the knees all the way up to the base of his neck.

EOD checked the body for wires or anything else suspicious. Corpses were often booby-trapped to kill other soldiers who came to remove them. One of the most common methods was to plant a live grenade underneath the dead soldier, the pin removed, so that it exploded as soon as someone disturbed the body.

Specialist Brandon Gray, the big, strong farm boy from Oklahoma, lay on top of Murphy, hugging his friend close, tears in his eyes, and rolled with the body to one side, using it as a shield in case something detonated. That was the only safe way to do it other than attaching a line to a foot or arm and dragging the soldier from a distance away. To Murphy's friends, that seemed too callous and disrespectful.

Someone checked for a pulse, a futile gesture fueled only by hope. Christopher Murphy from Lynchburg, Virginia, was dead. Sammy Rhodes and

Sergeant Alan Ecle stood and looked down on the young GI. He lay with his hands folded across his chest the way Gray had arranged them. His unmarred baby face looked serene and peaceful in the sunrise. Rhodes felt the urge to reach down and shake him out of sleep.

"Hey, Murphy, wake up. We gotta go, man."

Specialist James Cook, now in Fourth Platoon but formerly a member of First, had been Murphy's best friend. He broke down and wept.

SIXTY

The attack on Malibu Road was the bloodiest single incident in the AO since the 101st Airborne lost its soldiers near the JSB nearly a year ago. It was also the second largest capture of American GIs so far during the Iraq War, the worst since the seizure of Jessica Lynch and five other soldiers when their convoy took a wrong turn into An Nasiriyah on 23 March 2003. Insurgents had pulled off one of the most successful and sophisticated operations the 4/31st had encountered so far. Brigade and Battalion S-2 (Intelligence) sections came down, measured and examined the site, and estimated that twenty or more fighters were responsible for the ambush, not counting support personnel and organizers.

The U.S. Army and all its components lived and fought by the creed, the promise, that no soldiers would be left behind. If you were wounded, killed, or captured in action, the army would do everything in its power to get you to a hospital, recover your body, or liberate you. Within an hour after the occurrence, virtually every unit in Iraq was mobilized to locate the missing Americans. That included the American embassy, Special Operations, and the CIA.

Inchon and the other two battle positions along Malibu teemed with the frenzied activity of a major military operation. Most of 4th Battalion that was available, as well as assets from Brigade, the 3rd ID, the 1st Cavalry, and other outfits in the region, blitzed into The Triangle of Death. An IA armored battalion and an American battalion of 19-ton Stryker battle wagons rumbled down Malibu to assist in the hunt. Outposts normally equipped to handle platoons overflowed with companies and even battalions.

Helicopters and jets filled the skies. Soldiers on checkpoints and roving patrols cordoned off the full swath of the 2nd BCT's 330-square-mile sector while handlers with dogs trained to find bodies or bombs picked through cattails from one end of the road to the other. Choppers dropped leaflets asking for help. Trucks with loudspeakers roamed the area urging people to come forward. Dismounted patrols of very pissed-off troops swept the roads, kicking in doors and herding anxious Iraqis to holding areas.

None of the locals dared protest. The gloves were off. Bare knuckles were showing. GIs were in no mood for more bullshit. It would not be a good day for an insurgent. Even Crazy Legs had gone underground and couldn't be found.

"I don't want a hole in the perimeter big enough for a gnat to get through," Colonel Infanti directed. "If they still have our soldiers, I don't want them to be able to move out of the AO."

Soldiers cleared entire villages, searching houses, bringing in even some women and children as well as males of military age as possible witnesses or potential accomplices, creating long files of dark, staring eyes. Anyone who hadn't already fled in fear of arrest found himself at Inchon or one of the other battle positions. They weren't exactly prisoners, not being flex-cuffed, but they still weren't going anywhere. Hard-eyed young American soldiers surrounded them and segregated them into two separate groups—women and children in one, men and older boys in another. A dozen IA police interrogators, the most trusted of them, along with U.S. Army Special Forces Green Berets wearing beards and ragged clothing in order to blend with the population, isolated the captives for questioning. Nobody asked about their methods. Time was crucial. After 48 hours at the latest, whatever information prisoners might possess would be useless. The bad guys would have gone into hiding or changed their routines.

While all this was going on, Sergeant Ronnie Montgomery's Second Platoon drew the grim task of cleaning up the ambush site. By now, the two trucks were incinerated, leaving nothing except blackened cabs dropped down onto wheel rims with the rubber burned off. The Joes wore gloves to rummage through the ruins to pick up body parts—shards of bone, charred flesh—and place them reverently into body bags. Grave Registrations people would have to sort through it all later to identify which belonged to which slain GI.

They worked mostly in sickened silence, the nauseating smell of burnt flesh and bones bringing tears to their eyes.

Hulls of 7.62 AK-47 cartridges strewn on the road attested to the swiftness and ferocity of the attack. Insurgents must have outnumbered the crater watch by at least three to one. No American bullet hulls lay about. The spate of rifle fire heard by soldiers at Inchon and at 152 was all from enemy weapons. Apparently, Sergeant Connell and his men had not gotten off a single shot in the surprise raid.

Evidence left at the scene and witness statements from those Iraqis who lived in the vicinity, and who could still be located, painted a dark portrait of stark terror compressed into a few short minutes. Wind and the darkness of the night would have contributed to it.

Murphy appeared to have been the only man with a chance at escape— and that a slim one before the insurgents picked him off with automatic rifle fire. Claw marks showed where he continued to pull himself through the weeds until he became entangled in concertina and his executioners caught up to him.

Blood trails, drag and scuffle marks, plus the smear of blood inside the farmhouse, indicated that the three Americans apparently taken captive were wounded. An Iraqi witness who fled his house out of fear of involvement was hiding in shrubbery, watching. One of the Americans, he said, a big man, was beating up on two of the insurgents and was getting the better of them when a third ran up and belted him from behind. He and the other two prisoners were thrown up onto the bed of a bongo truck and hauled away.

Unlike World War II or Vietnam, where mutilated corpses had to be identified using dental records, fingerprints, and dog tags, modern DNA technology made identification faster and more certain. There was no problem with Chris Murphy since his body remained relatively intact. Hard as it was for them, platoon members confirmed his identity.

The other victims took longer. Still, Delta Company knew within a relatively short period of time the names of those slain in the action and those whose status became known as DUSTWUN (Duty Status and Whereabouts Unknown). In addition to Christopher E. Murphy, 21, the others found slaughtered were SFC James D. Connell, 40; PFC Daniel W. Courneya, 19; Sergeant Anthony J. Schober, 23; and IA interpreter Sabah Barak, about 30.

Missing in action were Specialist Alexander R. Jimenez, 25; PFC Byron W. Fouty, 19; and Joseph Anzak Jr., 20.

Probably no non-urban terrain in Iraq posed more challenge in conducting a search than that in The Triangle. Criss-crossed by irrigation ditches and canals flowing from the Euphrates River, dotted with family farms growing barley and wheat and goats, studded with villages and towns, it afforded enough hiding places and safe houses into which a thousand insurgents might vanish. Even if they were cornered, it was unlikely they would surrender peacefully after what they had done. Previous patterns revealed how, turning suicidal and even more homicidal, they would first execute their captives, then take as many other Americans with them as they could before they committed suicide by blowing themselves up.

Soldiers in Iraq knew only too well what awaited GIs if they were taken alive by radical Islamic extremists, to whom life was cheap and who thought nothing of torturing and executing their victims. The worst nightmare an American commander could have was of his soldiers being kidnapped and beheaded live on television for the world and their families to see. Colonel Infanti added five more casualty cards to his collection. Three of his soldiers remained missing, unknown whether they were dead or whether they were alive and being held in some moldy basement while savage Islamics sharpened their big knives and prepared to present their next macabre feature to Al Jazeera TV.

SIXTY-ONE

The massacre occurred before dawn on Sunday. Information about it remained sketchy most of the day throughout The Triangle of Death, except for those soldiers and outfits chopped down to Malibu Road who were actually involved in the search. Future history professor Big Willy Hendrickson had been temporarily assigned to Brigade at Mahmudiyah to pull tower guard for a battery of field artillery. Another soldier relieved him before sunrise. He was standing outside on the sprawling compound, smoking a cigarette before he hit the rack for some sleep, when another Bravo Company Joe rushed up with news he picked up at the chow hall.

"They've killed a bunch of our guys!" he blurted out.

Hendrickson dropped his cigarette, freaking out because he thought it might be some of his buddies in Bravo.

"Who?" he demanded, unable to get out more past the stricture in his throat.

"I don't know. They say the ragheads kidnapped some of them."

Hendrickson forgot all about sleep. The two GIs broke for Brigade TOC, the nerve center for 2nd BCT in Iraq. The whole place seemed to be going ape shit. Off-duty soldiers not tapped for immediate duties hung around outside the TOC trying to pick up what information they could. The air was full of aircraft coming and going.

Piecemeal, Hendrickson learned that the victims were with Delta Company down on Malibu Road, not from his Bravo. He felt relieved that the dead weren't some of his own friends. Better they be from some other outfit than from one's own.

Guilt followed relief. How could he feel better about the deaths of some Joes over others? History in the making could be so fucked up.

Chaplain Jeff Bryan was on his way to Delta Company to be with Captain Gilbreath's grieving soldiers when Hendrickson got a chance to speak with him. The chaplain knew only that five had been killed and three were missing. The only name Hendrickson knew was Specialist Alex Jimenez', that because of its connection with the battalion CSM.

"This is a chaplain's nightmare," Chaplain Bryan said. "I have to ask them to trust in God and His wisdom after a disaster like this."

"Chaplain, do you believe there really is a Big Plan for the universe?"

"Don't you, my son?"

Sometimes Hendrickson didn't know what he believed. History was full of mankind's follies; foolishness and cruelty repeated endlessly.

An hour after the chaplain departed, a headquarters sergeant burst into the tent where Hendrickson and the other Joes on tower detail were bivouacked.

"Gather up all your shit and get on the flight line," he said. "You got one hour. You guys are flying out."

A Black Hawk dropped them off in Yusufiyah at 4th Battalion's compound. By noon, Hendrickson found himself reassigned as a replacement for one of Delta's dead and missing. It gave him a funny feeling, taking a KIA's place. He also felt like an intruder when he linked up with First Platoon's surviving members at Inchon. They were supposed to be getting some rest following the chaplain's visit. None of them could sleep. The hate fest among them was something palpable and contagious. Some were crying from anger, loss, and frustration; others were cursing. Even Cookie Urbina's Brown Dog went around alternately whimpering and growling with his tail tucked between his legs, as though he sensed First Platoon's loss. Some of the guys were talking up some pretty wild stuff.

"Them motherfuckers living in their little shacks . . . They know who did it. We ought to burn every damn house and village along the river until somebody starts talking. I wouldn't trade all them cocksuckers' lives for one of our guys."

Most of the Iraqi captives rounded up were simple farmers trying to stay out of the way of both sides. Hear no evil, see no evil . . . Either that, or they *pretended* to be farmers. It was sometimes hard to ferret out the truth.

"I was in my cucumber field when I heard a big explosion and shooting. I ran to my house because I was afraid I would be arrested if someone spotted me in the field. I've been arrested four times. The real attackers run off and innocent people like me get arrested."

"You were in your cucumber field at four in the morning?"

SpecOps brought in a wounded man they caught hiding in a house. Hands cuffed behind his back, he was a scruffy-looking character in his early twenties with an even scruffier beard and a dished turban. Interrogators took him off into a room and spent hours with him. Word soon circulated that he may have participated in the attack.

"Stand him up against a wall and shoot out his eyes," Specialist Brandon Gray proposed.

"That's too easy," Sammy Rhodes counter-suggested. "Basically, stake him out in the sun, pour gas on him, and light a match. Burn him the way he did our guys. Doesn't the Koran and the Bible say an eye for an eye?"

Civilians tended to think American soldiers had a switch that could turn their emotions on and off at will. It wasn't that simple. It sometimes went beyond their ability to immediately back off and exercise restraint and maturity after some of their fellow soldiers had been killed or maimed. Specialist Shaun Gopaul, Jimenez' best friend, was so angry and devastated that the chaplain and mental health counselors pulled him off the combat line before he did something he and everyone else would regret. Psychiatrists prescribed antidepressants and sleeping pills and sent him to a desk job at Battalion HQ.

Hendrickson found himself working with a "search and clear" team, experiencing the gut-churning fear that comes with kicking in doors to confront whatever might be inside. Never knowing if the welcome would come from an armed fedayeen or a child huddling in fear with his mother. On the way out from Inchon, his caravan stopped to look over the wreckage at the ambush site.

He sat in his humvee with some of the other Joes of First Platoon and looked silently out at the shadows of rapidly approaching nightfall and the burnt-out hulls where his fellow soldiers had died. During daylight, the land could be attractive, even idyllic. It must have been a little ghostly last night with the wind blowing.

Another line of military vehicles with their lights blacked out whisked past without warning. A breeze blew the sounds of their engines the other way.

SIXTY-TWO

War mostly claimed the lives of young men and kids, who went out every day as they did on Malibu Road with the singular purpose of keeping faith with their buddies, of not letting them down in the face of danger or death. Of every war in which America has become embroiled, it can truthfully be said that soldiers rarely fight for God, country, and Mom's apple pie. Rather, they fight for each other, for their buddies.

Lieutenant Colonel Michael Infanti considered the toughest part of his job to be notifying a family that it had lost a son, husband, father, or brother in combat. A personal phone call was the least he could do, during which he strove to be reassuring, comforting, and complimentary in conveying his and, by extension, the army's sincerest condolences and appreciation for the job the soldier performed. Each time he finished such a call, the lump in his throat was so big he could hardly talk. He limped outside his TOC at Yusufiyah with his bad back and, standing alone, lifted his head to the stars until he recovered.

After the memorials, after the placement of boots and helmets and more photographs of the dead or missing on the walls, after Chaplain Jeff Bryan did what he could to ease the suffering, some of the "old hands" of First Platoon packed the gear of the dead and missing in boxes for shipment Stateside. The ritual was a somber one, with long-faced soldiers almost reverently handling shaving kits, wallets, photos, papers, books, letters, and other belongings before carefully placing them in boxes. New guys were not invited to participate. PFC Big Willy Hendrickson stood back and watched respectfully, feeling temporarily outcast. It was tough for a replacement to come into an outfit where bonds had already been formed. Many combat soldiers would not make new friends for fear of losing them as they had the old ones.

It seemed to medic Specialist Michael Morse that, in the sudden deaths of so many, First Platoon was losing its spiritual cohesion, its soul. Practical jokesters and teasers like Alex Jimenez and Joe Anzak had kept morale high and the men laughing. Someone in the platoon deflated Brenda the Bitch and took her off and either buried her or, if rumors were correct, stuffed her in a wag bag and burned her. She was never seen again lounging around half-dressed on the old sofa at Inchon. The Joes simply weren't in the mood for Saturday night dances or impromptu strip teases anymore after DUSTWUN.

"If we could just move time back to last week," Morse lamented.

Everyone blamed the crater watches; sooner or later T-Rex was bound to have come for the tethered goat.

During World War II, what family members waiting at home feared most was receiving the dreaded telegram, sometimes delivered by a local taxi company, followed by the Ladies Auxiliary. Before the war ended, the army adopted the practice of dispatching officers and NCOs to the home of the deceased to break the sad news. Which was most distressing, the taxi or grim soldiers arriving in a staff car, was difficult to measure.

With Iraq, as with Vietnam and Korea, an officer attended the funeral of every soldier killed in action. His job was to oversee all the military aspects of the funeral service—pall bearers, military escort, Honor Guard, taps, firing of the 21-gun salute, folding and presentation of the flag to the next of kin . . . He comforted where he could and read tributes from the soldier's buddies and commanders, those who knew him, who lived with him, loved him, and fought beside him. Voices from war-deployed units transcended distance and spoke with an eloquence no civil service could ever hope to match.

PFC Daniel W. Courneya was nineteen years old when he died. His stepfather, Army Specialist David Thompson, also serving in Iraq, flew home for the funeral. During the previous Thanksgiving/Christmas holidays, Courneya had been granted leave to come home to Vermontville, Michigan, where he married his longtime girlfriend Jennifer in a civil ceremony. They had planned to have a "real" wedding after he returned from Iraq.

Jennifer was a war bride and a war widow before she turned nineteen.

On 14 May, Maple Valley High School's public address system had announced Courneya's death and asked for a moment of silence throughout the school. Students put together a memorial of photographs, posters, and plaques surrounding a portrait of the 2005 graduate. The school's flag flew at half-mast until after his funeral.

"I always called him 'my bright eyes,'" said his grandmother. "He was my hero."

PFC Christopher E. Murphy was twenty-one. Memorial services were held in his school gymnasium at William Campbell High School near Lynchburg, Virginia, followed by a funeral ceremony at Arlington National Cemetery. Mourners stood at attention under a blazing afternoon sun while Major General Michael Oates, commander of the 10th Mountain Division, presented a folded flag to Murphy's mother. She looked toward the sky while a bugler played "Taps," wiping tears from her eyes with one hand and clutching the flag with the other.

"He was just one of those kids everyone enjoyed being around," said James Rinella, his school's assistant principal. "A very hardworking kid, a very humble kid."

Murphy was the most recent of 340 members of the military killed in Iraq to be buried at Arlington.

Sergeant Anthony J. Schober was twenty-three. He would never own the ranch he dreamed about. Nevada Governor Jim Gibbons and Nevada Congressman Dean Heller spoke at his service, held at the Vietnam War Memorial in Carson City. The local chapter of the Veterans of Foreign Wars vowed to erect a bench and a plaque bearing his name at the site.

Congressman Heller read quotes posted by readers on the message board of the Nevada *Appeal* newspaper.

"Rest easy, soldier . . ."

"You are a hero and will forever walk with heroes . . ."

"Anthony is not going to be forgotten . . ."

The congressman presented a flag that had flown over the nation's capitol to Schober's father Edward. "I believe someday you will be together again," he said.

Sergeant First Class James D. Connell, forty, received a hero's welcome upon his return to his small east Tennessee hometown of Lake City, where he had spent his leave a few weeks ago. A motorcade met him at the airport and escorted him home for the last time. Community members lined the street. Men, women, and children displaying tiny American flags stood at silent attention. The motorcade paused in front of his parents' home for a moment of silence before proceeding to memorial ceremonies at the Air National Guard Base. The same motorcade escorted his body on to Arlington National Cemetery for burial.

"We don't want another soldier to come back like they did from Vietnam," said Duane Romine, part of the escort for the Patriot Guard Riders. "We want them to come back with honor whether alive or deceased."

"I'm proud of my dad," said Connell's fourteen-year-old daughter Courtney, "because he didn't really fight for himself, he fought for his country."

SIXTY-THREE

The operation to recover the DUSTWUN men grew so massive that the soldiers of Delta Company, who had a personal stake in the outcome, felt they were little more than very small cogs in a big machine. They seldom saw the Big Picture. What they saw instead were raids and patrols, the daily grind of jumping across ditches and wading through muck in the difficult terrain searching for clues.

Sammy Rhodes' heart leaped when he came across a shred of camouflage caught on a bush. Disappointment followed when it turned out to be from the uniform of an IA who had passed through previously.

Grim-faced troops drained a canal along the Euphrates after local villagers reported seeing body parts floating. Nothing.

Second Platoon soldiers dug for the missing soldiers' bodies along another stretch of river. Either their information was bad, or they weren't in the right place.

The search that initially centered around the Kharghouli area soon began to widen. Not a good sign. Night and day throughout The Triangle of Death, GIs operating on the best intelligence available launched scores of raids against the houses of potential witnesses and suspects, rounding up more than 250 people with suspected ties to the attack. Gradually, the effort began to pay off. It was like piecing together a complicated puzzle.

Acting on a tip from a Shiite elder, Major Bob Griggs, Lieutenant Colonel Infanti's operations officer, took a squad of Polar Bears into the unfriendly 109 Mosque on Malibu to snap mug shots of thirty-nine men there with their prayer rugs. One or two of them, the elder said, might have been involved. Local Iraqis helping in the case behind the scenes identified one of the pictures as a man named Al Jasma, whom they said might know the missing soldiers' whereabouts. The guy took off before troops could arrest him. Raiders hit Al Jasma's house from then on every time they thought he might have slipped back into the AO.

Two apprehended suspects under harsh interrogation by Iraqi Army intelligence officers, who didn't always play by Geneva rules, confessed to having taken part in the attack. They said the insurgents split into two groups afterwards. The ringleader took the kidnapped soldiers with his band of men to turn them over to al-Qaeda in Iraq, whose leadership demanded live U.S. soldiers be turned over for use as hostages and bargaining chips.

U.S. forces stormed a storefront in Amiriyah, a Sunni stronghold with close tribal ties to Kharghouli, and captured nine more Iraqis suspected of some form of involvement in the attack. Under questioning, they confirmed information obtained by the IA intelligence officers. They believed one of the three captives was killed shortly after his capture, while the other two remained prisoner.

On May 18, six days after the incident, General David Petraeus gave a press conference. "Somebody has given us the names of all the guys that participated in it and told us how they did it. We have to verify it, but it sounds spot-on. We've had all kinds of tips down there. We just tragically haven't found any of the individuals. As of this morning, we thought there were at least two that were probably still alive. At one point of time there was a sense that one of them might have died, but again we just don't know."

Not a day passed but that the men of Delta Company didn't have their missing friends on their minds and on the day's schedule. In spite of gains made in hunting down players, any trail that might have been left by Fouty, Jimenez, and Anzak grew colder day by day, leaving their platoon mates with faint hope that they were still alive.

"We're not going to stop what we're doing," declared Colonel Mike Kershaw, 2nd BCT's commander. "We're not going to stop searching. We'll not leave any of our men behind."

A sentiment the White House echoed. "I'm confident that the military is doing everything it can to find the missing soldiers," President George W. Bush said during a press conference. "We're using all the intelligence and all the troops we can to find them. It's a top priority of our people there in Iraq."

Anzak and Jimenez, with their senses of irreverent humor and propensity for wisecracks, would undoubtedly have had a few witty comments to make had they known the President of The United States was talking about them. *Hey, Alex. You hear that? We are impo'tent.*

Bad guys started disappearing off Malibu Road, fleeing to a better climate, when they discovered the Americans knew who they were. Malibu Road had never been so safe. At the same time, insurgents in the Baghdad enclave initiated a Surge of their own in response to beefed-up, more aggressive ops by American troops.

Jihadists disguised as Iraqi soldiers massacred fifteen men in a Kurdish Shiite village northeast of Baghdad. The next day, a Saturday, about fifty insurgents assaulted a U.S. FOB in the center of Baghdad, sparking a battle that left at least six militants dead. Later that same day, mortar shells rained down into the Green Zone, wounding one American soldier, when British Prime Minister Tony Blair arrived for talks with Iraqi Prime Minister Nouri al-Maliki.

Two American soldiers were killed and nine wounded in separate ambushes and IED attacks in the capital, apparently to counter the continuing search for the captured soldiers of the 10th Mountain Division. Two Iraqi journalists working for ABC News were also slain as they drove home from work, bringing the toll of journalists killed in the war to more than one hundred.

Allahu Akbar—God is Great!

Videotapes usually made their way to Al Jazeera TV within a day or so after any incident in which insurgents scored what they considered a victory, especially if it entailed hostages who could be executed for the edification of the world. So far, however, the silence coming from Jihadists had been deafening, perhaps due to the fact that couriers bearing the tapes hadn't been able to slip through the cordon the Americans threw up around The Triangle. The only contact the insurgents attempted came via a brief message on a terrorist website.

It said the ambush and abductions were in retaliation for the rape and murder of 15-year-old Abeer Hamza and the slaying of her parents and sister by rogue troops of the 101st Airborne in Mahmudiyah in March 2006.

"What you are doing in searching for your soldiers will lead to nothing but exhaustion and headaches," the message warned. "Your soldiers are in our hands. If you want their safety, do not look for them."

SIXTY-FOUR

Unlike in previous wars, when hundreds of troops sometimes went missing from chaotic battlefields, only three U.S. soldiers were listed as missing in action in Iraq from the 1991 Gulf War through Operation *Iraqi Freedom*, up until the current DUSTWUN. The last U.S. soldier known to have been captured by the enemy was Sergeant Ahmed Qusai al-Taayie, an Iraqi-born GI from Ann Arbor, Michigan, who was snatched from the home of his Iraqi wife on 23 October 2006 while visiting her in Baghdad.

Sergeant Keith Maupin of Batavia, Ohio, was abducted on 9 April 2004 after insurgents ambushed a fuel convoy. Two months later, tapes on Al Jazeera showed a hooded man in U.S. ACUs being shot. Purportedly, it was Maupin, although no body had ever been recovered.

Maupin and al-Taayie remained listed as MIA, along with U.S. Navy pilot Michael Speicher, whose jet fighter was shot down during Operation *Desert Storm* sixteen years previously. The three soldiers from Delta Company had not yet formally been reclassified from DUSTWUN to MIA.

The round-the-clock hunt for the Americans continued despite warnings from the Islamic State of Iraq, now claiming responsibility for the abductions, that the search, if pursued, could end only with the soldiers being executed. No one really believed anything the U.S. did would affect the soldiers' fate one way or another. They were going to be publically executed sooner or later—unless they were rescued first.

Nearly every day, Lieutenant Colonel Infanti and CSM Alex Jimenez went out into the field to check on progress. When night fell, the tall commander of 4/31st often could not sleep because of back pain and the weight of responsibility upon his shoulders. Lines of concern and pain etched into his rough countenance, he stood outside his shipping container and gazed up at the sky, as though seeking a brighter, more hopeful tomorrow.

On 23 May, eleven days after the ambush on Malibu Road, the first confirmed news of the missing men reached 4/31st headquarters.

An Iraqi farmer named Ali Abbas al-Fatlawi and some of his neighbors were looking for a lost goat on the outskirts of the little village of Musayyib a dozen miles or so south of FOB Inchon when they saw something large bobbing in the gentle current of the Euphrates River. Whatever it was had hung up in some reeds near the bank. Approaching it out of curiosity, they discovered the body of a big man clad in a U.S. military uniform.

Using shepherd's staffs, they pulled the partly decomposed corpse from the brown water. Two point-blank gunshot wounds punctured the face, with more gunshots visible in the left side of the abdomen. That the hands were not tied nor the eyes blindfolded, a common procedure found on executed men recovered in The Triangle, seemed to indicate that the man may have been fighting his captors when he had to be shot and tossed from a boat crossing the river. Al-Fatlawi notified the local Iraqi police.

That afternoon, Captain John Gilbreath and First Platoon leader Lieutenant Springlace drove to Brigade at Mahmudiyah. A Graves Registration officer escorted them to a small room where a body lay on a table. He unzipped the bag to reveal the decomposing remains of what had once been a muscular young man. Not enough of the face remained to be sure, but Springlace recognized the distinctive tattoo on the man's arm. He nodded, sighed deeply, and looked up.

"It's Joe Anzak," he said. "Damn them all to hell."

SIXTY-FIVE

Something astonishing began to happen in the month following the DUST-WUN incident, a remarkable change that the Joes on Malibu Road found hard to explain. Sure, they had started to make progress in winning the people away from the homicidal maniacs in their midst, but nothing like the sudden acceleration that occurred now. Not a single IED had ruined anyone's day along the entire length of the road since 12 May.

One afternoon, Lieutenant John Dudish and Sergeant Ronnie Montgomery dashed out of the Company TOC at Inchon to where Second Platoon was catching a breather smoking 'n joking around their trucks in the yard. Second was acting as Company QRF for the week.

"Load 'em up. Move 'em out."

Some local farmers had spotted a group of Jihadists at a weapons cache along a drainage canal near Kharghouli. Far from remaining pacifist observers, the farmers had taken matters in their own hands and chased off the bad guys with scythes, farm tools, and legally owned AK-47s. When American soldiers arrived, the angry farmers were guarding the site and had spread a fluorescent marking cloth to alert U.S. helicopters that they were not hostile.

The interpreter grinned. "They are—how do you say it?—*fed up and pissed off*."

The cache contained one of the largest repositories of enemy ordnance ever recovered in The Triangle: over 200 57mm rockets; fifteen 82mm rockets; eight 120mm rockets; bags of homemade explosives; and a 5.56 Squad Automatic Weapon (SAW) that had been issued to Specialist Alex Jimenez before his capture. Although most of the rockets and mortars found were unsuitable for firing as intended, they made excellent IEDs.

A few days later, Second Platoon was on its way by four-vehicle convoy from 152 to a rural village in the direction of al Taqa to check on a tip that a terrorist named Maloof might be hiding out there. That was something else that was changing: ordinary Iraqis were coming forward in increasing numbers to inform on insurgents.

It was a true scorcher of a desert midday, when most Iraqis liked to find someplace cool to sleep off the heat. Almost no one was out and about. The convoy sped into the S-curve where the attack against the crater watch had occurred. By now, most of the wreckage had been removed. Little remained to mark the site other than a single crude wooden cross some of the Joes had tapped into the ground roadside.

Not everyone, it seemed, was trying to escape the heat. Cruising out of the curve, the soldiers saw several locals chasing another man down the middle of the road. They were armed with sticks, switches, and clubs and were whaling hell out of their victim at every step. Wearing a dished turban, dirty gray robe over baggy trousers and combat boots, the guy was running as fast as he could with his head down and his shoulders bunched against the merciless beating he was receiving. Apparently, it was the Iraqi version of being tarred and feathered and run out of town on a rail.

Chiva Lares driving the lead vehicle keyed his mike. "L.T., you getting a load of this?"

"*Roger that,*" Lieutenant Dudish responded. "*Pull up. Let's see what's going on.*"

The American trucks broke up the ruckus. The victim kept going, bounding and leaping off the road and into a field without so much as casting a backwards glance. His sweating persecutors gathered around Dudish and Montgomery and an IA interpreter.

"They say he is al-Qaeda and does not belong in this community," the terp translated. "They are chasing him away."

Montgomery looked at Lieutenant Dudish. They looked at the hajji who was doing a credible impersonation of the Road Runner on his way out of the country as fast as he could go. Montgomery gave his platoon leader a sly grin before turning to the interpreter.

"Tell them to carry on," he said. The Americans climbed into their trucks and left.

These days, a convoy could drive the length of Malibu Road without encountering anything more hazardous than an old IED scar on what, only a few short weeks ago, had been the most dangerous strip of highway in the world. Sammy Rhodes and Brandon Gray stood outside the two-story house at Inchon smoking cigarettes. The conversation turned to their missing comrades.

"I can't imagine what they must be going through if they're still alive," Rhodes said. "We can't leave them behind, we just can't."

They could see through the gate and past the concrete blast walls a length of the now-peaceful road that ran by. The two Joes went silent for a long time, contemplating the road and its history they had endured.

"We paid for that road in blood," Rhodes said.

The United States had put up a $200,000 reward for information on the whereabouts of Fouty and Jimenez. That was a lot of money in Iraq, roughly equivalent to making the recipient a millionaire. However, the prospect of riches failed to account for the overwhelming swell of helpfulness in the local population after DUSTWUN. Ironically, it took a major incident and loss of life to bring about that change.

Kidnapping the Americans may have been the worst mistake insurgents could have made in The Triangle of Death. Military presence in the AO became intense, forcing the bad guys to get out of Dodge and thereby provide a breathing spell for the population to cooperate with the U.S. to make sure the Jihadists stayed out. The true turning point in the war, Lieutenant Colonel Infanti believed, or at least in his battalion's part of the war, began when his companies occupied their AOs and proved they were there to stay. DUSTWUN was the catalyst that capped off everything the Americans were trying to accomplish, the DUSTWUN search a test of how far the good Iraqis were willing to go to bring peace and stability to their country.

So far, they seemed to be passing the test. In a savage tribal land of blood feuds and revenge pacts, many Iraqis were becoming infatuated with the American military not only for its fighting abilities but also for its patience and restraint in its ongoing efforts to help Iraq recover from decades of tyranny and terrorism. Until Operation *Iraqi Freedom*, the country had languished for almost six decades under a series of megalomaniac tyrants. Although the popular press back in the United States failed to acknowledge it, U.S. soldiers and the Surge were changing the country at a fundamental level.

There was still shooting and dying, but nothing like it was before. Instead of sneaking around at night to provide a tip or scrap of information, many locals now discovered the courage to openly and boldly come forward. People were turning in weapons caches in tribal areas that had formerly been a tight-lipped source of IEDs and munitions for terrorist attacks. Thanks to informants, six suspects from the crater watch had been caught and were being held at a U.S. military prison near the Baghdad airport.

The insurgents were losing friends fast. It was a real coup for the Americans when Khalil, a sheikh leader at the 109 Mosque, offered his militia to patrol the Malibu Road area. Wearing reflective vests and carrying clubs and sticks, with which they presumably beat any stranger who didn't belong in the community, they set up Concerned Citizens Checkpoints throughout The Triangle. Even the 1920s Revolutionary Brigade, which had opposed the American "invaders" in the beginning, now turned against the insurgents and became Concerned Citizens. Men who only weeks before were accepting al-Qaeda cash to plant IEDs or snipe at American soldiers now patrolled the roads and villages armed with clubs and wearing their badges of authority—reflective vests.

At first, the Joes of Delta Company were still suspicious of their new allies, but they began to come around when the number of attacks against them fell to almost zero. Even Crazy Legs vanished, never to be seen again.

"They aren't *insurgents* anymore," Corporal Mayhem quipped of their new friends. "They're *consurgents*."

The name stuck.

In spite of the metamorphosis, however, the search for Byron Fouty and Alex Jimenez continued to encounter a frustrating number of dead ends.

On 4 June, a video smuggled out by the so-called Islamic State of Iraq found its way to a terrorist website and, naturally, to Al Jazeera TV. The eleven-minute tape showed armed, hooded men allegedly planning the pre-dawn strike against the crater watch. Following a display of sketches, maps, and schematics of the ambush came shots of the missing soldiers' military-issued IDs, credit cards bearing their names, and a small golden cross thought to have belonged to Jimenez.

The soldiers were not shown. An unidentified voice claimed that the two abducted GIs were dead. "Their end will be underground, Allah willing," the voice said in a cold tone. "The bodies will not be returned to their families because you refused to deliver the bodies of our killed people."

No matter Lieutenant Colonel Infanti's vow of "no soldier left behind," many Joes in Delta began to fear they would have to do the unthinkable when their tour of duty ended after October: return home without two of their own.

"I'm actually scared to go home," lamented Specialist Shaun Gopaul, whose wife Caridad was as close to Jimenez' wife as Gopaul and Jimenez were to each other. "How can I look her in the face? What am I supposed to say? I was just down the road when it happened."

At Lieutenant Colonel Infanti's Battalion TOC in Yusufiyah, only ten miles from where the assault occurred, color photos of the two MIAs were tacked to a board at his desk. The edges of the pictures were starting to curl. Someone had scrawled an inscription at the top of Jimenez' likeness: *Never give up. We will find you. Keep fighting.*

SIXTY-SIX

Roberta Infanti and all six children were waiting for Lieutenant Colonel Infanti when he stepped off the Freedom Bird in Virginia in June 2007 on a short leave home to attend his son's high-school graduation. His nine-year-old daughter threw herself into his arms and hugged him so tightly he thought she would never let him go. He had departed Iraq with reluctance. The hunt for his two missing soldiers continued. In his pocket he carried casualty cards bearing their names.

Major Mark Manns, his XO, could handle anything that came up during the CO's short absence. The war in his AO had quieted down until crime and evil in The Triangle, it seemed, were no worse than a wild Saturday night in New York City or Detroit. In fact, he felt as safe these days driving down Malibu Road where he had been blown up and wounded only months ago as he would have felt walking alone at night in Times Square.

He returned home to a nation even more divided and at war with itself than when the 2nd BCT had left on deployment the previous August. The next year was election year, in which Americans would choose a new President and quite probably a new direction. The campaigns for nomination were already loud, strident, partisan, and confrontational, in many ways more savage than the fighting in Iraq.

A military officer owed it to his nation, to his commander-in-chief, and to his uniform to remain apolitical and outside the process, loyal to his country no matter what it demanded of him. That didn't mean he wasn't allowed to form personal opinions and to express them. Having a few days' liberty to reflect on the "Big Picture" of what was happening to the United States of America while he was away left Infanti feeling discouraged and disgusted.

Even discounting a terrorist connection, U.S. goals to remove a dangerous and murderous dictator from power and establish a base of freedom in the Middle East had been laudable ones. If these goals were met, history would record them as some of the world's most notable accomplishments. The initial reaction to the war when it began in 2003 was immediate and positive. Middle Eastern dictators and strongmen warily watched and wondered how far the U.S. would go to create a free nation while they pondered their own fates if they continued to support Islamic terror against the West. Libya's dictator Muammar al-Qaddafi suddenly announced he would end his nuclear program and establish closer diplomatic ties with the United States. The House of Saud broadened voting privileges in Saudi Arabia. Syria tried to break all ties with Iraqi insurgents. Even Iran stepped back to take a more cautious look at developments.

Tragically, a certain amount of death and mutilation was the unavoidable cost of combat. Almost from the first day, pundits in the media began decrying the loss of life. Network newscasts flooded American living rooms with bombings and death, emphasizing U.S. failures and ignoring its successes, suggesting in the process that America was losing the war since its soldiers were taking hits. Politicians began calling for an exit strategy before the smoke had cleared from the initial blitz to Baghdad.

Infanti knew from personal experience that America *was* winning in its effort to bring peace, economic liberty, and a freely elected representative government to Iraq. If the media and certain politicians hadn't been so hell-bent on destroying President Bush's administration, if they had truly got behind the nation in a non-partisan unity, chances were the war would have been over and won long before the 10th Mountain Division deployed to Iraq for the second time. The Arab world feared and respected a determined enemy.

Islamic fascists watched and learned. It didn't take them long to realize the U.S. was split, demoralized, less than determined, and as unlikely to stick this one out as it had in Vietnam or, for that matter, Somalia. They knew that if they could just maintain a steady stream of American soldier deaths while exploiting American misdeeds and atrocities, whether real or manufactured, the American people led by self-serving politicians and Western news outlets would eventually throw in the towel.

"When people stand up for a political sound bite and say they support the troops but don't support the war, I have questions," Infanti responded to a news interview while he was home on leave. "Politicians are the ones that allowed what happened to go on. They're the ones who authorized the President to go to war against Iraq. The question I would ask, not as a soldier, but as a citizen, is when did they change their minds? We've had 3,700 soldiers killed. Did they change their minds at 1,999, at 2,999? Or did they change their minds when a poll said the American people were losing support for the war. That's the question I want to ask them: 'Did you change your mind when a poll said you weren't going to be re-elected?'"

Would the next election encourage the Islamic radicals by revealing a lack of American resolve, a weakness to be exploited by those already planning their next terrorist attack on American soil? To cut and run at this crucial point, as so many political hacks were advocating if it would win them a few more votes, meant that everything American soldiers had achieved in Iraq would be thrown out like yesterday's garbage. To have won the war, then abandoned it and the country's people back to tyranny, was nothing more than a betrayal of sacrifices made by American soldiers like Chris Messer, Joe Given, Sergeant Connell, Courneya, Schober, Murphy, Fouty, Jimenez, Anzak, and all the others.

Damn them! Damn the lily-livered politicians who would treat the lives of young soldiers as though they meant nothing.

The prospect of what the next election likely foretold broke Lieutenant Colonel Infanti's heart, all the more so when he and his wife visited wounded and maimed soldiers from the 10th Mountain at Bethesda's Walter Reed Army Medical Center. Here were young men who had given so much and were still willing to give in a cause they believed in. A twenty-year-old soldier who had lost most of one leg and part of his arm to an IED grinned at his former commander.

"Sir, as soon as this arm gets better," he said, "I'm ready to go back to work. I think I can operate a machine gun."

A sniper had shot another soldier in the leg, shattering it so that he could no longer straighten it. Units of the 2ⁿᵈ BCT had finally nailed the sniper, who was being paid 500,000 dinars a month, about $490, to take shots at American soldiers, with a bonus of another $490 for each hit.

"It's really a shame because he's not getting any more money," Infanti told the soldier. "He took three rounds in his chest from an Apache helicopter."

"Sir, what about our guys still missing from the 4/31ˢᵗ?"

The greatest thing about American soldiers, Infanti once observed, "is that they will do whatever you ask them to do. They'll go without food, without family, without a bed to sleep on other than the hard ground. They'll shave out of a canteen cup and take a bath in a mud puddle. They'll wear filthy clothes, get body sores, go without a break while they wait for the next bullet or the next explosion, waiting to die or waiting to get wounded, hoping that if they do get it their buddies won't get it too. They always think of each other first before they think of themselves. If only the world were made up of more men like them."

All too soon, still limping, still in constant pain, Michael Infanti was on his way back to Iraq and his 4ᵗʰ Battalion. He had a job to finish. Two of his men were still missing.

"I'm going to search until they kill me or they send me home," he pledged. "That's just the bottom line. And when I find them, I'm going to keep running down the guys who did it like they were dogs—until they kill me or send me home. The bad guys know I'm coming. And they're going to put up a fight. And that's okay."

SIXTY-SEVEN

Almost from its inception, the American military had nurtured the myth that it would leave none of its wounded, dead, or missing behind on the battlefield. That was the ideal. Hard reality, however, did not always follow the myth. More than 78,000 GIs remained MIA from World War II, their bodies long gone and decomposed in the jungles of Borneo or on the battlefields of France and Germany. Korea added another 8,100 missing in the Frozen Chosin, along the Yalu, or in the hills near the DMZ where some of the most savage fighting occurred. Nearly 1,800 more had never been recovered from the tropical forests of Vietnam.

Compared to such staggering numbers, the five missing in Iraq, including the pilot from 1991's *Desert Storm*, appeared paltry indeed. However, the impact of numbers meant nothing when one of the MIAs was your best buddy, your platoon or squad member with whom you had shared everything for months, down to your last pair of clean socks. The prospect of going home was proving bittersweet for the Joes of Delta Company 4/31st. Unfortunately, real war was not like a movie in which a dramatic rescue at the end resolved everything and wrapped it up neatly. Real life was messy, inconclusive, and often heartbreaking.

Days and nights in the patrol bases were dull, long, and gloomy. It took a long time for a small, tightly knit outfit like Delta to recover from the losses it suffered in the S-curves. The raucous days of Brenda the Bitch and chasing chickens for a barbecue were long gone. Sometimes twenty-two-year-old Specialist Brandon Gray or twenty-four-year-old Specialist Sammy Rhodes thought their youth was also long gone.

First Platoon's "old hands" recalled how the roof at Inchon had been Byron Fouty's favorite place, where he went days to read books or at night to lean on the roof's lip with his chin in his hands to think. Brandon Gray sometimes wondered what he was thinking, this retiring, gentle kid who had pretty much been on his own from the time he was sixteen until the army took him into its "family."

In contrast, Alex Jimenez had been big and gregarious, sometimes loud and profane, always ready for a prank in the safety of a battle position or for a fight in the S-curves. He had made CSM Jimenez proud to share the name.

Despite Herculean efforts to rescue the two soldiers, or to recover their bodies, few clues as to their whereabouts had surfaced in the five months since their disappearance. In June, a month after the abductions, a raid on an al-Qaeda safe house near Samarra, more than one hundred miles north of the ambush site, turned up their military ID cards. In October 2007, just as the 2nd BCT was preparing to redeploy to Fort Drum, Coalition Forces recovered a weapon that had been issued to Joe Anzak. Other than that, the search had gone down a black hole, all incoming intelligence about them proving to be little more than red herring. Now, in spite of Lieutenant Colonel's Infanti's vow that no soldier would be left behind, in spite of searching up until the last minute, it appeared Fouty and Jimenez would not be going home with the other Polar Bears.

"We are not leaving them behind," Infanti tried to reassure his men. "One of the things we're talking to the 101st about is continuing the search for our missing soldiers. We've not forgotten them. The search will go on until they're found."

The 10th Mountain had relieved the 101st Airborne Division in The Triangle in September 2006. When the 3rd BCT of the 101st returned to reassume control of the AO in November 2007, it found the area much more settled than when it left. Iraqi consurgents manned checkpoints the length of the road; they had proved themselves and now carried AK-47s instead of clubs. Delta Company 4/31st had opened the road to civilian traffic and began issuing driver's permits to legal vehicle owners. Economic conditions were improving and children who had been required to work went back to school. People waved and smiled from their doorsteps.

Thousands of Iraqis were openly aligning themselves with the Coalition; many had applied to join the Iraqi police forces.

Colonel Infanti and Major Mark Manns became comfortable with driving Malibu Road to have dinner or tea with sheikhs and mosque elders. One night, Manns' host began to laugh. He was a skinny little guy suspected of having been an insurgent for hire. Now he was leader of a group of Concerned Citizens fighting against Jihadists. He pulled up his trouser leg to reveal a nasty scar not quite healed.

"You know," he said, "your people shot me one time. Now we are friends and together we will rebuild Iraq."

CSM Alexander Jimenez liked to say that the soldiers of the 10th went into The Triangle of Death and did something people said would never happen—they turned it around.

By the time the "most deployed" division in the U.S. Army redeployed to Fort Drum from its extended 15-month tour, the 2nd BCT had served overseas forty months since December 2001. During that time the 10th Mountain Division had lost 157 soldiers killed in action in Iraq and Afghanistan, 52 of them during the current tour, with another 270 wounded.

That task force built around Colonel Infanti's 4th Battalion in The Triangle conducted over 50 air assaults and three amphibious operations on the Euphrates River. It fired nearly 400 counter-fire artillery missions against enemy forces and in support of troops in contact, killed or wounded 51 enemy fighters, and captured or aided in the capture of some 1,600 insurgents. Members of the battalion won two Silver Stars for gallantry. The battalion was nominated for a Valorous Unit Award.

The battalion also suffered 26 men killed, 109 wounded in action, and 2 whose status had been changed from DUSTWUN to MIA—missing in action. Colonel Infanti's pocket bulged with casualty cards.

Over fourteen months ago, Sergeant Ronnie Montgomery had stood at the JSB with his counterpart from the 101st Airborne and looked down untamed Malibu Road. "You will never control that road," the 101st sergeant predicted.

That same sergeant was back again. With a great sense of pride bordering on smugness, Montgomery drove him from JSB past all three Delta Company outposts—without a single incident. The sergeant's jaw dropped as they completed the uneventful drive.

"We paid a price," Montgomery said, "but we control the road. We're giving The Triangle of Death back to you as simply The Triangle."

EPILOGUE

Balad, Iraq, Dec. 27, 2007 (AMERICAN FORCES PRESS SERVICES)—
Iraqi police and U.S. special operations forces seized two suspected extremists believed to be complicit in the kidnapping of
three U.S. soldiers in early May, U.S. military officials said today.
The suspects were detained during Dec. 24–25 operations in
Ramadi, officials said. The raids were prompted by intelligence
reports linking the two individuals to the May 12 abduction of
three U.S. 10th Mountain Division soldiers after an insurgent
ambush near Mahmudiyah in which four U.S. soldiers were
killed.

Reports indicate the two detainees are linked to al-Qaeda in
Iraq. One of the suspected terrorists is believed to have facilitated
the kidnapping and is reported to have used his home to aid in
the hiding and transporting of captured soldiers.

The Ramadi raids were part of a series of operations conducted to detain individuals believed complicit in the abduction
of the soldiers, officials said . . .

During a previous operation, a weapon belonging to one of
the missing soldiers was recovered at a residence of one of the
suspects . . .

Both suspects are allegedly involved in terrorist cells responsible for several roadside bomb and mortar attacks against Iraqi
and Coalition forces, as well as the kidnapping and murder of
Iraqi citizens and members of the Iraqi security forces . . .

Four other individuals seized during the operations are being
detained for questioning . . .

Baghdad, July 12, 2008 (MCCLATCHY NEWSPAPERS)—The remains
of two U.S. soldiers kidnapped during a military patrol last year
were found after a U.S.-captured suspect led soldiers to their location, the Pentagon announced Friday.

Spec. Alex. R. Jimenez, 25, of Lawrence, Mass., and Pvt. Byron W. Fouty, 19, of Waterford, Michigan, members of the 10th Mountain Division based at Fort Drum, N.Y., were captured when insurgents overran their observation post . . .

Jimenez' and Fouty's remains were found buried together in the open desert west of Jurf al-Sakhr, a one-time al-Qaeda and Sunni insurgent hotbed, after a suspect pointed out their location during a U.S. military interrogation . . .

Their remains were recovered July 8 and flown to Dover, Delaware . . . where they were positively identified . . .

Detroit, July 12, 2008 (YAHOO NEWS)—The bodies of two U.S. soldiers missing in Iraq for more than a year have been found . . .

Jim Waring of the Family Support Group . . . said he spoke to Jimenez' and Fouty's families Thursday night.

"It's going to be tough on them," he said. "They really had hoped they were alive."

Waring said his group had a banner for the missing soldiers: *Together They Serve Our Nation and Together They Will Come Home.*

"They did come home together, just not the way we wanted," Waring said . . .

At Fort Drum, New York, Sergeant Ronnie Montgomery stood in front of the big glass case at 4th Battalion headquarters that contained the photographs of soldiers in the battalion who had sacrificed their lives in Afghanistan and Iraq. Other than the case with its growing number of photos, Fort Drum seemed to have a life of its own that continued through soldiers coming and going. Nothing changed. *Manticore* was still playing on the SciFi channel and an infusion of new Joes was already talking about deployment, the Sandbox, and monsters that come out at night.

Among the photographs in the case were those of Chris Messer, Nathan Given, James Connell, Anthony Schober, Chris Murphy, Dan Courneya, Joe Anzak, Byron Fouty, Alex Jimenez . . . Their faces in better times floated in front of the sergeant's eyes. They were all good men, good soldiers.

The eternal mystery of dying, of death, took an even more mysterious twist in the preserved images of James Connell, Chris Messer, Joe Anzak, and, to a lesser extent, Nathan Given. Chris Messer had died almost exactly the way he dreamed it months in advance, his legs blown off. Somehow, Sergeant Connell knew he would never return home alive and had tried to prepare his brother for it. The marquee of his old high school back home strangely foretold Joe Anzak's death. Given's and Messer's lives seemed inextricably enmeshed during their final days and hours, to the point that Given even switched places with Specialist Jared Isbell in a move that led to his death at Messer's side.

Perhaps, and Sergeant Montgomery could never reject the hypothesis, there really was a Great Plan in the universe to which man's fate was sealed and through the portals of which he sometimes caught glimpses of what lay ahead. It was not a soldier's privilege to understand, but instead merely to accept.

He felt the presence of someone next to him. Startled, he glanced up and saw Lieutenant Colonel Michael Infanti. The two career warriors stood there side by side in front of the case, not having to speak. Montgomery would remain with the 10th as it trained and refitted for its next mission somewhere in the world. Infanti was on his way to a staff position at the Pentagon, where he would finally undergo surgery for his fractured back. He still carried his soldiers' casualty cards in his pocket. It had taken time, but none was left behind.

"Sergeant Montgomery," Colonel Infanti said, "do you remember in *Band of Brothers* when Dick Winters' grandson asks him, 'Grandpaw, were you a hero?'"

"No," Winters had said, "but I served with a lot of them."

"Sometimes it's easy for us to convince ourselves that the United States is a decadent society," Infanti said, as much to himself as to the sergeant beside him, "that our young people have gone soft and that we'll never produce another generation like the one that stormed Normandy on D-day. Anyone who thinks that wasn't in The Triangle of Death."

He went quiet. The two soldiers looked at the faces in the glass case.

"One day my grandchildren will ask me about the 4th Battalion in Iraq," Infanti continued at last. "I'll tell them these men weren't heroes because they died. They were heroes because of the way they lived."